PREP

PSAT®
READING AND WRITING

300
PRACTICE EXERCISES

ADVANCED
PRACTICE
SERIES

250
QUESTIONS

BEST USED IN CONJUNCTION WITH A TUTOR OR PSAT PREP COURSE

3
TIMED SECTIONS

◆ Contains **Answer Keys** (no explanations)

◆ Time-Saving **Advice**, Proven **Strategies**

◆ Essential PSAT **Tips and Tricks**

Authors
Khalid Khashoggi, Co-Founder IES
Arianna Astuni, Co-Founder IES

Editorial
Christopher Carbonell, Editorial Director
Patrick Kennedy, Executive Editor
Megan Caldwell, Editor
Rajvi Patel, Editor

Design
Christopher Carbonell

Contributors
Danielle Barkley   Nathaniel Hunt
Nancy Hoffman   Johnna Landau
Chris Holliday   Cassidy Yong
Caitlyn Hoynes-O'Connor

Published by IES Publications
www.IESpublications.co
© IES Publications, 2020

ON BEHALF OF

Integrated Educational Services, Inc.
355 Main Street
Metuchen, NJ 08840
www.iestestprep.com

We would like to thank the IES Publications team as well as the teachers and students at IES Test Prep who have contributed to the creation of this book.

The SAT® is a registered trademark of the College Board, which was not involved in the production of, and does not endorse, this product.

ISBN-13: 9798645918941

QUESTIONS OR COMMENTS? Visit us at iestestprep.com

TABLE OF CONTENTS

Timed Sections

INTRODUCTION

OVERVIEW

This book is divided into four main units regarding the PSAT:

1) Reading

2) Writing (Grammar)

3) Graphics

4) Timed Practice

HOW TO USE THIS BOOK

Accuracy. Precision. Speed.

To improve your **Accuracy**, the Reading, Writing, and Graphics areas all offer specific IES techniques for each question-type. After you learn the steps per question-type, you will apply those steps to "blank" questions.

These "blank" questions will only have the question itself (*no answer choices*). By focusing on the question ONLY, you will AVOID the common PITFALL of evaluating each answer choice, wasting time, and possibly being tricked by false words. With these "blank" questions, you will practice applying the IES techniques to find the EVIDENCE that best SUPPORTS the CORRECT answer. Lastly, you will apply the IES techniques on FULL questions (with answer choices) to practice your **Precision** during the Process of Elimination.

After you have completed learning the IES techniques from the first three areas, continue onto the timed practice sections. Here, you will focus on your **Speed** using the IES techniques under a time constraint. Remember to apply the IES techniques to **every single question**! Good luck!

DISCLAIMER

- The *PSAT Reading and Writing Book* does **NOT** contain answer explanations.

- Answer keys are provided within each unit and at the end of each timed section.

- This course book is best used with a tutor or PSAT Prep Course.

6

PSAT
Structure

PSAT Structure

Reading Test

Each **Reading Test** will follow exactly the same positioning and roughly the same structure. Reading is the very first section that test-takers will encounter on the PSAT, and will always adhere to the following content and timing standards:

PSAT 8/9

55 MINUTES to complete Five Passages

42 QUESTIONS at 8-9 Questions per Passage

PSAT 10/N

60 MINUTES to complete Five Passages

47 QUESTIONS at 8-9 Questions per Passage

The different passages themselves will also break down in a manner that should be familiar to test-takers well in advance:

◆ FIVE Passages per test, each passage between 500 and 750 words. The total word count for all passages will be 2800 words

◆ FOUR Topic Areas, which typically occur in the following order: 1) Fiction, 2) Social Science, 3) Natural Science (first), 4) Global Conversation, 5) Natural Science (second)

◆ ONE Paired Passage reading and TWO Passages with graphics. A Paired Passage may occur in any of the Topic Areas except for Fiction; a graphic may occur in any of the Topic Areas except for Fiction and Global Conversation.

The Four Topic Areas for the PSAT Reading

Fiction: excerpts from novels and short stories, published between the eighteenth century and the present. The PSAT has prioritized written works that feature discernible conflicts or objectives and only a few principal characters.

Social Science: short essays and excerpts on economics, urban studies, transportation and infrastructure, careers and occupations, ethics and morality. A reading in this area will typically have a strong thesis supported by data, case studies, observed trends, and other evidence.

Natural Science: articles and excerpts discussing experiments and data, often with an emphasis on new knowledge or changing theories, in biology, chemistry, ecology, physics, astronomy, psychology, and related topics

Global Conversation: thesis-oriented documents, speeches, and excerpts from major politicians and important historical figures. These readings can range in date from the eighteenth to the twenty-first century.

> ✔ **Remember**
>
> When answering questions, always try to use effective process of elimination. Even if you ultimately need to guess on your answer, guessing between two decent-looking answers is better than randomly picking from four answers that you have not really examined.

8

Major Reading Question Types

Primary Purpose or Main Idea

These questions require you to give an accurate synopsis of the entire passage, often with a focus on the position or situation described.

Which choice best summarizes the passage?

A) A young man accepts a job that proves to be unexpectedly rewarding.

B) A young man achieves new insights by making a dramatic lifestyle change.

C) A young man deals with the whims of an unfair employer.

D) A young man questions the value and utility of his university education.

Content and Characterization

You may be asked, for these questions, to identify what is explicitly stated or asserted by the author. You may also need to give a summary of the tone of a portion of the passage.

Ms. Kurimoto addresses the narrator in a manner that can best be characterized as

A) bewildered.

B) cautious.

C) downcast.

D) amused.

Word in Context

For these questions, you will need to consider four possible meanings of a single word or phrase and decide which meaning is logically appropriate to the context given by the passage.

As used in line 16, "deliver" most nearly means

A) provide.

B) fulfill.

C) rescue.

D) transport.

Purpose, Function, and Developmental Pattern

These questions require attention to the fine points of device and structure, both for individual lines and for the passage as a whole.

The main purpose of the fifth paragraph (lines 45-57) is to

A) summarize an argument that the author rejects.

B) offer statistical evidence for an unpopular view.

C) describe an experiment that is inherently flawed.

D) question the methods used in a recent study.

Inference and Suggestion

Questions such as these require you to draw logical conclusions from passage content. Do NOT misread these as opportunities to interpret the passage or use outside knowledge.

Based on information in the passage, it can reasonably be inferred that the Goblin Shark

A) has only recently been studied by ecologists.

B) inhabits ecosystems that are difficult to explore.

C) has altered its behavior in response to natural disasters.

D) is of greater interest to non-specialists than to trained biologists.

Command of Evidence

Often linked to specific Content or Inference questions, Command of Evidence questions ask you to provide evidence for previous answers by choosing specific, justifying line references.

Which choice provides the best evidence for the answer to the previous question?

A) Lines 2-3 ("It was . . . statistics")

B) Lines 18-20 ("Despite such . . . Goblin Shark")

C) Lines 47-51 ("When Leary . . . Goblin Shark")

D) Lines 68-72 ("Ecologists . . . after all")

Graphics and Evidence

These questions may ask you to analyze a graphic (chart, table, map, diagram) on its own, or may ask you to compare the content of a graphic to the content of the passage it accompanies.

Do the data in the chart support the author's claims about "online merchandising" (line 39)?

A) Yes, because the data show that such merchandising is unregulated.

B) Yes, because the data indicate a proliferation of small online merchants.

C) No, because the data only account for merchants based in the United States.

D) No, because the data indicate a decrease in merchandising revenues.

PSAT Structure

Writing Test (Grammar)

Officially known as the **Writing and Language** test, this portion of the PSAT deals with grammar fundamentals such as verb tense, pronoun use, sentence structure, and standard English idioms. In addition, each Writing Test will include questions on style, coherence, and the use of visual resources (charts, maps, tables, etc).

To succeed on the PSAT Writing, you will need to work within the following time and content requirements in order to complete **four nonfiction passages**:

PSAT 8/9

30
MINUTES
to complete
Four Passages

40
QUESTIONS
at 10 Questions
per Passage

PSAT 10/N

35
MINUTES
to complete
Four Passages

44
QUESTIONS
at 10 Questions
per Passage

On each Writing Test, you will need to answer questions for **four different passage types**. Each passage will be approximately **325-400 words long**. The passage types will not always occur in the same order, but the passages themselves will always be written in similarly clear and informative styles. The four types are:

Careers: Passages that discuss work, employment, and related issues in culture and society. Workplace conditions, the economics of employment, changes to certain industries over time, the skills required for a certain career, and the modernization of older careers are all possible topics here.

Social Science: Similar in content to the Social Science passages found on the Reading Test. The major difference is that, in the Writing Test, the passages in this topic category tend to survey situations, scenarios, and phenomena, rather than arguing strong theses or taking on highly personal tones.

Humanities: Passages that discuss issues in literature, visual art, the performing arts, philosophy, theater, hobbies, entertainment, and related areas. Some history passages will also be considered Humanities rather than Social Science.

Natural Science: Similar in content to the Natural Science passages found on the Reading Test. Due to space constraints, the author will often provide an overview of a scientific sub-field or describe a single experiment, rather than evaluating the perspectives and ramifications that are frequently of interest on the Reading Test.

Major Writing (Grammar) Question Types

Essential Grammar Usage
Fundamental flaws in wording and syntax, including subject-verb disagreement, pronoun choice, adverb and adjective disagreement, and confusion involving contractions and possessives (it's/its, etc.)

because there was nine

cats in the basket.

8
A) NO CHANGE
B) there were
C) they was
D) they were

Sentence Structure
Overarching errors including parallelism, misplaced modifiers, comma splices, sentence fragments, standard phrases that use conjunctions, and improper comma and dash placement.

that it was not only

impressive but also

original.

9
A) NO CHANGE
B) and also original
C) but also it was original
D) and also it was original

Style and Concision
Departures from common English idioms, redundant phrases, excessively informal speech, improper diction (effect/affect, etc.), excessively wordy and non-concise phrasing.

were part of the annual

exhibition of patterns

that were floral every year,

10
A) NO CHANGE
B) yearly floral patterns.
C) patterns, each year, and made with flowers.
D) floral patterns.

Topic and Coherence
Finding appropriate transitions from sentence to sentence and paragraph to paragraph, deciding which information is most relevant to the author's intent, theme, or argument.

unless you go to Russia

 and attend the

Moscow Circus for

yourself.

11
Which choice most effectively transitions from the previous paragraph?
A) NO CHANGE
B) as a member of a team of cultural anthropologists.
C) when the weather is relatively mild.
D) and avoid the difficulties I encountered.

Graphics and Response
Incorporating information from a graphic, deciding which reading of statistics is most accurate, deciding which information from a graphic is most relevant to the passage.

although the giant tapir

 cannot accurately

discern objects more than

200 feet away.

12
Which choice offers the most accurate and relevant information from the data in the chart?
A) NO CHANGE
B) cannot accurately discern objects more than 100 feet away.
C) appears to have much sharper eyesight than the giant anteater.
D) appears to have much weaker eyesight than the giant anteater.

Ordering, Insertion, Deletion
Deciding whether to add or delete a sentence, where to place a new sentence, how to order sentences in a paragraph, how to order the paragraphs in a passage.

Question 13 asks about the previous passage as a whole.

13
To make the passage most logical, paragraph 2 should be placed
A) where it is now.
B) before paragraph 1.
C) after paragraph 3.
D) after paragraph 4.

PSAT
Reading

QUICK READ

In order to master the reading section on the PSAT, you must know how to read different kinds of passages with different complexity levels and determine quickly what is generally implied and what is directly stated.

To cover both needs, IES has created a two-fold technique that consists of a **QUICK READ** and **MARGIN ANSWERS**.

A **QUICK READ** will give you a general overview of the passage. You will use this to answer any non- line reference questions. The **QUICK READ** preparation will help you stay on theme when answering these questions and will allow you to avoid trap answers with little time and without excessive rereading of the passage.

First, you will apply a **QUICK READ**. Here are the steps:

1. READ the entire passage at a quick pace.
2. A QR is primarily done with little to no marking or stopping on a passage. BUT if you find that you need to go back to the passage in order to answer questions, then you may need an <u>annotated</u> QR.
3. DO read for OVERALL Main Idea (MI)/ Supporting Points (SP)/ Tone (+/–).
4. WRITE the Main Idea/Supporting Points and Tone at the bottom of the passage.

NOTE: Paired passages will have **TWO** MI/SP/TN. Having MI/SP/TN delineated at the bottom of the page will help you answer the compare and contrast questions quickly and aptly.

EXERCISES: PASSAGE EXCERPTS

Read the short passage excerpts in the next section, and find the MAIN IDEA (MI), SUPPORTING POINTS (SP), and TONE (+/–) for each passage. Then, check your ideas against the answers on page 11.

CONTINUE

PASSAGE 1

While you have probably learned how to graph shapes and lines in your algebra classes, chances are that you have not learned anything about what is called "graph theory" in
Line modern mathematics. In fact, you probably wouldn't call
5 the diagrams studied by this theory "graphs" at all! These interconnected dots and lines, while mysterious to most secondary mathematics students, are extremely useful for mapping delivery routes, managing interpersonal connections in an organization, and efficiently scheduling business
10 meetings. Despite a few applications in chemistry, the fact that graph theory has little connection to traditional secondary science education seems to keep it out of the high school curriculum.

Quick Read (QR)

What is the Main Idea?

What Supporting Points can you find?

What is the Tone (+/-)?

PASSAGE 2

This year, the public was graced with the first ever YouTube Music Awards, where the judges aggregated posts and hash-tags and clicks galore to determine which artist had
Line the most popular music videos. The South Korean pop group
5 Girls' Generation won Video of the Year, earning nearly ten times as many "votes" as a few other, primarily English-language, artists (the nine members of the group perform in Korean, Japanese, and English in sold-out concerts around the world). Many North American fans complained that their
10 favorites had lost (again, by a factor of ten) to "unknowns."

Quick Read (QR)

What is the Main Idea?

What Supporting Points can you find?

What is the Tone (+/-)?

CONTINUE

PASSAGE 3

Before plants, most of the oxygen on Earth was bound up in compounds such as water and carbon dioxide. As part of photosynthesis, plants take in carbon dioxide and release
Line oxygen into the air, which animals can then breathe in. This
5 complex system of life has kept the atmospheric concentration of oxygen around 21%, up from basically zero before life. Some scientists postulate that methane gas, produced by certain bacteria, combines with excess oxygen gas to create more carbon dioxide, keeping oxygen concentration where it
10 needs to be in order to maintain favorable conditions for life to continue.

Quick Read (QR)

What is the Main Idea?

What Supporting Points can you find?

What is the Tone (+/-)?

PASSAGE 4

Toys represent more than a plaything to their child owners, which results in the child's infuriation at the flippant attitudes most adults have towards toys. Just the other day I
Line was cleaning my son's Lego blocks and he responded with
5 such ardent venom that I forgot we were arguing over toys! It hadn't occurred to me—all the worlds he had built, the friendships he had made amongst his tiny people. Now I let my son decide when to tear down his worlds, when to end his friendships. In the indelible words of the prominent child
10 psychologist Albert Emmington, "Give the children toys. What are all things that matter most to us in life but toys?"

Quick Read (QR)

What is the Main Idea?

What Supporting Points can you find?

What is the Tone (+/-)?

CONTINUE ➡

PASSAGE 5

Although the Humboldt squid isn't nearly as giant as the giant squid, it still grows to the length of an adult human—instead of legs, though, it has tentacles with razor-sharp teeth
Line on its suckers, which can flay flesh from bone in seconds! The
5 Humboldt squid, which normally lives in deep water off the western coast of Central and South America, has recently been seen close to the shore as far north as Canada. Some people blame overfishing of its predators, while others blame climate change for this spread; either way, this ruthless killer is getting
10 farther from its own habitat—and closer to ours.

Quick Read (QR)

What is the Main Idea?

What Supporting Points can you find?

What is the Tone (+/-)?

FULL PASSAGES

Now that you have figured out how to perform an effective Quick Read for shorter texts, it is time to apply your skills to full-length PSAT Passages. Remember: full passages will run between 500 and 750 words, and will fall (on average) in the range of 560 words each.

Keep the following tips in mind as you perform longer Quick Reads:

1.   **DO NOT re-read the passage.** Even with the longest readings, a Quick Read is your tool for rapidly pulling out as much information as you can, NOT for pulling out tiny details.
2.   **DO NOT over-think tone.** Even if an overall positive passage has a few negative tones, or vice versa, note this information and keep moving. Qualifications such as these can be accounted for in your Supporting Points with the right amount of practice.
3.   **DO NOT try to formulate an elaborate Main Idea.** Even though the passages are longer, tone and thesis should still be very straightforward, and your notes should reflect this quality of the passages.

CONTINUE

PASSAGE 6

Perform a Quick Read of the following passage.

Adapted from Grant Allen, *The Woman Who Did* (1895).

From that day forth, Alan and Herminia met frequently. Alan was given to sketching, and he sketched a great deal in his idle times on the common. He translated the cottages
Line from real estate into poetry. On such occasions, Herminia's
5 walks often led her in the same direction. For Herminia was frank; she liked the young man, and, the truth having made her free, she knew no reason why she should avoid or pretend to avoid his company. She had no fear of that sordid impersonal goddess who rules Philistia; it mattered not to her what
10 "people said," or whether or not they said anything about her. "Aiunt: quid aiunt? aiant," was her motto. Could she have known to a certainty that her meetings on the common with Alan Merrick had excited unfavorable comment among the old ladies of Holmwood, the point would have seemed to her
15 unworthy of an emancipated soul's consideration. She could estimate at its true worth the value of all human criticism upon human action.

So, day after day, she met Alan Merrick, half by accident, half by design, on the slopes of the Holmwood. They talked
20 much together, for Alan liked her and understood her. His heart went out to her. Compact of like clay, he knew the meaning of her hopes and aspirations. Often as he sketched he would look up and wait, expecting to catch the faint sound of her light step, or see her lithe figure poised breezy against the sky on the
25 neighboring ridges. Whenever she drew near, his pulse thrilled at her coming,—a somewhat unusual experience with Alan Merrick. For Alan, though a pure soul in his way, and mixed of the finer paste, was not quite like those best of men, who are, so to speak, born married. A man with an innate genius for
30 loving and being loved cannot long remain single. He MUST marry young; or at least, if he does not marry, he must find a companion, a woman to his heart, a help that is meet for him. What is commonly called prudence in such concerns is only another name for vice and cruelty. The purest and best of men
35 necessarily mate themselves before they are twenty. As a rule, it is the selfish, the mean, the calculating, who wait, as they say, "till they can afford to marry." That vile phrase scarcely veils hidden depths of depravity. A man who is really a man, and who has a genius for loving, must love from the very first,
40 and must feel himself surrounded by those who love him. 'Tis the first necessity of life to him; bread, meat, raiment, a house, an income, rank far second to that prime want in the good man's economy.

But Alan Merrick, though an excellent fellow in his way,
45 and of noble fibre, was not quite one of the first, the picked souls of humanity. He did not count among the finger-posts who point the way that mankind will travel. Though Herminia always thought him so. That was her true woman's gift of the highest idealizing power.

Quick Read (QR)

What is the Main Idea?

What Supporting Points can you find?

What is the Tone (+/-)?

18

CONTINUE ➡

PASSAGE 7

Perform a Quick Read of the following passage.

Adapted from Chris Holliday, "Prosperity and Its Discontents."

The fundamental ideal of American democracy is enshrined in the Declaration of Independence: "All men are created equal, endowed by their creator with certain
Line unalienable rights... Life, Liberty and the Pursuit of
5 happiness." A century later, a brass plate pinned to the base of the Statue of Liberty proclaimed "Give me your tired, your poor, / Your huddled masses, yearning to breathe free." These two quotations entwine to form the basis of what came to be known as the American Dream. Yet ironically, the life of many
10 of the new arrivals in this Promised Land turned out to be very similar to the life they had left behind in other countries. Even prosperous Americans, those who approach the "Dream," can find themselves trapped in lives of emptiness and longing. Pursuing happiness was one thing, but capturing it and keeping
15 it was something else altogether.
American dramatist Arthur Miller, particularly in the plays he wrote between 1947 and 1955, attempted to analyze this apparent dilemma. *In All My Sons* (1947) it seems that Miller's protagonist, Joe Keller, has achieved many of the possibilities
20 suggested by the American Dream: a house and a yard with a freshly felled apple tree, family life and relative wealth. As the play unfolds, Joe comes to the realization that, in the apparent fulfilment of his dream, he has in truth compromised his integrity as an individual man. Miller appears to suggest that
25 the irony of "unalienable rights" lies in the fact that, although these rights are tantalizingly desirable to the individual, they are impossible to achieve without loss of the sense of self. Keller's own wife puts the case thus: "Certain things have to be—certain things cannot be. Otherwise anything could
30 happen." Is this really what the Founding Fathers intended? At the end of the play, Joe leaves the stage and shoots himself. Nothing is left but the empty yard and the demolished apple tree, symbols of the tragic effect of the American Dream on the individual.
35 In *Death of a Salesman* (1949), Miller's analysis goes even farther. Here, Miller considers the bewilderment of the individual faced with the ideal of the American dream by depicting the character of Willy Loman, a travelling salesman. In a series of flashbacks, Willy examines his life-long failure
40 to discover the route that leads to happiness. He thought he had pursued all the correct goals, yet all that remains for him is the fear of abandonment: in particular, there is a sense of alienation between Willy and his son, Biff, who ignores all the demands of conformity that Willy's version of the American
45 Dream entails. The suggestion, perhaps, is that the American Dream is irrelevant to the individual's life, that ambition can compromise the most important of family bonds.

Miller's plays force us to consider the true intent of the Declaration of Independence. The sense that we have of the
50 American Dream may not have been what the Founding Fathers envisioned when they forged the United States of America. These men were, after all, radically different individuals, each with his own agenda, each with his own view of life. However, they did have one thing in common:
55 they wanted to create a society free from the demands, restrictions, and overbearing class privileges imposed by European culture. The wanted to forge a country where any person could find the opportunity to advance according to individual ability, education, or talent. Although they could
60 not root out prejudice—or even, at the time, really rein in slavery—these men were not naïve to try to create, at the very least, a more level playing field. No one can deny the worthiness of that ideal, no matter how far American society may remain from perfecting either "liberty" or "life." Miller
65 reminds us of the pitfalls of that dream, and of the progress that we have yet to make.

Quick Read (QR)

What is the Main Idea?

What Supporting Points can you find?

What is the Tone (+/-)?

CONTINUE

PASSAGE 8

Perform a Quick Read of the following passage.

Adapted from Nathaniel Hunt, "The Zika Virus: When Science and Public Health Collide."

Three Latin American countries (Colombia, Ecuador, and El Salvador) made international headlines in January 2016 when they warned women not to get pregnant. It seems absurd
Line to advise women to avoid building families, but these countries
5 were desperate to stop a viral outbreak that was threatening their unborn citizens. The culprit? The mosquito-borne Zika virus, which is relatively minor for adults, but can have disastrous consequences for children in the womb. Alarmingly, there is currently no specific treatment for the Zika virus. As
10 this new viral threat spreads over South, Central, and even North America, public health agencies are scrambling to combat it.

The Zika virus is related to the dengue, yellow fever, and West Nile viruses. It was first identified in 1947 in Nigeria,
15 but wasn't involved in any major human outbreaks until 2007, when there was a major outbreak in Micronesia. Symptoms of Zika infection include fever, headache, red eyes, rash, and muscle and joint pain. These are very similar to the symptoms of dengue and chikungunya, which can make diagnosis
20 difficult based on symptoms alone. Zika may also be linked to Guillain-Barré syndrome, which can cause paralysis, but further research is needed to definitively say how they're related, or if Zika can actually cause Guillain-Barré syndrome.

Zika infection is usually quite minor for adults. In fact,
25 most infected adults have very few symptoms—or even none at all. Zika is most dangerous for expectant mothers, because of the severe birth defects and abnormalities it can cause. These include scarring, fluid accumulation, and even miscarriage. The most common serious abnormality it can
30 cause is microcephaly, however. Microcephaly is a serious, lifelong condition caused by a smaller than normal brain and skull size. Babies born with microcephaly are often intellectually disabled, with impaired motor function and facial feature abnormalities. People with this disorder can also suffer
35 from chronic seizures. Microcephaly appears in approximately 29% of pregnant women who are infected with the Zika virus.

Zika is spread through several different vectors. First of all, it is carried by several different species of mosquitoes— much like dengue, to which it is related. Secondly, the virus
40 can be transmitted between humans in several different ways, including by sexual transmission. It can also be transmitted from pregnant women to their children in the womb. Like other viruses, it can also be spread by blood transfusion.

Zika's largest outbreak, which is still ongoing, began
45 in August, 2014 in Brazil. Researchers in the state of Natal noticed an outbreak of a mysterious fever. The illness spread to several other states of Brazil, and in May 2015 researchers identified it as the Zika virus. From there, Zika spread widely, with confirmed cases appearing in 35 countries in
50 South America, Central America, and the Caribbean. Other outbreaks have been reported in Pacific nations and at least one African country.

Efforts to combat the spread of Zika are mostly focused on mosquito control, because Zika is primarily a
55 mosquito-borne disease. Unfortunately, the specific species of mosquitoes that spread Zika can be found throughout most of the US, and the World Health Organization has warned that the virus is likely to spread through most of the Americas by the end of 2016.

Quick Read (QR)

What is the Main Idea?

What Supporting Points can you find?

What is the Tone (+/-)?

CONTINUE

PASSAGE 9

Perform a Quick Read of the following passage.

Adapted from the 2016 State of the Union Address delivered by President Barack Obama.

We live in a time of extraordinary change—change that's reshaping the way we live, the way we work, our planet, our place in the world. It's change that promises amazing medical
Line breakthroughs, but also economic disruptions that strain
5 working families. It promises education for girls in the most remote villages, but also connects terrorists plotting an ocean away. It's change that can broaden opportunity, or widen inequality. And whether we like it or not, the pace of this change will only accelerate.
10 America has been through big changes before—wars and depression, the influx of new immigrants, workers fighting for a fair deal, movements to expand civil rights. Each time, there have been those who told us to fear the future; who claimed we could slam the brakes on change; who promised to restore past
15 glory if we just got some group or idea that was threatening America under control. And each time, we overcame those fears. We did not, in the words of Lincoln, adhere to the "dogmas of the quiet past." Instead we thought anew, and acted anew. We made change work for us, always extending
20 America's promise outward, to the next frontier, to more people. And because we did—because we saw opportunity where others saw only peril—we emerged stronger and better than before.
What was true then can be true now. Our unique strengths
25 as a nation—our optimism and work ethic, our spirit of discovery, our diversity, our commitment to rule of law—these things give us everything we need to ensure prosperity and security for generations to come.
In fact, it's that spirit that made the progress of these past
30 seven years possible. It's how we recovered from the worst economic crisis in generations. It's how we reformed our health care system, and reinvented our energy sector; how we delivered more care and benefits to our troops and veterans, and how we secured the freedom in every state to marry the
35 person we love.
But such progress is not inevitable. It's the result of choices we make together. And we face such choices right now. Will we respond to the changes of our time with fear, turning inward as a nation, turning against each other as a
40 people? Or will we face the future with confidence in who we are, in what we stand for, in the incredible things that we can do together? . . .
For the past seven years, our goal has been a growing economy that works also better for everybody. We've made
45 progress. But we need to make more. And despite all the political arguments that we've had these past few years, there are actually some areas where Americans broadly agree.

We agree that real opportunity requires every American to get the education and training they need to land a good-
50 paying job. The bipartisan reform of No Child Left Behind was an important start, and together, we've increased early childhood education, lifted high school graduation rates to new highs, boosted graduates in fields like engineering. In the coming years, we should build on that progress,
55 by providing Pre-K for all and offering every student the hands-on computer science and math classes that make them job-ready on day one.

Quick Read (QR)

What is the Main Idea?

What Supporting Points can you find?

What is the Tone (+/-)?

21

CONTINUE

ANSWERS: QUICK READ

EXERCISES: PASSAGE EXCERPTS

Passage 1
MI: Graph Theory; **SP:** Unlike school mathematics (-), Still has useful applications (+); **TONE:** Positive overall

Passage 2
MI: YouTube Music Awards; **SP:** Korean pop group won (+), Complaints from North American voters (-); **TONE:** Mixed

Passage 3
MI: Plants; **SP:** Generate oxygen (+), Maintain needed levels for animal life (+); **TONE:** Positive overall

Passage 4
MI: Toys; **SP:** Children become strongly attached to toys (+), Story about author's child (-); **TONE:** Mixed

Passage 5
MI: Humboldt squid; **SP:** Potentially dangerous (-), New geographic range (-); **TONE:** Negative overall

EXERCISES: FULL PASSAGES

Passage 6
MI: Romantic connection (Alan and Herminia); **SP:** Meet during sketching excursions (+), Alan is pleasant (+), Alan is not one of the "best men" (-); **TONE:** Positive overall

Passage 7
MI: American Dream; **SP:** Arthur Miller's depictions of the Dream (-), Dream is hard to achieve in reality (-); **TONE:** Negative overall

Passage 8
MI: Zika Virus; **SP:** Recent outbreaks (-), Transmitted by mosquitoes (-), Impact on pregnant women (-); **TONE:** Negative overall

Passage 9
MI: Change; **SP:** Americans chose change over fear (+), progress in the economy and education (+); **TONE:** Positive Overall

CONTINUE

MARGIN ANSWERS: LINE REFERENCES

On the PSAT, you will see that some of the questions ask about a:

specific line (*lines 12-17...*)
OR
specific place in the passage (*the description of the bridge, during the telephone conversation...*)

These are **LINE REFERENCE** questions. For these answers you will utilize a **MARGIN ANSWER**. A margin answer is, very simply, the answer to the question! It is an answer based on actual, factual, and VISUAL clues that you will **pull from the passage** to answer a specific question. It will NOT come from a quick read or from your mind. You will apply it to any question that sends you to a specific place or word.

MARGIN ANSWER STEPS:

1. Read question #1. If it is a line reference question (a question that sends you to an exact area by line number, paragraph, reference or context clue), then you are ready to use a MARGIN ANSWER.
2. Read the question carefully. What are they asking you to do or look for? (This distinction is important because it determines how much you have to read)
3. Go to the passage, read, and bracket the line reference. (Always bracket full sentences!)
4. Ask yourself the following:

    Who is my answer about?
    What is my answer about?
    Tone of my answer?

The above questions make up your MARGIN ANSWER. You may prefer to use three words to indicate the above information or you may use a full sentence. It is up to the individual test taker. What is most important is that you **use the facts from the passage to answer the question** and thus create a MARGIN ANSWER.

5. WRITE YOUR MARGIN ANSWER <u>IN THE MARGIN</u>. This information should be placed NEXT to the question. This placement will remind you to use these FACTS to do a thorough process of elimination.
6. Apply POE (Process of Elimination; see POE Lesson)

EXERCISES: USING THE QUICK READ

Now, try the passages on the next page, which already appeared as Passage 8 and Passage 9 of the Quick Read section. You should return to your Quick Read and use it, as needed, to help you arrive at accurate Margin Answers.

CONTINUE

PASSAGE 8 (REVISITED)

Directions: Create Accurate Margin Answers

Questions 1-5 are based on the following passage.

Adapted from Nathaniel Hunt, "The Zika Virus: When Science and Public Health Collide."

Three Latin American countries (Colombia, Ecuador, and El Salvador) made international headlines in January 2016 when they warned women not to get pregnant. It seems absurd
Line to advise women to avoid building families, but these countries
5 were desperate to stop a viral outbreak that was threatening their unborn citizens. The culprit? The mosquito-borne Zika virus, which is relatively minor for adults, but can have disastrous consequences for children in the womb. Alarmingly, there is currently no specific treatment for the Zika virus. As
10 this new viral threat spreads over South, Central, and even North America, public health agencies are scrambling to combat it.

The Zika virus is related to the dengue, yellow fever, and West Nile viruses. It was first identified in 1947 in Nigeria,
15 but wasn't involved in any major human outbreaks until 2007, when there was a major outbreak in Micronesia. Symptoms of Zika infection include fever, headache, red eyes, rash, and muscle and joint pain. These are very similar to the symptoms of dengue and chikungunya, which can make diagnosis
20 difficult based on symptoms alone. Zika may also be linked to Guillain-Barré syndrome, which can cause paralysis, but further research is needed to definitively say how they're related, or if Zika can actually cause Guillain-Barré syndrome.

Zika infection is usually quite minor for adults. In fact,
25 most infected adults have very few symptoms—or even none at all. Zika is most dangerous for expectant mothers, because of the severe birth defects and abnormalities it can cause. These include scarring, fluid accumulation, and even miscarriage. The most common serious abnormality it can
30 cause is microcephaly, however. Microcephaly is a serious, lifelong condition caused by a smaller than normal brain and skull size. Babies born with microcephaly are often intellectually disabled, with impaired motor function and facial feature abnormalities. People with this disorder can also suffer
35 from chronic seizures. Microcephaly appears in approximately 29% of pregnant women who are infected with the Zika virus.

Zika is spread through several different vectors. First of all, it is carried by several different species of mosquitoes— much like dengue, to which it is related. Secondly, the virus
40 can be transmitted between humans in several different ways, including by sexual transmission. It can also be transmitted from pregnant women to their children in the womb. Like other viruses, it can also be spread by blood transfusion.

Zika's largest outbreak, which is still ongoing, began
45 in August, 2014 in Brazil. Researchers in the state of Natal noticed an outbreak of a mysterious fever. The illness spread to several other states of Brazil, and in May 2015 researchers identified it as the Zika virus. From there, Zika spread widely, with confirmed cases appearing in 35 countries in
50 South America, Central America, and the Caribbean. Other outbreaks have been reported in Pacific nations and at least one African country.

Efforts to combat the spread of Zika are mostly focused on mosquito control, because Zika is primarily a
55 mosquito-borne disease. Unfortunately, the specific species of mosquitoes that spread Zika can be found throughout most of the US, and the World Health Organization has warned that the virus is likely to spread through most of the Americas by the end of 2016.

1

In the first paragraph, the author mentions "Three Latin American countries" (line 1) as examples of

Margin Answer

Who?

What?

Tone (+/-)?

CONTINUE

2

The main purpose of the passage as a whole is to

Margin Answer

Who?

What?

Tone (+/-)?

3

According to the passage, one group that is especially vulnerable to the Zika virus is

Margin Answer

Who?

What?

Tone (+/-)?

4

In the fourth and fifth paragraphs (lines 37-52), the author transitions from

Margin Answer

Who?

What?

Tone (+/-)?

5

How, according to the author, is the Zika virus currently being fought?

Margin Answer

Who?

What?

Tone (+/-)?

CONTINUE

PASSAGE 9 (REVISITED)
Directions: Create Accurate Margin Answers

Questions 6-10 are based on the following passage.

Adapted from the 2016 State of the Union Address delivered by President Barack Obama.

We live in a time of extraordinary change—change that's reshaping the way we live, the way we work, our planet, our place in the world. It's change that promises amazing medical
Line breakthroughs, but also economic disruptions that strain
5 working families. It promises education for girls in the most remote villages, but also connects terrorists plotting an ocean away. It's change that can broaden opportunity, or widen inequality. And whether we like it or not, the pace of this change will only accelerate.
10   America has been through big changes before—wars and depression, the influx of new immigrants, workers fighting for a fair deal, movements to expand civil rights. Each time, there have been those who told us to fear the future; who claimed we could slam the brakes on change; who promised to restore past
15 glory if we just got some group or idea that was threatening America under control. And each time, we overcame those fears. We did not, in the words of Lincoln, adhere to the "dogmas of the quiet past." Instead we thought anew, and acted anew. We made change work for us, always extending
20 America's promise outward, to the next frontier, to more people. And because we did—because we saw opportunity where others saw only peril—we emerged stronger and better than before.
What was true then can be true now. Our unique strengths
25 as a nation—our optimism and work ethic, our spirit of discovery, our diversity, our commitment to rule of law—these things give us everything we need to ensure prosperity and security for generations to come.
In fact, it's that spirit that made the progress of these past
30 seven years possible. It's how we recovered from the worst economic crisis in generations. It's how we reformed our health care system, and reinvented our energy sector; how we delivered more care and benefits to our troops and veterans, and how we secured the freedom in every state to marry the
35 person we love.
But such progress is not inevitable. It's the result of choices we make together. And we face such choices right now. Will we respond to the changes of our time with fear, turning inward as a nation, turning against each other as a
40 people? Or will we face the future with confidence in who we are, in what we stand for, in the incredible things that we can do together? . . .

For the past seven years, our goal has been a growing economy that works also better for everybody. We've made
45 progress. But we need to make more. And despite all the political arguments that we've had these past few years, there are actually some areas where Americans broadly agree.
We agree that real opportunity requires every American
50 to get the education and training they need to land a good-paying job. The bipartisan reform of No Child Left Behind was an important start, and together, we've increased early childhood education, lifted high school graduation rates to new highs, boosted graduates in fields like engineering.
55 In the coming years, we should build on that progress, by providing Pre-K for all and offering every student the hands-on computer science and math classes that make them job-ready on day one.

___

6

The main purpose of the passage is to

Margin Answer

Who?

What?

Tone (+/-)?

CONTINUE

7

According to Obama, how did "America" (line 10) react to earlier changes?

Margin Answer

Who?

What?

Tone (+/-)?

8

It can be inferred that Obama mentions the "dogmas of the quiet past" (line 18) in order to

Margin Answer

Who?

What?

Tone (+/-)?

9

In the fifth paragraph (lines 36-42), Obama promotes

Margin Answer

Who?

What?

Tone (+/-)?

10

The "progress" that Obama mentions in line 55 was made possible by

Margin Answer

Who?

What?

Tone (+/-)?

CONTINUE

PROCESS OF ELIMINATION (POE)

Process of elimination should be done on EVERY question. It will utilize both the QUICK READ NOTES and the MARGIN ANSWERS.

Facts from the QR and MA can help you pick up great speed and precision by applying this technique. It will also help you avoid the pitfalls of subjective test taking habits.

POE STEPS:

1.   Eliminate all answers that are **off theme (QR)**
2.   Eliminate all answers that have the **wrong WHO**
3.   Eliminate all answers that have the **wrong WHAT**
4.   Eliminate all answers that have the **wrong TONE (+,-)**

A POE application should be quick and ruthless! Do NOT get attached to answers that appeal to you on a general basis. **FIND FALSE WORDS and FALSE TONES to eliminate actual words in each answer.**

If you are unsure, skip the answer and do NOT eliminate. NEVER cross something out if you can not actually cross out a FALSE WORD.

If you cannot make your final decision, you may have to return to the passage in order to add to your MARGIN ANSWER.

EXERCISES: APPLYING MARGIN ANSWERS AND POE

Use Margin Answers and POE to address the answer choices for Passage 8 and Passage 9 on the following page.

CONTINUE

PASSAGE 8 (REVISITED)

1

In the first paragraph, the author mentions "Three Latin American countries" (line 1) as examples of

A) nations that took precautions against the Zika virus.
B) nations with abnormally large mosquito populations.
C) nations where the Zika virus was first identified.
D) nations that have successfully eliminated the Zika virus.

2

The main purpose of the passage as a whole is to

A) compare a dangerous virus to other diseases.
B) present a recent experiment in cell biology.
C) describe a threat that may grow more severe.
D) advocate a new medical procedure.

3

According to the passage, one group that is especially vulnerable to the Zika virus is

A) the elderly and infirm.
B) otherwise healthy toddlers.
C) mature adults.
D) unborn children.

4

In the fourth and fifth paragraphs (lines 37-52), the author transitions from

A) showing how the Zika virus can be prevented to showing why people ignore such warnings.
B) defining the Zika virus's geographical range to defining the virus's most common symptons.
C) explaining how the Zika virus is transmitted to describing a recent outbreak.
D) explaining the source of the Zika virus to comparing the Zika virus to other viruses.

5

How, according to the author, is the Zika virus currently being fought?

A) Through efforts to contain or eliminate mosquito populations
B) Through quarantining the nations that have been most strongly affected
C) Through the creation of new medicines
D) Through increased hospital funding

PASSAGE 9 (REVISITED)

6

The main purpose of the passage is to

A) summarize different periods from American history and encourage Americans to seek new role models.
B) explain that society is being transformed and encourage Americans to be proactive.
C) connect the idea of change to the work of a single political party.
D) attack specific groups that do not embrace American social changes.

7

According to Obama, how did "America" (line 10) react to earlier changes?

A) With hostility
B) With confusion
C) With acceptance
D) With disinterest

8

It can be inferred that Obama mentions the "dogmas of the quiet past" (line 18) in order to

A) argue that these dogmas are praiseworthy.
B) argue that these dogmas are undesirable.
C) criticize the Americans of his own era.
D) show why Abraham Lincoln became famous.

9

In the fifth paragraph (lines 36-42), Obama promotes

A) debate.
B) radicalism.
C) cooperation.
D) education.

10

The "progress" that Obama mentions in line 55 was made possible by

A) Obama's own election.
B) improvements in the economy.
C) a Pre-K for all initiative.
D) the No Child Left Behind act.

CONTINUE

Questions 11-15 are based on the following passage.

Adapted from Charles Dickens, *Hard Times*. Published in book format in 1854.

Mr. Gradgrind walked homeward from the school, in a state of considerable satisfaction. It was his school, and he intended it to be a model. He intended every child in it to be a
Line model—just as the young Gradgrinds were all models.
5   There were five young Gradgrinds, and they were models every one. They had been lectured at, from their tenderest years; coursed, like little hares. Almost as soon as they could run alone, they had been made to run to the lecture-room. The first object with which they had an association, or of which
10 they had a remembrance, was a large black board with a dry Ogre chalking ghastly white figures on it.
    Not that they knew, by name or nature, anything about an Ogre Fact forbid! I only use the word to express a monster in a lecturing castle, with Heaven knows how many heads
15 manipulated into one, taking childhood captive, and dragging it into gloomy statistical dens by the hair.
    No little Gradgrind had ever seen a face in the moon; it was up in the moon before it could speak distinctly. No little Gradgrind had ever learnt the silly jingle, Twinkle, twinkle,
20 little star; how I wonder what you are! No little Gradgrind had ever known wonder on the subject, each little Gradgrind having at five years old dissected the Great Bear like a Professor Owen, and driven Charles's Wain like a locomotive engine-driver. No little Gradgrind had ever associated a cow
25 in a field with that famous cow with the crumpled horn who tossed the dog who worried the cat who killed the rat who ate the malt, or with that yet more famous cow who swallowed Tom Thumb: it had never heard of those celebrities, and had only been introduced to a cow as a graminivorous ruminating
30 quadruped with several stomachs.
    To his matter-of-fact home, which was called Stone Lodge, Mr. Gradgrind directed his steps. He had virtually retired from the wholesale hardware trade before he built Stone Lodge, and was now looking about for a suitable
35 opportunity of making an arithmetical figure of himself and be arithmetically elected to Parliament. Stone Lodge was situated on a moor within a mile or two of a great town—called Coketown in the present faithful guide-book.
    A very regular feature on the face of the country, Stone
40 Lodge was. Not the least disguise toned down or shaded off that uncompromising fact in the landscape. A great square house, with a heavy portico darkening the principal windows, as its master's heavy brows overshadowed his eyes. A calculated, cast up, balanced, and proved house. Six windows
45 on this side of the door, six on that side; a total of twelve in this wing, a total of twelve in the other wing; four-and-twenty carried over to the back wings. A lawn and garden and an infant avenue, all ruled straight like a botanical account-book. Gas and ventilation, drainage and water-service, all of
50 the primest quality. Iron clamps and girders, fire-proof from top to bottom; mechanical lifts for the housemaids, with all their brushes and brooms; everything that heart could desire.

11

The passage indicates that Mr. Gradgrind is

A) a businessman who cares only about empty pleasures.

B) a father preoccupied with the education of his children.

C) an architect with a very unusual style.

D) a teacher who has recently been disgraced.

12

Which of the following best describes the structure of the passage?

A) A description of a memorable conflict in the life of Mr. Gradgrind

B) A recollection of the unpleasant childhood of Mr. Gradgrind

C) An overview of the day-to-day lifestyle promoted by Mr. Gradgrind

D) An account of the business successes achieved by Mr. Gradgrind

13

As described in the fourth paragraph (lines 17-30), the educational system developed for the little Gradgrinds prioritizes

A) ancient myths over modern principles.

B) artistic pursuits over scientific knowledge.

C) dry analysis over whimsical enjoyment.

D) abstract theory over practical pursuits.

CONTINUE

14

The author suggests that Mr. Gradgrind aspires to

A) become active in politics.
B) begin work as a professor.
C) help the poor in his town.
D) start a new hardware company.

15

The narrator characterizes Mr. Gradgrind's house, Stone Lodge, as

A) ugly and unclean.
B) enormous and exciting.
C) oppressive and chaotic.
D) orderly and efficient.

Questions 16-20 are based on the following passage.

Adapted from a recent magazine article on the role of the automobile in American society.

In the 20th century, the automobile quickly went from a luxury item in America to a necessity. The car transformed the way Americans worked, traveled, and, perhaps most
Line importantly, the way Americans built. As cars made longer
5 and longer commutes possible, suburbs began to grow in rings around most American cities. And one of the most defining characteristics of suburbs is their single-use nature—residential areas are segregated from commercial and industrial areas. However, older Main Streets and downtown areas are
10 usually centers of mixed-use, which integrates various kinds of construction and usage into cohesive neighborhoods. Though America's construction trends embraced single-use construction in the 20th century, a renaissance of mixed-use is gathering steam.
15   The American urban landscape changed dramatically during the 20th century. President Eisenhower's Interstate Highway System criss-crossed the country with high-capacity, high-speed freeways. When these freeways were built through cities, the result was often the destruction or division of entire
20 neighborhoods. One of the leading proponents of suburbia and large freeways was Robert Moses, who was New York City's "master builder" from the 1920s into the 1960s. Though he never held any elected office, Moses wielded enormous power to reshape the city, building new bridges and new expressways.
25   Moses met his fiercest opponent, however, in Jane Jacobs, who resisted his efforts to build an expressway through Greenwich Village. Jacobs, in her seminal book *The Death and Life of Great American Cities*, argued that what made a neighborhood (and, by extension, a city) great was the degree
30 to which it incorporated mixed uses. Mixing together different types of buildings, different ages of buildings, and different kinds of buildings has hugely important implications for the safety and well-being of a city.
    Integrating residential and commercial uses can make a
35 neighborhood more safe, because it has the effect of gathering more people on the sidewalk at more hours during the day. For instance, in purely residential areas, most people leave for work early in the morning and return in the evening. The streets are empty for large stretches of the day. Mixed-use
40 neighborhoods, on the other hand, draw people in, which provides an automatic social safety net, and usually means lower crime. The more "eyes on the street" there are, the safer the neighborhood is.
    Mixing uses can have important effects beyond the
45 boundaries of the city too, particularly in the environmental impact a city has. Mixed-use neighborhoods are typically much more dense than single-use areas, and denser

CONTINUE

neighborhoods promote sustainability, from more walking to better public transit. With cars and trucks being the
50 #2 contributor to greenhouse gases, reducing traffic will be extremely important for lowering America's carbon footprint. Not only that, but MIT has shown that up to 53,000 Americans die prematurely each year from car and truck pollution. Fewer cars on the road would mean fewer
55 deaths for other reasons, too: car crashes are the #1 killer for Americans between the ages of 1 and 39. In 2015 alone, there were more than 3,000 traffic fatalities each month.
        Many of America's cities are experiencing new life as more Americans are drawn to high-density, mixed-use
60 neighborhoods. Some argue that we're experiencing the renaissance of cities such as New York and San Francisco, which are also becoming centers of lucrative in start-up scenes. A large part of the draw of these revitalized cities is the presence of mixed-use neighborhoods.

16

The passage is written from the perspective of an author who is

A) openly supportive of mixed-use projects.
B) unsure of the benefits of mixed-use projects.
C) worried that mixed-use projects are unpopular.
D) completely hostile to mixed-use projects.

17

Which of the following would be an example of a mixed-use neighborhood?

A) A former industrial area that is now the site of apartment buildings
B) A commercial district with several different types of stores
C) An area that combines major businesses with small homes
D) An office complex situated close to a major highway

18

In the first paragraph, the author explains that mixed-use neighborhood planning

A) was facilitated by cars.
B) is increasingly popular.
C) was once universal.
D) is difficult to define.

19

According to the author, who, out of the following choices, most clearly supported mixed-use planning?

A) "President Eisenhower" (line 16)
B) "Robert Moses" (line 21)
C) "Jane Jacobs" (line 25)
D) "most people" (line 37)

20

The fifth paragraph (lines 44-57) serves primarily to

A) indicate that creating more mixed-use neighborhoods could help to address various problems.
B) argue that mixed-use planning has negligible effects on public safety but has a significant effect on the environment.
C) explain a recent controversy that relates to mixed-use neighborhoods.
D) record the results of a single influential study.

CONTINUE

Questions 21-25 are based on the following passage.

Adapted from a recent article on marine biology.

A pale complexion might be a sign that someone is physically unwell, or emotionally agitated. Deep under the sea, coral also changes colour when responding to stress.
Line These changes, however, are caused not by blood flow, but by
5 disruptions to the vital relationship between coral and algae.
Algae are single-celled organisms that live within the tissues of the coral. The algae engage in photosynthesis, converting light from the sun into the energy they need to survive and grow. When they do so, they produce carbon
10 compounds that the coral rely on for nutrients. As Stephanie Wear, the Nature Conservancy's director of coral reef conservation, explains, "These tiny organisms live in harmony with coral animals, and they basically share resources. For example, the most important thing that the algae do is provide
15 food to the corals through carbohydrates they produce during photosynthesis." In exchange, the algae receive a sheltered living environment. The two organisms are so interlinked that the characteristic of one is often mistaken as a property of the other: coral is actually clear, and its trademark rosy color is
20 caused by the presence of the algae living within it.
Coral, however, are highly sensitive. Changes and stressors in the surrounding environment lead coral to expel algae. When this happens, the coral lose colour, hence the term "bleaching." Bleached coral is not dead, though it is
25 threatened. Coral may recover from bleaching, particularly if the stressful factor in the environment is eliminated. However, if the stress persists, the coral will die. This can have a number of consequences, ranging from impact on biodiversity to economic decline. Although they make up less than 1% of
30 underwater ecosystems, coral reefs shelter approximately 25% of aquatic species. Damage to coral can rapidly affect a vast number of other organisms, resulting in negative consequences for the fishing industry. The presence of coral reefs can also contribute positively to tourist industries, resulting in lost
35 income and jobs if those reefs disappear.
Often, elevated water temperatures are the most frequent cause of coral bleaching. Pollution can also result in chemical disruptions and bleaching, especially for coral located close to the shoreline. In shallow waters where coral
40 are located not far below the surface, intense sunlight may trigger bleaching. There is also evidence that sharp decreases in water temperature can cause bleaching. Coral bleaching events can range in size from relatively isolated to widespread occurrences: in fact, global coral bleaching events have
45 occurred several times. In 1998, an oceanic heatwave triggered widespread coral bleaching that wiped out 16% of the global coral population. Similarly elevated ocean temperatures led to more bleaching in 2010. The US National Oceanic

& Atmospheric Administration announced a third global
50 bleaching event in October 2015. Nor has the danger passed. For example, Australia's Great Barrier Reef, the world's largest coral reef, faces significant threats, and inspections carried out in spring 2016 reveal that up to 93% of the reef has been affected by some degree of bleaching.
55 During past mass bleaching events, some especially resilient coral did show the ability to regenerate rapidly after bleaching. It is not understood exactly why some coral is able to recover, but scientists and conservationists are working to understand how bleaching can be reversed, and
60 what recovery measures can be put in place.

21

It can be reasonably inferred that coral bleaching is a sign that

A) marine animals are destroying the coral.

B) too much algae has entered the bleached coral.

C) a particular group of coral is in danger.

D) a particular group of coral is over-producing carbon compounds.

22

In the second paragraph, the author quotes Stephanie Wear primarily in order to

A) indicate the ecological threat posed by coral bleaching.

B) compare coral and algae to other symbiotic organisms.

C) clarify a point about the biology of coral.

D) promote the study of marine biology.

23

According to the author, the "fishing industry" (line 33) is similar to "tourist industries" (line 34) in that it

A) can be harmed by coral bleaching events.

B) contributes to the spread of coral bleaching.

C) has worked in collaboration with marine biologists.

D) is raising awareness of coral bleaching.

CONTINUE

24

The author argues that coral formations are significant because

A) they are one of today's most popular tourist destinations.

B) several new species have been discovered recently in coral reefs.

C) they can prevent sea temperatures from rising.

D) other sea organisms rely on them for shelter.

25

The "scientists and conservationists" (line 58) would be most likely to participate in

A) an effort to quickly and dramatically lower sea temperatures.

B) an experiment that clarifies the relationship between coral and algae.

C) an initiative to rehabilitate bleached coral populations.

D) a campaign to increase tourism to coral reefs.

Questions 26-30 are based on the following passage.

Adapted from a 1947 speech to Congress delivered by president Harry S. Truman. In this address, Truman set forward what became known as the "Truman Doctrine," an approach to international affairs that involved the defense of international democracy.

The peoples of a number of countries of the world have recently had totalitarian regimes forced upon them against their will. The Government of the United States has made
Line frequent protests against coercion and intimidation in violation
5 of the Yalta agreement in Poland, Rumania, and Bulgaria. I must also state that in a number of other countries there have been similar developments.

At the present moment in world history nearly every nation must choose between alternative ways of life. The
10 choice is too often not a free one. One way of life is based upon the will of the majority, and is distinguished by free institutions, representative government, free elections, guarantees of individual liberty, freedom of speech and religion, and freedom from political oppression. The
15 second way of life is based upon the will of a minority forcibly imposed upon the majority. It relies upon terror and oppression, a controlled press and radio, fixed elections, and the suppression of personal freedoms.

I believe that it must be the policy of the United States to
20 support free peoples who are resisting attempted subjugation by armed minorities or by outside pressures.

I believe that we must assist free peoples to work out their own destinies in their own way.

I believe that our help should be primarily through
25 economic and financial aid which is essential to economic stability and orderly political processes.

The world is not static, and the status quo is not sacred. But we cannot allow changes in the status quo in violation of the Charter of the United Nations by such methods as coercion,
30 or by such subterfuges as political infiltration. In helping free and independent nations to maintain their freedom, the United States will be giving effect to the principles of the Charter of the United Nations.

It is necessary only to glance at a map to realize that the
35 survival and integrity of a free country, such as the Greek nation, are of grave importance in a much wider situation. If Greece should fall under the control of an armed minority, the effect upon its neighbor, Turkey, would be immediate and serious. Confusion and disorder might well spread throughout
40 the entire Middle East. Moreover, the disappearance of Greece as an independent state would have a profound effect upon those countries in Europe whose peoples are struggling against great difficulties to maintain their freedoms and their independence while they repair the damages of war. . .

CONTINUE

45   This is a serious course upon which we embark. I would not recommend it except that the alternative is much more serious. The United States contributed $341,000,000,000 toward winning World War II. This is an investment in world freedom and world peace. The assistance that I am
50 recommending for Greece and Turkey amounts to little more than 1 tenth of 1 percent of this investment. It is only common sense that we should safeguard this investment and make sure that it was not in vain. The seeds of totalitarian regimes are nurtured by misery and want. They spread and
55 grow in the evil soil of poverty and strife. They reach their full growth when the hope of a people for a better life has died.

     We must keep that hope alive.

26

The "developments" that Truman refers to in line 7 are cases in which

A) the United States has intervened to completely eliminate oppressive regimes.

B) opposition from American voters has prevented the United States from intervening.

C) new international treaties have been developed to improve upon the Yalta agreement.

D) nations have been forced to adopt totalitarian government.

27

Truman's main purpose in this passage is to

A) commemorate the peacekeeping efforts of the United Nations.

B) formulate a policy and criticize complacent Americans.

C) explain how World War II created a new system of international alliances.

D) call attention to a crisis and promote a new endeavor.

28

In lines 19-26 ("I believe . . . processes") Truman does which of the following

A) attacks his political enemies.

B) praises past accomplishments.

C) states a series of convictions.

D) expresses pity for oppressed people.

29

Why does Truman mention World War II in line 48?

A) To explain that the United States must reward Greece and Turkey for their cooperation during the war

B) To highlight the economic prosperity that has characterized American life after the war

C) To indicate that his present plan of action could have more important results than America's victory in the war

D) To call attention to a United States commitment that was much more costly than Truman's present proposal

30

Throughout the passage, Greece and Turkey are mentioned as examples of nations that

A) are in drastic need of assistance.

B) have appealed to the United Nations for assistance.

C) fought alongside the United States in World War II.

D) cannot be rescued from totalitarian rule.

CONTINUE

ANSWERS: MARGIN ANSWERS
LINE REFERENCE QUESTIONS

1. A	16. A
2. C	17. C
3. D	18. B
4. C	19. C
5. A	20. A
6. B	21. C
7. C	22. C
8. B	23. A
9. C	24. D
10. D	25. C
11. B	26. D
12. C	27. D
13. C	28. C
14. A	29. D
15. D	30. A

CONTINUE

MARGIN ANSWERS: WORD IN CONTEXT

As you become adept at using MARGIN ANSWERS you will begin to see the nuances of each question-type. The popular **WORD IN CONTEXT (WIC)** question is an example of this minor difference.

WIC is not asking about the main idea of the passage or the author's purpose but instead, WIC is determining if a student can understand the meaning of a word that is being used in an unusual context. This is NOT vocabulary. You are NOT defining the word in question.

EXAMPLES:

1

As used in line 24, "high" most nearly means

A) inaccessible.
B) unsafe.
C) authoritative.
D) unaware.

2

As used in line 67, "shore up" most nearly means

A) support.
B) prolong.
C) guarantee.
D) increase.

WIC MARGIN ANSWER STEPS

In Detail:

1. Go to the passage and **cross out the word** in the sentence that is being asked about in the question. DO NOT circle. Eliminate from sight.
2. Replace that word with a **new word that you determine from the context clues** in the immediate sentence or surrounding sentences.
3. **Write** this new word/ context clue **in the MARGIN of your question**.
4. Next, write in the margin, **what you mean by the new word**. Why did you choose it? Why does it work? How does it work? **Include the tone (+/-) of the new word**.
5. Now you are ready to **put a simple definition next to each answer choice**. Be simple and literal.
6. You should see your match almost immediately. If you are stuck at two choices, you can use step 2 in MA to see which answer works better.

NOTE: steps 2 and 3, while not needed on easy questions, are advisable to apply. They help avoid the common WIC pitfall that causes a student to be stuck at two choices.

Essentially (based on above):
1. NEW WORD
2. WHAT YOU MEAN, IN CONTEXT, BY THAT NEW WORD?
3. TONE (+/-) OF NEW WORD?
4. DEFINE ANSWER CHOICES

EXERCISES:

Using the steps above, complete the Word in Context questions that follow. Begin with Margin Answers, and move on to consider full Multiple Choice Answers.

CONTINUE

PASSAGE 1: MARGIN ANSWER

Whenever I hear an announcer proclaim that such-and-
such a play has only happened five times in Major League
Baseball history, I am impressed to have witnessed something
Line so remarkable. But how can the word "history" properly
5 denote a record that has only existed for little more than a
century? Even American history, if we include the Colonial
period, is barely more than four hundred years old. Egypt has
a cultural history that spans millennia of recorded facts. Speak
to a paleontologist or geologist, and you'll be regaled with a
10 "history" where a million years is treated as an instant.

1 As used in line 3, "witnessed" most nearly means

Word?

What you mean by that "word"?

Tone (+/-)?

2 As used in line 8, "spans" most nearly means

Word?

What you mean by that "word"?

Tone (+/-)?

PASSAGE 1: MULTIPLE CHOICE

Whenever I hear an announcer proclaim that such-and-
such a play has only happened five times in Major League
Baseball history, I am impressed to have witnessed something
Line so remarkable. But how can the word "history" properly
5 denote a record that has only existed for little more than a
century? Even American history, if we include the Colonial
period, is barely more than four hundred years old. Egypt has
a cultural history that spans millennia of recorded facts. Speak
to a paleontologist or geologist, and you'll be regaled with a
10 "history" where a million years is treated as an instant.

1 As used in line 3, "witnessed" most nearly means

Define answer choices:
A) observed. _____
B) described. _____
C) defended. _____
D) testified to. _____

2 As used in line 8, "spans" most nearly means

Define answer choices:
A) stretches above. _____
B) brings into agreement. _____
C) takes into account. _____
D) enables communication between. _____

CONTINUE

PASSAGE 2: MARGIN ANSWER

The human ear is an amazing mechanism. The visible
part of the ear, the auricle, acts as a conical amplifier, picking
up sounds and funneling them into our ear. The system works
Line based on the same structure as a shell. If a shell had an opening
5 at its pinnacle, and the pinnacle were placed gently into the ear,
it would greatly amplify the surrounding sounds. But that's not
all when it comes to the ear. While many think of it as merely
an organ concerned with listening, hearing is actually the ear's
ancillary purpose: keeping the body in equilibrium is a more
10 difficult, but more essential, task.

3
As used in lines 2-3, "picking up" most nearly means

Word?

What you mean by that "word"?

Tone (+/-)?

4
As used in line 9, "purpose" most nearly means

Word?

What you mean by that "word"?

Tone (+/-)?

PASSAGE 2: MULTIPLE CHOICE

The human ear is an amazing mechanism. The visible
part of the ear, the auricle, acts as a conical amplifier, picking
up sounds and funneling them into our ear. The system works
Line based on the same structure as a shell. If a shell had an opening
5 at its pinnacle, and the pinnacle were placed gently into the ear,
it would greatly amplify the surrounding sounds. But that's not
all when it comes to the ear. While many think of it as merely
an organ concerned with listening, hearing is actually the ear's
ancillary purpose: keeping the body in equilibrium is a more
10 difficult, but more essential, task.

3
As used in lines 2-3, "picking up" most nearly means

Define answer choices:
A) helping. _____
B) lifting. _____
C) rescuing. _____
D) detecting. _____

4
As used in line 9, "purpose" most nearly means

Define answer choices:
A) career. _____
B) function. _____
C) meaning. _____
D) belief. _____

CONTINUE

PASSAGE 3: MARGIN ANSWER

The decision to move from a densely populated city to the wide-open suburbs is a natural one for a growing family. The availability of larger homes with private yards around them
Line attracts parents with young children, leading to a more family-
5 oriented society with better schools and more efficient public services. Parents have the ability to rear their children at a comfortable pace, introducing them to the less desirable realities of life when they decide the time is right. Most importantly, young parents have numerous options for the type of community
10 they want to settle in.

5

As used in line 2, "natural" most nearly means

Word?

What you mean by that "word"?

Tone (+/-)?

6

As used in line 3, "private" most nearly means

Word?

What you mean by that "word"?

Tone (+/-)?

PASSAGE 3: MULTIPLE CHOICE

The decision to move from a densely populated city to the wide-open suburbs is a natural one for a growing family. The availability of larger homes with more private yards around
Line them attracts parents with young children, leading to a more
5 family-oriented society with better schools and more efficient public services. Parents have the ability to rear their children at a comfortable pace, introducing them to the less desirable realities of life when they decide the time is right. Most importantly, young parents have numerous options for the type of community
10 they want to settle in.

5

As used in line 2, "natural" most nearly means

Define answer choices:
A) easygoing. _____
B) appropriate. _____
C) talented. _____
D) inspired. _____

6

As used in line 3, "private" most nearly means

Define answer choices:
A) business-oriented. _____
B) highly secretive. _____
C) individually owned. _____
D) unusually sensitive. _____

CONTINUE ➡

Questions 7-11 are based on the following passage.

Adapted from Virginia Woolf, "The Mark on the Wall," a short story first published in 1919.

Perhaps it was the middle of January in the present year that I first looked up and saw the mark on the wall. In order to fix a date it is necessary to remember what one saw. So now I
Line think of the fire; the steady film of yellow light upon the page
5 of my book; the three chrysanthemums in the round glass bowl on the mantelpiece. Yes, it must have been the winter time, and we had just finished our tea, for I remember that I was smoking a cigarette when I looked up and saw the mark on the wall for the first time. I looked up through the smoke of my cigarette
10 and my eye lodged for a moment upon the burning coals, and that old fancy of the crimson flag flapping from the castle tower came into my mind, and I thought of the cavalcade of red knights riding up the side of the black rock. Rather to my relief the sight of the mark interrupted the fancy, for it is an old
15 fancy, an automatic fancy, made as a child perhaps. The mark was a small round mark, black upon the white wall, about six or seven inches above the mantelpiece.
How readily our thoughts swarm upon a new object, lifting it a little way, as ants carry a blade of straw so
20 feverishly, and then leave it. . . If that mark was made by a nail, it can't have been for a picture, it must have been for a miniature—the miniature of a lady with white powdered curls, powder-dusted cheeks, and lips like red carnations. A fraud of course, for the people who had this house before us would
25 have chosen pictures in that way—an old picture for an old room. That is the sort of people they were—very interesting people, and I think of them so often, in such queer places, because one will never see them again, never know what happened next. They wanted to leave this house because they
30 wanted to change their style of furniture, so he said, and he was in process of saying that in his opinion art should have ideas behind it when we were torn asunder, as one is torn from the old lady about to pour out tea and the young man about to hit the tennis ball in the back garden of the suburban villa as
35 one rushes past in the train.
But as for that mark, I'm not sure about it; I don't believe it was made by a nail after all; it's too big, too round, for that. I might get up, but if I got up and looked at it, ten to one I shouldn't be able to say for certain; because once a thing's
40 done, no one ever knows how it happened. Oh! dear me, the mystery of life; The inaccuracy of thought! The ignorance of humanity! To show how very little control of our possessions we have—what an accidental affair this living is after all our civilization—let me just count over a few of the things lost
45 in one lifetime, beginning, for that seems always the most mysterious of losses—what cat would gnaw, what rat would nibble—three pale blue canisters of book-binding tools? Then

there were the bird cages, the iron hoops, the steel skates, the Queen Anne coal-scuttle, the bagatelle board, the hand
50 organ—all gone, and jewels, too. Opals and emeralds, they lie about the roots of turnips.

7

As used in line 3, "fix" most nearly means
A) repair.
B) immobilize.
C) assign.
D) fascinate.

8

As used in line 18, "swarm upon" most nearly means
A) disorient.
B) gravitate to.
C) cover up.
D) stampede past.

9

As used in line 25, "chosen" most nearly means
A) selected.
B) appointed.
C) honored.
D) befriended.

10

As used in line 43, "affair" most nearly means
A) condition.
B) scandal.
C) romance.
D) episode.

11

As used in line 51, "lie" most nearly means
A) recline.
B) live.
C) are relaxing.
D) are located.

CONTINUE

Questions 12-16 are based on the following passage.

Adapted from Chris Holliday, "Prosperity and Its Discontents."

The fundamental ideal of American democracy is enshrined in the Declaration of Independence: "All men are created equal, endowed by their creator with certain
Line unalienable rights... Life, Liberty and the Pursuit of
5 happiness." A century later, a brass plate pinned to the base of the Statue of Liberty proclaimed "Give me your tired, your poor, / Your huddled masses, yearning to breathe free." These two quotations entwine to form the basis of what came to be known as the American Dream. Yet ironically, the life of many
10 of the new arrivals in this Promised Land turned out to be very similar to the life they had left behind in other countries. Even prosperous Americans, those who approach the "Dream," can find themselves trapped in lives of emptiness and longing. Pursuing happiness was one thing, but capturing it and keeping
15 it was something else altogether.

American dramatist Arthur Miller, particularly in the plays he wrote between 1947 and 1955, attempted to analyze this apparent dilemma. *In All My Sons* (1947) it seems that Miller's protagonist, Joe Keller, has achieved many of the possibilities
20 suggested by the American Dream: a house and a yard with a freshly felled apple tree, family life and relative wealth. As the play unfolds, Joe comes to the realization that, in the apparent fulfilment of his dream, he has in truth compromised his integrity as an individual man. Miller appears to suggest that
25 the irony of "unalienable rights" lies in the fact that, although these rights are tantalizingly desirable to the individual, they are impossible to achieve without loss of the sense of self. Keller's own wife puts the case thus: "Certain things have to be—certain things cannot be. Otherwise anything could
30 happen." Is this really what the Founding Fathers intended? At the end of the play, Joe leaves the stage and shoots himself. Nothing is left but the empty yard and the demolished apple tree, symbols of the tragic effect of the American Dream on the individual.
35 In *Death of a Salesman* (1949), Miller's analysis goes even farther. Here, Miller considers the bewilderment of the individual faced with the ideal of the American dream by depicting the character of Willy Loman, a travelling salesman. In a series of flashbacks, Willy examines his life-long failure
40 to discover the route that leads to happiness. He thought he had pursued all the correct goals, yet all that remains for him is the fear of abandonment: in particular, there is a sense of alienation between Willy and his son, Biff, who ignores all the demands of conformity that Willy's version of the American
45 Dream entails. The suggestion, perhaps, is that the American Dream is irrelevant to the individual's life, that ambition can compromise the most important of family bonds.

Miller's plays force us to consider the true intent of the Declaration of Independence. The sense that we have of the
50 American Dream may not have been what the Founding Fathers envisioned when they forged the United States of America. These men were, after all, radically different individuals, each with his own agenda, each with his own view of life. However, they did have one thing in common:
55 they wanted to create a society free from the demands, restrictions, and overbearing class privileges imposed by European culture. The wanted to forge a country where any person could find the opportunity to advance according to individual ability, education, or talent. Although they could
60 not root out prejudice—or even, at the time, really rein in slavery—these men were not naïve to try to create, at the very least, a more level playing field. No one can deny the worthiness of that ideal, no matter how far American society may remain from perfecting either "liberty" or "life." Miller
65 reminds us of the pitfalls of that dream, and of the progress that we have yet to make.

12

As used in line 13, "emptiness" most nearly means
A) dissatisfaction.
B) spaciousness.
C) scarcity.
D) irresponsibility.

13

As used in line 28, "puts" most nearly means
A) ranks.
B) explains.
C) stores.
D) arranges.

14

As used in line 44, "version of" most nearly means
A) copy of.
B) edition of.
C) performance of.
D) interpretation of.

CONTINUE

15

As used in line 52, "radically" most nearly means

A) starkly.

B) overconfidently.

C) angrily.

D) artistically.

16

As used in line 60, "root out" most nearly means

A) find.

B) explore.

C) eliminate.

D) transplant.

Questions 17-21 are based on the following passage.

Adapted from Grant Allen, *The Woman Who Did* (1895).

From that day forth, Alan and Herminia met frequently. Alan was given to sketching, and he sketched a great deal in his idle times on the common. He translated the cottages
Line from real estate into poetry. On such occasions, Herminia's
5 walks often led her in the same direction. For Herminia was frank; she liked the young man, and, the truth having made her free, she knew no reason why she should avoid or pretend to avoid his company. She had no fear of that sordid impersonal goddess who rules Philistia; it mattered not to her what
10 "people said," or whether or not they said anything about her. "Aiunt: quid aiunt? aiant," was her motto. Could she have known to a certainty that her meetings on the common with Alan Merrick had excited unfavorable comment among the old ladies of Holmwood, the point would have seemed to her
15 unworthy of an emancipated soul's consideration. She could estimate at its true worth the value of all human criticism upon human action.

So, day after day, she met Alan Merrick, half by accident, half by design, on the slopes of the Holmwood. They talked
20 much together, for Alan liked her and understood her. His heart went out to her. Compact of like clay, he knew the meaning of her hopes and aspirations. Often as he sketched he would look up and wait, expecting to catch the faint sound of her light step, or see her lithe figure poised breezy against the sky on the
25 neighboring ridges. Whenever she drew near, his pulse thrilled at her coming,—a somewhat unusual experience with Alan Merrick. For Alan, though a pure soul in his way, and mixed of the finer paste, was not quite like those best of men, who are, so to speak, born married. A man with an innate genius for
30 loving and being loved cannot long remain single. He MUST marry young; or at least, if he does not marry, he must find a companion, a woman to his heart, a help that is meet for him. What is commonly called prudence in such concerns is only another name for vice and cruelty. The purest and best of men
35 necessarily mate themselves before they are twenty. As a rule, it is the selfish, the mean, the calculating, who wait, as they say, "till they can afford to marry." That vile phrase scarcely veils hidden depths of depravity. A man who is really a man, and who has a genius for loving, must love from the very first,
40 and must feel himself surrounded by those who love him. 'Tis the first necessity of life to him; bread, meat, raiment, a house, an income, rank far second to that prime want in the good man's economy.

But Alan Merrick, though an excellent fellow in his way,
45 and of noble fibre, was not quite one of the first, the picked souls of humanity. He did not count among the finger-posts who point the way that mankind will travel. Though Herminia always thought him so. That was her true woman's gift of the highest idealizing power.

CONTINUE

17

As used in line 2, "a great deal" most nealy means

A) with many consequences.

B) in an exaggerated way.

C) a great amount.

D) an ideal negotiation.

18

As used in line 19, "design" most nearly means

A) decoration.

B) intention.

C) structure.

D) deception.

19

As used in line 23, "faint" most nearly means

A) hopeless.

B) whitish.

C) soft.

D) weakened.

20

As used in line 36, "calculating" most nearly means

A) deceptively manipulative.

B) mathematically precise.

C) strategically intelligent.

D) unpleasantly cautious.

21

As used in line 45, "first" most nearly means

A) earliest.

B) youngest.

C) most noble.

D) most essential.

Questions 22-26 are based on the following passage.

Adapted from Nancy Hoffman, "I Am Iron Microbe: New Research in Biochemistry."

Microbiologists have discovered bacteria in the unlikeliest of places—bacteria ranging from the thermophiles that live in superheated deep-sea sulfur vents to the halophiles that
Line thrive in environments too salty for any other organisms.
5 Researchers have also encountered certain bacteria that breathe metal the way that humans breathe oxygen, although until recently the mechanism by which they do so has been poorly understood. A team from the University of East Anglia and the U.S. Department of Energy's Pacific Northwest National
10 Laboratory (PNNL), however, has achieved a breakthrough that not only sheds light on these bacteria, but opens up intriguing possibilities for using bacteria to remove dangerous pollutants, like uranium, from the environment.

The PNNL team hypothesized that some bacteria, known
15 as Shewanella oneidensis, have proteins protruding from their surfaces that, when brought into contact with a mineral, produce an electric current that allows the bacteria to breathe the iron in the mineral. To test this hypothesis, the team created a "simulated bacterium" by inserting the proteins they
20 believed to be producing the current into lipid bubbles, which are similar to the membranes of bacterial cells. These proteins protruded from the lipid bubbles, and they transmitted an electric current—in the form of individual electrons—at a high enough rate to make cellular respiration sustainable.
25 Dr. Tom Clarke, lead researcher from the University of East Anglia, suggested several possible applications for these findings: "These bacteria show great potential as microbial fuel cells, where electricity can be generated from the breakdown of domestic or agricultural waste products. Another possibility
30 is to use these bacteria as miniature factories on the surface of an electrode, where chemical reactions take place inside the cell using electrical power supplied by the electrode through these proteins." Another researcher, Dr. Liang Shi from PNNL, pointed to the importance of this research for understanding
35 the ways that carbon cycles through the environment, since when bacteria consume iron one of the byproducts is carbon dioxide. "If we understand electron transfer, we can learn how bacteria control the carbon cycle." This is especially important to climate scientists who are seeking and testing
40 ways to reduce the amount of carbon dioxide released into the environment.

The underlying knowledge about bacterial metabolism may also soon lead to advances in the disposal and treatment of toxic materials, including nuclear waste. A Rutgers
45 University team funded by the U.S. Department of Energy has discovered a strain of bacteria that take electrons from uranium and render it "immobile," harmless to the

CONTINUE

surrounding organisms. The team's experiments were aimed at determining the effect of radiation pollution on
50 microorganisms. They added uranium, dissolved into water, to samples of water from polluted areas, which already contained immobilized uranium. When the concentration of radioactive uranium reached a high enough benchmark, the bacteria proliferated to detectable levels.

55 Radiation can linger in the environment for many, many years. In some places, people still live in contaminated areas, such as the regions affected by the Chernobyl or Fukushima Daiichi catastrophes, areas near nuclear mining or testing, or parts of the Middle East where depleted
60 uranium in munitions has polluted groundwater and soil. With a better understanding of these bacteria, scientists may be able to develop a biological tool for removing dangerous radioactive metals from the environment.

22

As used in line 7, "mechanism" most nearly means

A) social theory.

B) specialized tool.

C) careful strategy.

D) natural process.

23

As used in line 24, "sustainable" most nearly means

A) infinite.

B) possible.

C) popularly accepted.

D) environmentally conscious.

24

As used in line 28, "breakdown" most nearly means

A) decomposition.

B) analysis.

C) disagreement.

D) panic.

25

As used in line 51, "areas" most nearly means

A) specialties.

B) calculations.

C) locations.

D) pursuits.

26

As used in line 62, "develop" most nearly means

A) explain.

B) nurture.

C) expand.

D) invent.

CONTINUE

Questions 27-31 are based on the following passage.

Adapted from the "Preface" to *Clotel* (1853), an anti-slavery novel written by William Wells Brown.

More than two hundred years have elapsed since the first cargo of slaves was landed on the banks of the James River, in the colony of Virginia, from the West coast of Africa. From
Line the introduction of slaves in 1620, down to the period of the
5 separation of the Colonies from the British Crown, the number had increased to five hundred thousand; now there are nearly four million. In fifteen of the thirty-one States, Slavery is made lawful by the Constitution, which binds the several States into one confederacy.
10   On every foot of soil, over which Stars and Stripes wave, the Negro is considered common property, on which any white man may lay his hand with perfect impunity. The entire white population of the United States, North and South, are bound by their oath to the constitution, and their adhesion to the Fugitive
15 Slaver Law, to hunt down the runaway slave and return him to his claimant, and to suppress any effort that may be made by the slaves to gain their freedom by physical force. Twenty-five millions of whites have banded themselves in solemn conclave to keep four millions of blacks in their chains. In all grades
20 of society are to be found men who either hold, buy, or sell slaves, from the statesmen and doctors of divinity, who can own their hundreds, down to the person who can purchase but one.
    Were it not for persons in high places owning slaves,
25 and thereby giving the system a reputation, and especially professed Christians, Slavery would long since have been abolished. The influence of the great "honours the corruption, and chastisement doth therefore hide his head." The great aim of the true friends of the slave should be to lay bare the
30 institution, so that the gaze of the world may be upon it, and cause the wise, the prudent, and the pious to withdraw their support from it, and leave it to its own fate. It does the cause of emancipation but little good to cry out in tones of execration against the traders, the kidnappers, the hireling overseers, and
35 brutal drivers, so long as nothing is said to fasten the guilt on those who move in a higher circle.
    The fact that slavery was introduced into the American colonies, while they were under the control of the British Crown, is a sufficient reason why Englishmen should feel
40 a lively interest in its abolition; and now that the genius of mechanical invention has brought the two countries so near together, and both having one language and one literature, the influence of British public opinion is very great on the people of the New World.
45   If the incidents set forth in the following pages should add anything new to the information already given to the Public through similar publications, and should thereby aid in bringing British influence to bear upon American slavery, the main object for which this work was written will have been
50 accomplished.

27

As used in line 4, "introduction" most nearly means
A) basic facts.
B) first arrival.
C) opening remarks.
D) formal greeting.

28

As used in line 18, "banded" most nearly means
A) harnessed.
B) pledged.
C) decorated.
D) chained.

29

As used in line 24, "high" most nearly means
A) inaccessible.
B) unsafe.
C) authoritative.
D) oblivious.

30

As used in line 36, "circle" most nearly means
A) social class.
B) pattern of behavior.
C) district.
D) repetition.

31

As used in line 49, "object" most nearly means
A) body.
B) goal.
C) device.
D) possession.

CONTINUE

ANSWERS ON THE NEXT PAGE

ANSWERS: Margin Answers
Word in Context Questions

1. A	17. C
2. C	18. B
3. D	19. C
4. B	20. D
5. B	21. C
6. C	22. D
7. C	23. B
8. B	24. A
9. A	25. C
10. A	26. D
11. D	27. B
12. A	28. B
13. B	29. C
14. D	30. A
15. A	31. B
16. C	

CONTINUE

COMMAND OF EVIDENCE

Some questions on the PSAT will be come in pairs. These are known as Command of Evidence (COE) questions. COE questions will ask you to select a specific line reference that **SUPPORTS** the answer to a **PREVIOUS** question.

At IES, each COE pair will have two parts: the **Actual Question (AQ)** and the **Evidence Question (EQ)**.

Take note of the key words (the effectiveness of the flu vaccine) in the AQ. We call this the **Topic**. ⇦**AQ**

Here are the COE technique steps:

1. **Identify** the **Topic** in the AQ.
2. Go to the EQ and go through choices to **look** for a **Topic Match**. Do <u>NOT</u> analyze the line reference, just check if it's ON TOPIC. If the line reference is **ON topic, put a check (✓)** on the left side of the choice. If the line reference is **OFF topic, put an "x" (×)** on the left side of the choice. (see example on right)
3. For those that have a topic match: analyze the line reference and write a **Line Reference Note** next to the answer choice. Each Line Reference Note should be a FACT. If the line reference says "the chair, the table, and the desk are beautiful", you must write "the chair, the table, and the desk are beautiful." Do NOT write "the furniture is beautiful." Do NOT summarize!
4. **Match** your Line Reference Note to choices in the AQ.
5. POE.

1
The author states that the effectiveness of the flu vaccine is

A) largely reduced when individuals are above 65 years old.
B) correlative to the time of year when the vaccine is administered.
C) no longer potent due to many generations of viral evolution.
D) highly dependent upon an individual's genetic makeup.

EQ

2
Which choice provides the best evidence for the answer to the previous question?

× A) Lines 49-53 ("Scientists . . . one-third")
× B) Lines 61-63 ("He found . . . CDC")
✓ C) Lines 66-69 ("Some . . . individuals") *individual genes*
✓ D) Lines 75-80 ("Pending . . . genetics") *scientists don't consider genetics*

EXERCISES:
Practice applying the COE technique for the questions on the following page.

CONTINUE

Questions 1-6 are based on the following passage.

Adapted from Theodore Dreiser, *Sister Carrie* (1900).

When Caroline Meeber boarded the afternoon train for Chicago, her total outfit consisted of a small trunk, a cheap imitation alligator-skin satchel, a small lunch in a paper box,
Line and a yellow leather snap purse, containing her ticket, a
5 scrap of paper with her sister's address in Van Buren Street, and four dollars in money. It was in August, 1889. She was eighteen years of age, bright, timid, and full of the illusions of ignorance and youth. Whatever touch of regret at parting characterised her thoughts, it was certainly not for advantages
10 now being given up. A gush of tears at her mother's farewell kiss, a touch in her throat when the cars clacked by the flour mill where her father worked by the day, a pathetic sigh as the familiar green environs of the village passed in review, and the threads which bound her so lightly to girlhood and home were
15 irretrievably broken.

To be sure there was always the next station, where one might descend and return. There was the great city, bound more closely by these very trains which came up daily. Columbia City was not so very far away, even once she was
20 in Chicago. What, pray, is a few hours—a few hundred miles? She looked at the little slip bearing her sister's address and wondered. She gazed at the green landscape, now passing in swift review, until her swifter thoughts replaced its impression with vague conjectures of what Chicago might be.
25 When a girl leaves her home to seek the metropolis at eighteen, she does one of two things. Either she falls into saving hands and becomes better, or she rapidly assumes the cosmopolitan standard of virtue and becomes worse. Of an intermediate balance, under the circumstances, there
30 is no possibility. The city has its cunning wiles, no less than the infinitely smaller and more human tempter. There are large forces which allure with all the soulfulness of expression possible in the most cultured human. The gleam of a thousand lights is often as effective as the persuasive
35 light in a wooing and fascinating eye. Half the undoing of the unsophisticated and natural mind is accomplished by forces wholly superhuman. A blare of sound, a roar of life, a vast array of human hives, appeal to the astonished senses in equivocal terms. Without a counsellor at hand to whisper
40 cautious interpretations, what falsehoods may not these things breathe into the unguarded ear! Unrecognised for what they are, their beauty, like music, too often relaxes, then weakens, then perverts the simpler human perceptions.

Caroline, or Sister Carrie, as she had been half
45 affectionately termed by the family, was possessed of a mind rudimentary in its power of observation and analysis. Self-interest with her was high, but not strong. It was, nevertheless, her guiding characteristic. Warm with the fancies of youth, pretty with the insipid prettiness of the formative period,
50 possessed of a figure promising eventual shapeliness and an eye alight with certain native intelligence, she was a fair example of the middle American class—two generations removed from the emigrant. Books were beyond her interest—knowledge a sealed book. In the intuitive graces
55 she was still crude. She could scarcely toss her head gracefully. Her hands were almost ineffectual. The feet, though small, were set flatly. And yet she was interested in her charms, quick to understand the keener pleasures of life, ambitious to gain in material things.

1

According to the passage, what is Caroline's destination?

A) The country village where she had spent her youth
B) The mill town where her father now lives
C) Her sister's residence in Columbia City
D) Her sister's residence in Van Buren Street

2

Which choice provides the best evidence for the answer to the previous question?

A) Lines 1-6 ("When . . . money")
B) Lines 8-10 ("Whatever . . . up")
C) Lines 10-15 ("A gush . . . broken")
D) Line 19 ("Columbia . . . away")

3

It can be reasonably inferred that the influence of a city on a young woman who leaves home will be

A) inevitably negative.
B) inevitably positive.
C) either strongly negative or positive.
D) completely negligible.

CONTINUE

4

Which choice provides the best evidence for the answer to the previous question?

A) Lines 22-24 ("She gazed . . . be")
B) Lines 26-28 ("Either . . . worse")
C) Lines 30-31 ("The city . . . tempter")
D) Lines 35-37 ("Half . . . superhuman")

5

The narrator suggests that "Caroline, or Sister Carrie" (line 44) is

A) disillusioned.
B) unsophisticated.
C) dishonest.
D) unreliable.

6

Which choice provides the best evidence for the answer to the previous question?

A) Lines 39-41 ("Without . . . ear!")
B) Lines 41-43 ("Unrecognised . . . perceptions")
C) Lines 53-55 ("Books . . . crude")
D) Lines 57-59 ("And yet . . . things")

Questions 7-12 are based on the following passage.

Adapted from Danielle Barkley, "Emergency Rooms: Whatever Happened to 'Ladies First'?"

Finding yourself in a hospital emergency room, suffering from intense pain, often without knowing the cause of the problem, is a terrifying and disorienting situation. Most of us would assume that, under these circumstances, we would
5 receive medical treatment as promptly as possible, with doctors and nurses working rapidly to diagnose and treat our ailment. However, in countries in both Europe and North America, reports emerge from patients left feeling neglected and ignored. They attest that their accounts of the pain they
10 were experiencing were minimized or brushed aside by emergency room staff. In some cases, there was a delay in diagnosis, leading to an increased risk of complications and to prolonged suffering.

Why might a patient reporting severe pain might not be
15 prioritized for treatment? One possibility might be gender. In 2001, a study by researchers at the University of Maryland argued that women presenting symptoms of pain were less likely to receive adequate health care than men. "There are gender-based biases regarding women's pain experiences,"
20 the researchers concluded. "These biases have led health-care providers to discount women's self-reports of pain at least until there is objective evidence for the pain's cause." The authors suggest a number of factors that may lead to women's pain being taken less seriously by a medical professional,
25 such as stereotypes that women express distress more readily than men, or that women can better tolerate physical pain and therefore require less urgent attention. The researchers also express concern that when they do receive treatment for pain, men and women tend to be treated differently. In a previous
30 study, men were more likely to receive pain medication while women tended to receive sedatives, which reduced their ability to articulate their symptoms rather than actually alleviating them.

However, despite allegations of inequality, it is currently
35 impossible to conclude whether women are less likely to receive medical attention when presenting symptoms of pain. Moreover, whether a dismissive attitude towards symptoms actually translates into longer emergency room wait times is even more complicated. Many factors, such as inadequate
40 staffing or lower hospital-to-population ratios, can influence how long a patient waits during a visit to the emergency room. A large scale study conducted in the United Kingdom in 2005 concluded that time of arrival, rather than individual patient characteristics, was the most influential factor in determining
45 wait time.

On the other hand, the characteristics of a specific patient do seem to have some impact on how rapidly he or she

CONTINUE

receives treatment. A 2015 study conducted at a hospital in Sweden found that patients who were more assertive
50 received care more quickly. For example, demanding patients that approached the counter were attended to more quickly than passive patients who quietly waited for their turn. The study also found that displays of assertiveness tended to correlate in gender. As a result, in many cases
55 male emergency room patients actually were treated more promptly, but this difference seemed to result from males' purposeful behaviour, rather than from gender alone. More research is clearly required to better understand how hospital staff can respond effectively to all patients—research that
60 must consider the complex dynamics at play in the provision of health care services.

7

Which of the following statements best represents the author's stance on whether emergency room neglect is based on gender?

A) The current research has not yielded a definitive answer.

B) The current research is completely inaccurate.

C) Gender is the main factor that determines emergency room neglect.

D) Gender does not in any way determine emergency room neglect.

8

Which choice provides the best evidence for the answer to the previous question?

A) Lines 1-3 ("Finding . . . situation")

B) Lines 7-9 ("However . . . ignored")

C) Lines 34-36 ("However . . . pain")

D) Lines 53-54 ("The study . . . gender")

9

The author indicates that the "researchers at the University of Maryland" (line 16) were

A) former emergency room physicians.

B) experts in sociological theory.

C) determined to propse reforms.

D) troubled by their findings.

10

Which choice provides the best evidence for the answer to the previous question?

A) Lines 14-15 ("Why might . . . treatment?")

B) Lines 27-29 ("The researchers . . . differently")

C) Lines 37-39 ("Moreover . . . complicated")

D) Lines 39-41 ("Many . . . room")

11

Why, according to the authors of the study described in the final paragraph, are women not prioritized in emergency room treatment?

A) Most emergency room patients are male.

B) Women inaccurately report the levels of pain they feel.

C) Men more aggressively called attention to pain.

D) Men spent more money obtaining healthcare services.

12

Which choice provides the best evidence for the answer to the previous question?

A) Lines 46-48 ("On the . . . treatment")

B) Lines 48-50 ("A 2015 . . . quickly")

C) Lines 54-57 ("As a . . . alone")

D) Lines 57-61 ("More . . . services")

CONTINUE

Questions 13-18 are based on the following passage.

Adapted from Nancy Hoffman, "I Am Iron Microbe: New Research in Biochemistry."

Microbiologists have discovered bacteria in the unlikeliest of places—bacteria ranging from the thermophiles that live in superheated deep-sea sulfur vents to the halophiles that
Line thrive in environments too salty for any other organisms.
5 Researchers have also encountered certain bacteria that breathe metal the way that humans breathe oxygen, although until recently the mechanism by which they do so has been poorly understood. A team from the University of East Anglia and the U.S. Department of Energy's Pacific Northwest National
10 Laboratory (PNNL), however, has achieved a breakthrough that not only sheds light on these bacteria, but opens up intriguing possibilities for using bacteria to remove dangerous pollutants, like uranium, from the environment.

The PNNL team hypothesized that some bacteria, known
15 as Shewanella oneidensis, have proteins protruding their surfaces that, when brought into contact with a mineral, produce an electric current that allows the bacteria to breathe the iron in the mineral. To evaluate this hypothesis, the team created an "artificial bacterium" by inserting the proteins they
20 believed to be producing the current into lipid bubbles, which are similar to the membranes of bacterial cells. These proteins protruded from the lipid bubbles, and they transmitted an electric current—in the form of individual electrons—at a high enough rate to sustain cellular respiration.
25 Dr. Tom Clarke, lead researcher from the University of East Anglia, suggested several possible applications for these findings: "These bacteria show great potential as microbial fuel cells, where electricity can be generated from the breakdown of domestic or agricultural waste products. Another possibility
30 is to use these bacteria as miniature factories on the surface of an electrode, where chemical reactions take place inside the cell using electrical power supplied by the electrode through these proteins." Another researcher, Dr. Liang Shi from PNNL, pointed to the importance of this research for understanding
35 the ways that carbon cycles through the environment, since when bacteria consume iron one of the byproducts is carbon dioxide. "If we understand electron transfer, we can learn how bacteria control the carbon cycle." This is especially important to climate scientists who are seeking and testing
40 ways to reduce the amount of carbon dioxide released into the environment.

The underlying knowledge about bacterial metabolism may also soon lead to advances in the disposal and treatment of toxic materials, including nuclear waste. A Rutgers
45 University team funded by the U.S. Department of Energy has discovered a strain of bacteria that take electrons from uranium and render it "immobile," harmless to the surrounding organisms. The team's experiments were aimed at determining the effect of radiation pollution on
50 microorganisms. They added uranium, dissolved into water, to samples of water from polluted areas, which already contained immobilized uranium. When the concentration of radioactive uranium reached a high enough concentration, the bacteria proliferated to detectable levels.
55 Radiation can linger in the environment for many, many years. In some places, people still live in contaminated areas, such as the regions affected by the Chernobyl or Fukushima Daiichi catastrophes, areas near nuclear mining or testing, or parts of the Middle East where depleted
60 uranium in munitions has polluted groundwater and soil. With a better understanding of these bacteria, scientists may be able to develop a biological tool for removing dangerous radioactive metals from the environment.

13

The research described in the passage is significant because

A) it offers new insights into how human respiration functions.

B) it has the potential to eliminate ecological hazards.

C) it will facilitate the discovery of new bacteria species.

D) it offers a sustainable new method of producing electric power.

14

Which choice provides the best evidence for the answer to the previous question?

A) Lines 5-8 ("Researchers . . . understood")

B) Lines 21-24 ("These . . . respiration")

C) Lines 25-27 ("Dr. Tom . . . findings")

D) Lines 42-44 ("The underlying . . . waste")

15

With which of the following statements about radiation would the author most clearly agree?

A) The activity of bacteria can cause the radiation level in an area to rise.

B) Once introduced into an area, radiation does not disappear quicky.

C) Radioactive materials are often stored in areas that are much too close to populous communities.

D) Catastrophes invoving radiation have been largely neglected by the public.

CONTINUE

16

Which choice provides the best evidence for the answer to the previous question?

A) Lines 27-29 ("These bacteria . . . products")
B) Lines 48-50 ("The team's . . . microorganisms")
C) Lines 55-56 ("Radiation . . . years")
D) Lines 56-60 ("In some . . . soil")

17

How did the PNNL team test its ideas about bacteria respiration?

A) By seeking out bacteria that live in extreme environments
B) By creating a simulation of a biological process
C) By revisiting older ideas about the origins of life
D) By introducing bacteria into toxic environments

18

Which choice provides the best evidence for the answer to the previous question?

A) Lines 1-4 ("Microbiologists . . . organisms")
B) Lines 5-8 ("Researchers . . . understood")
C) Lines 18-21 ("To evaluate . . . cells")
D) Lines 33-37 ("Another . . . dioxide")

Questions 19-24 are based on the following passage.

Adapted from the "Preface" to *Clotel* (1853), an anti-slavery novel written by William Wells Brown.

More than two hundred years have elapsed since the first cargo of slaves was landed on the banks of the James River, in the colony of Virginia, from the West coast of Africa. From
Line the introduction of slaves in 1620, down to the period of the
5 separation of the Colonies from the British Crown, the number had increased to five hundred thousand; now there are nearly four million. In fifteen of the thirty-one States, Slavery is made lawful by the Constitution, which binds the several States into one confederacy.
10   On every foot of soil, over which Stars and Stripes wave, the Negro is considered common property, on which any white man may lay his hand with perfect impunity. The entire white population of the United States, North and South, are bound by their oath to the constitution, and their adhesion to the Fugitive
15 Slaver Law, to hunt down the runaway slave and return him to his claimant, and to suppress any effort that may be made by the slaves to gain their freedom by physical force. Twenty-five millions of whites have banded themselves in solemn conclave to keep four millions of blacks in their chains. In all grades
20 of society are to be found men who either hold, buy, or sell slaves, from the statesmen and doctors of divinity, who can own their hundreds, down to the person who can purchase but one.
    Were it not for persons in high places owning slaves,
25 and thereby giving the system a reputation, and especially professed Christians, Slavery would long since have been abolished. The influence of the great "honours the corruption, and chastisement doth therefore hide his head." The great aim of the true friends of the slave should be to lay bare the
30 institution, so that the gaze of the world may be upon it, and cause the wise, the prudent, and the pious to withdraw their support from it, and leave it to its own fate. It does the cause of emancipation but little good to cry out in tones of execration against the traders, the kidnappers, the hireling overseers, and
35 brutal drivers, so long as nothing is said to fasten the guilt on those who move in a higher circle.
    The fact that slavery was introduced into the American colonies, while they were under the control of the British Crown, is a sufficient reason why Englishmen should feel
40 a lively interest in its abolition; and now that the genius of mechanical invention has brought the two countries so near together, and both having one language and one literature, the influence of British public opinion is very great on the people of the New World.
45   If the incidents set forth in the following pages should add anything new to the information already given to the Public through similar publications, and should thereby aid in

CONTINUE

bringing British influence to bear upon American slavery, the main object for which this work was written will have been
50 accomplished.

19

Brown indicates that the slave population in the United States

A) has grown larger over time.
B) has grown smaller over time.
C) has remained the same over time.
D) has never been accurately measured.

20

Which choice provides the best evidence for the answer to the previous question?

A) Lines 3-7 ("From . . . million")
B) Lines 7-9 ("In fifteen . . . confederacy")
C) Lines 17-19 ("Twenty-five . . . chains")
D) Lines 28-32 ("The great . . . fate")

21

According to Brown, the practice of owning slaves is

A) not protected by the Constitution.
B) common in both the North and the South.
C) not confined to a single social class.
D) disliked even by slaveowners themselves.

22

Which choice provides the best evidence for the answer to the previous question?

A) Lines 12-17 ("The entire . . . force")
B) Lines 19-23 ("In all . . . one")
C) Lines 32-36 ("It does . . . circle")
D) Lines 40-44 ("and now . . . World")

23

In criticizing slavery, Brown voices his hope that

A) British writers will do more to analyze the situation in America.
B) British politicians will urge Americans to change laws related to slaves.
C) Americans will follow the example set by the British.
D) Americans will reflect on their own country's founding.

24

Which choice provides the best evidence for the answer to the previous question?

A) Lines 1-3 ("More . . . Africa")
B) Lines 10-12 ("On every . . . impunity")
C) Lines 37-40 ("The fact . . . abolition")
D) Lines 45-50 ("If the . . . accomplished")

CONTINUE

ANSWERS: COMMAND OF EVIDENCE

1. D

2. A

3. C

4. B

5. B

6. C

7. A

8. C

9. D

10. B

11. C

12. C

13. B

14. D

15. B

16. C

17. B

18. C

19. A

20. A

21. C

22. B

23. C

24. D

CONTINUE

DOUBLE PASSAGES

Each PSAT Reading section will include one "double" or "paired" passage. For each of these, you will be given two closely-related passages on a single topic. It will be up to you to answer questions that ask about each passage individually, as well as questions that compare the two passages.

To master PSAT Double Passages, simply adapt the techniques that you already know and perform a modified Quick Read that takes BOTH passages into account.

Here is how to do a **Double Passage QR**:

1. Perform a standard QR of the first passage.
2. Once you have completed this read, write the **Main Idea and Tone (+/-)** of the passage as a whole right below the last line of the passage. You will need this information readily available for questions that COMPARE the two passages.
3. Repeat the process for the second passage, and make sure to write the **Main Idea and Tone** (+/-) at the end of this passage as well.
4. Use strong Margin Answers and Process of Elimination to complete the questions IN ORDER. Do not attempt to divide up the questions by passage, as this will only consume time.

shells increases), there are several periodic trends. The radius of the atom increases, while the elements' ionization energy and electronegativity both decrease. Electron affinity also generally decreases. Organizing the elements in this way provides us with a powerful insight into the underlying patterns of how matter works, and how we can manipulate it.

Passage 2
    The periodic table now has a new look. In January of 2016, scientists from Russia, Japan and the United States succeeded in discovering four new elements. All of these super-heavy new substances will be added to the seventh row or "period" of the famed table: students reading right-to-left across the period will now be greeted by elements 113, 115,

Location for Main Idea and Tone (+/-)

Make sure that you do not provide your own views or opinions on Double Passages under any circumstances. You may be accustomed to comparing two readings or two viewpoints from your schoolwork. However, PSAT Double Passage questions are **purely content and evidence based**. Keep this in mind for questions that ask about BOTH Passage 1 and Passage 2: these ask you to consider the **Main Ideas, Tones, and Line References** of the passages, NOT any other factors.

EXERCISES:

Practice Quick Read and Margin Answers for Double Passages on the following pages.

CONTINUE

NATURAL SCIENCE DOUBLE
Directions: Create Accurate Margin Answers

Questions 1-5 are based on the following passages.

These two passages are adapted from recent articles on the periodic table, which offers a means of classifying elements according to the properties of their atoms. The periodic table is widely used both by chemistry students and specialists in chemistry.

Passage 1

The periodic table is the foundational tool of chemistry, encompassing all the known elements. As scientists in the 18th and 19th centuries began discovering the basic elements, they
Line also searched for ways to categorize them and organize them
5 into coherent systems. It was in 1862 that a French chemist named Alexandre-Emile Béguyer de Chancourtois noticed that elements tend to show discernible patterns. These are the namesake periods of the periodic table, and they are one of the factors that elevate the periodic table above a random
10 arrangement. These, along with the vertical columns called "groups," give the periodic table its elegance and power.

In the periodic table, each horizontal row align elements with similar properties together. Each period is arranged according to the number of electron "shells" that its elements
15 share: according to modern quantum mechanics, each atom is surrounded by a certain number of possible orbits or "shells" that electrons can inhabit. Each shell also encompasses smaller sub-shells, and the shell number for each element in the periodic table also corresponds to that element's period
20 number. For example, both hydrogen and helium are in period 1, because they each have 1 electron shell. Radium, on the other hand, is in period 7, because it has 7 electron shells.

Interestingly, these electron shells have important implications for how elements behave. As the periods go
25 from 1 to 7 (and the corresponding number of electron shells increases), there are several periodic trends. The radius of the atom increases, while the elements' ionization energy and electronegativity both decrease. Electron affinity also generally decreases. Organizing the elements in this way provides us
30 with a powerful insight into the underlying patterns of how matter works, and how we can manipulate it.

Main Idea:

Passage 2

The periodic table now has a new look. In January of 2016, scientists from Russia, Japan and the United States succeeded in discovering four new elements. All of these
35 super-heavy new substances will be added to the seventh row or "period" of the famed table: students reading right-to-left across the period will now be greeted by elements 113, 115, 117, and 118, which all have yet to be named.

It should be noted, though, that "discovered" may not
40 be the best term for these four periodic table additions. According to an article in *The Guardian* that announced the revised periodic table, "the four new elements, all of which are synthetic, were discovered by slamming lighter-nuclei into each other and tracking the following decay of the
45 radioactive superheavy elements." These elements, unlike higher-period entries such as carbon and oxygen, cannot really be discovered anywhere on Earth (or at least anywhere outside a lab with a very good particle collider) and must be "produced" instead. Moreover, all of these new elements
50 are extremely short-lived and decompose rapidly into earlier-period substances even under controlled laboratory conditions.

Yet researchers are gearing up to find elements beyond 118. "There are a couple of laboratories that have already
55 taken shots at making elements 119 and 120 but with no evidence yet of success," notes Paul Karol, the chair of the international initiative that added the four elements to the periodic table. With any luck, future endeavors will continue to slot new entries a classification system that, over
60 a century and a half after its creation, continues to provide an invaluable framework for understanding the world of chemistry.

Main Idea:

1

Which statement best describes the relationship between Passage 1 and Passage 2?

Margin Answer

Who?

What?

Tone (+/-)?

CONTINUE

2

The tone of both Passage 1 and Passage 2 can best be described as

Margin Answer

Who?

What?

Tone (+/-)?

4

How does the use of quotation marks in Passage 2 differ from the use of quotation marks in Passage 1?

Margin Answer

Who?

What?

Tone (+/-)?

3

Which of the following individuals or groups of individuals is discussed in Passage 1 but not in Passage 2?

Margin Answer

Who?

What?

Tone (+/-)?

5

On the basis of the information provided in Passage 1, which of the four elements described in Passage 2 would have the largest atom radius?

Margin Answer

Who?

What?

Tone (+/-)?

CONTINUE

NATURAL SCIENCE CONTINUED
Directions: Answer the Questions Using Your Margin Answers

Questions 1-5 are based on the following passages.

These two passages are adapted from recent articles on the periodic table, which offers a means of classifying elements according to the properties of their atoms. The periodic table is widely used both by chemistry students and specialists in chemistry.

Passage 1

The periodic table is the foundational tool of chemistry, encompassing all the known elements. As scientists in the 18th and 19th centuries began discovering the basic elements, they
Line also searched for ways to categorize them and organize them
5 into coherent systems. It was in 1862 that a French chemist named Alexandre-Emile Béguyer de Chancourtois noticed that elements tend to show discernible patterns. These are the namesake periods of the periodic table, and they are one of the factors that elevate the periodic table above a random
10 arrangement. These, along with the vertical columns called "groups," give the periodic table its elegance and power.

In the periodic table, each horizontal row align elements with similar properties together. Each period is arranged according to the number of electron "shells" that its elements
15 share: according to modern quantum mechanics, each atom is surrounded by a certain number of possible orbits or "shells" that electrons can inhabit. Each shell also encompasses smaller sub-shells, and the shell number for each element in the periodic table also corresponds to that element's period
20 number. For example, both hydrogen and helium are in period 1, because they each have 1 electron shell. Radium, on the other hand, is in period 7, because it has 7 electron shells.

Interestingly, these electron shells have important implications for how elements behave. As the periods go
25 from 1 to 7 (and the corresponding number of electron shells increases), there are several periodic trends. The radius of the atom increases, while the elements' ionization energy and electronegativity both decrease. Electron affinity also generally decreases. Organizing the elements in this way provides us
30 with a powerful insight into the underlying patterns of how matter works, and how we can manipulate it.

Passage 2

The periodic table now has a new look. In January of 2016, scientists from Russia, Japan and the United States succeeded in discovering four new elements. All of these
35 super-heavy new substances will be added to the seventh row or "period" of the famed table: students reading right-to-left across the period will now be greeted by elements 113, 115, 117, and 118, which all have yet to be named.

It should be noted, though, that "discovered" may not
40 be the best term for these four periodic table additions. According to an article in *The Guardian* that announced the revised periodic table, "the four new elements, all of which are synthetic, were discovered by slamming lighter-nuclei into each other and tracking the following decay of the
45 radioactive superheavy elements." These elements, unlike higher-period entries such as carbon and oxygen, cannot really be discovered anywhere on Earth (or at least anywhere outside a lab with a very good particle collider) and must be "produced" instead. Moreover, all of these new elements
50 are extremely short-lived and decompose rapidly into earlier-period substances even under controlled laboratory conditions.

Yet researchers are gearing up to find elements beyond 118. "There are a couple of laboratories that have already
55 taken shots at making elements 119 and 120 but with no evidence yet of success," notes Paul Karol, the chair of the international initiative that added the four elements to the periodic table. With any luck, future endeavors will continue to slot new entries a classification system that, over
60 a century and a half after its creation, continues to provide an invaluable framework for understanding the world of chemistry.

1

Which statement best describes the relationship between Passage 1 and Passage 2?

A) Passage 1 presents a theory in chemistry; Passage 2 discusses a recent argument against that theory.

B) Passage 1 describes a classification system; Passage 2 records a recent development involving that system.

C) Passage 1 offers a historical narrative; Passage 2 presents a new perspective on the same narrative.

D) Passage 1 predicts that the periodic table will become usesless; Passage 2 demonstrates that the periodic table is still useful.

2

The tone of both Passage 1 and Passage 2 can best be described as

A) uncertain.
B) impassioned.
C) objective.
D) idealistic.

CONTINUE

3

Which of the following individuals or groups of individuals is discussed in Passage 1 but not in Passage 2?

A) A modern-day scientist
B) The creator of the periodic table
C) A few prominent science journalists
D) The students who use the periodic table

4

How does the use of quotation marks in Passage 2 differ from the use of quotation marks in Passage 1?

A) Passage 2 uses quotation marks for excerpts from specific sources; Passage 1 only uses quotation marks to emphasize scientific terms.
B) Passage 2 only uses quotation marks to define obscure concepts; Passage 1 uses quotation marks to quote historical documents.
C) Only Passage 1 uses quotation marks to express sarcasm and irony.
D) Only Passage 2 uses quotation marks to express sarcasm and irony.

5

On the basis of the information provided in Passage 1, which of the four elements described in Passage 2 would have the largest atom radius?

A) Element 113
B) Element 115
C) Element 117
D) Element 118

CONTINUE

HISTORY DOCUMENTS DOUBLE
Directions: Create Accurate Margin Answers

Questions 6-10 are based on the following passages.

Passage 1 is from *Up from Slavery: An Autobiography* (1901) by Booker T. Washington; Passage 2 is from "Of Mr. Booker T. Washington and Others," a section of *The Souls of Black Folk* (1903) by W.E.B. du Bois. Both passages discuss Washington's efforts to establish the Tuskegee Institute, a school designed to aid African Americans in the American South.

Passage 1
I confess that what I saw during my month of travel and investigation left me with a very heavy heart. The work to be done in order to lift these people up seemed almost beyond
Line accomplishing. I was only one person, and it seemed to me
5 that the little effort which I could put forth could go such a short distance toward bringing about results. I wondered if I could accomplish anything, and if it were worth while for me to try.

Of one thing I felt more strongly convinced than ever,
10 after spending this month in seeing the actual life of the coloured people, and that was that, in order to lift them up, something must be done more than merely to imitate New England education as it then existed. I saw more clearly than ever the wisdom of the system which General Armstrong had
15 inaugurated at Hampton. To take the children of such people as I had been among for a month, and each day give them a few hours of mere book education, I felt would be almost a waste of time.

After consultation with the citizens of Tuskegee, I set
20 July 4, 1881, as the day for the opening of the school in the little shanty and church which had been secured for its accommodation. The white people, as well as the coloured, were greatly interested in the starting of the new school, and the opening day was looked forward to with much earnest
25 discussion. There were not a few white people in the vicinity of Tuskegee who looked with some disfavour upon the project. They questioned its value to the coloured people, and had a fear that it might result in bringing about trouble between the races.

Main Idea:

Passage 2
30   To gain the sympathy and cooperation of the various elements comprising the white South was Mr. Washington's first task; and this, at the time Tuskegee was founded, seemed, for a black man, well-nigh impossible. And yet ten years later

it was done in the word spoken at Atlanta: "In all things
35 purely social we can be as separate as the five fingers, and yet one as the hand in all things essential to mutual progress." This "Atlanta Compromise" is by all odds the most notable thing in Mr. Washington's career. The South interpreted it in different ways: the radicals received it as
40 a complete surrender of the demand for civil and political equality; the conservatives, as a generously conceived working basis for mutual understanding. So both approved it, and to-day its author is certainly the most distinguished Southerner since Jefferson Davis, and the one with the
45 largest personal following.

Next to this achievement comes Mr. Washington's work in gaining place and consideration in the North. Others less shrewd and tactful had formerly essayed to sit on these two stools and had fallen between them; but as Mr. Washington
50 knew the heart of the South from birth and training, so by singular insight he intuitively grasped the spirit of the age which was dominating the North. And so thoroughly did he learn the speech and thought of triumphant commercialism, and the ideals of material prosperity, that the picture of a
55 lone black boy poring over a French grammar amid the weeds and dirt of a neglected home soon seemed to him the acme of absurdities.

Main Idea:

6

Which choice accurately describes the relationship between the two passages?

Margin Answer
Who?

What?

Tone (+/-)?

CONTINUE

7

Unlike Passage 1, Passage 2 considers

Margin Answer

Who?

What?

Tone (+/-)?

8

In explaining Washington's efforts to improve education, both passages describe

Margin Answer

Who?

What?

Tone (+/-)?

9

According to Passage 2, how did Washington respond to the "white people" (line 25) who encoutered his projects?

Margin Answer

Who?

What?

Tone (+/-)?

10

According to Passage 1, which of the following would Washington most likely see as one of the "absurdities" (line 57) described in Passage 2?

Margin Answer

Who?

What?

Tone (+/-)?

CONTINUE

HISTORY DOCUMENTS CONTINUED
Directions: Answer the Questions Using Your Margin Answers

Questions 6-10 are based on the following passages.

Passage 1 is from *Up from Slavery: An Autobiography* (1901) by Booker T. Washington; Passage 2 is from "Of Mr. Booker T. Washington and Others," a section of *The Souls of Black Folk* (1903) by W.E.B. du Bois. Both passages discuss Washington's efforts to establish the Tuskegee Institute, a school designed to aid African Americans in the American South.

Passage 1

I confess that what I saw during my month of travel and investigation left me with a very heavy heart. The work to be done in order to lift these people up seemed almost beyond
Line accomplishing. I was only one person, and it seemed to me
5 that the little effort which I could put forth could go such a short distance toward bringing about results. I wondered if I could accomplish anything, and if it were worth while for me to try.

Of one thing I felt more strongly convinced than ever,
10 after spending this month in seeing the actual life of the coloured people, and that was that, in order to lift them up, something must be done more than merely to imitate New England education as it then existed. I saw more clearly than ever the wisdom of the system which General Armstrong had
15 inaugurated at Hampton. To take the children of such people as I had been among for a month, and each day give them a few hours of mere book education, I felt would be almost a waste of time.

After consultation with the citizens of Tuskegee, I set
20 July 4, 1881, as the day for the opening of the school in the little shanty and church which had been secured for its accommodation. The white people, as well as the coloured, were greatly interested in the starting of the new school, and the opening day was looked forward to with much earnest
25 discussion. There were not a few white people in the vicinity of Tuskegee who looked with some disfavour upon the project. They questioned its value to the coloured people, and had a fear that it might result in bringing about trouble between the races.

Passage 2

30   To gain the sympathy and cooperation of the various elements comprising the white South was Mr. Washington's first task; and this, at the time Tuskegee was founded, seemed, for a black man, well-nigh impossible. And yet ten years later it was done in the word spoken at Atlanta: "In all things purely
35 social we can be as separate as the five fingers, and yet one as the hand in all things essential to mutual progress." This "Atlanta Compromise" is by all odds the most notable thing in Mr. Washington's career. The South interpreted it in different ways: the radicals received it as a complete
40 surrender of the demand for civil and political equality; the conservatives, as a generously conceived working basis for mutual understanding. So both approved it, and to-day its author is certainly the most distinguished Southerner since Jefferson Davis, and the one with the largest personal
45 following.

Next to this achievement comes Mr. Washington's work in gaining place and consideration in the North. Others less shrewd and tactful had formerly essayed to sit on these two stools and had fallen between them; but as Mr. Washington
50 knew the heart of the South from birth and training, so by singular insight he intuitively grasped the spirit of the age which was dominating the North. And so thoroughly did he learn the speech and thought of triumphant commercialism, and the ideals of material prosperity, that the picture of a
55 lone black boy poring over a French grammar amid the weeds and dirt of a neglected home soon seemed to him the acme of absurdities.

6

Which choice accurately describes the relationship between the two passages?

A) Passage 1 depicts Washington's early life, while Passage 2 recounts Washington's old age.

B) Passage 1 surveys a period of Washington's life, while Passage 2 explains Washington's principles.

C) Passage 1 argues that Washington's efforts were doomed to fail, while Passage 2 argues that those efforts were successful.

D) Passage 1 indicates that Washington was enormously influential, while Passage 2 downplays Washington's role.

7

Unlike Passage 1, Passage 2 considers

A) the phyical appearance of the Tuskegee Institute.

B) specific educators who influenced Washington.

C) those who criticized Washington's projects.

D) Washington's reputation in the North.

CONTINUE

8

In explaining Washington's efforts to improve education, both passages describe

A) considerable challenges that Washington faced.

B) the schools inspired by the Tuskegee Institute.

C) the importance of the "Atlanta Compromise."

D) the schools that Washington himself attended.

9

According to Passage 2, how did Washington respond to the "white people" (line 25) who encountered his projects?

A) He persisted in his efforts despite mounting hostility.

B) He adopted positions that enabled him to avoid conflict.

C) He eventually relocated his school to the North.

D) He abandoned projects in an unpredictable fashion.

10

According to Passage 1, which of the following would Washington most likely see as one of the "absurdities" (line 57) described in Passage 2?

A) The "work to be done" (lines 2-3)

B) A "few hours of mere book education" (lines 16-17)

C) The "consultation" (line 19)

D) An "earnest discussion" (lines 24-25) involving the school

CONTINUE

Questions 11-15 are based on the following passages.

Passage 1 is adapted from Charles Darwin, *The Expression of the Emotions in Man and Animals* (1899); Passage 2 is adapted from Patrick Kennedy, "Goodnight, Moon. Goodnight, Oxytocin: The Chemistry of Maternal Instincts" (2016).

Passage 1

Infants whilst young do not shed tears or weep, as is well known to nurses and medical men. This circumstance is not exclusively due to the lacrymal glands being as yet incapable
Line of secreting tears. I first noticed this fact from having
5 accidentally brushed with the cuff of my coat the open eye of one of my infants, when seventy-seven days old, causing this eye to water freely; and though the child screamed violently, the other eye remained dry, or was only slightly suffused with tears. A similar slight effusion occurred ten days previously
10 in both eyes during a screaming-fit. The tears did not run over the eyelids and roll down the cheeks of this child, whilst screaming badly, when 122 days old. This first happened 17 days later, at the age of 139 days. A few other children have been observed for me, and the period of free weeping appears
15 to be very variable. In one case, the eyes became slightly suffused at the age of only 20 days; in another, at 62 days. With two other children, the tears did NOT run down the face at the ages of 84 and 110 days; but in a third child they did run down at the age of 104 days. In one instance, as I was
20 positively assured, tears ran down at the unusually early age of 42 days. It would appear as if the lacrymal glands required some practice in the individual before they are easily excited into action, in somewhat the same manner as various inherited consensual movements and tastes require some exercise before
25 they are fixed and perfected. This is all the more likely with a habit like weeping, which must have been acquired since the period when man branched off from the common progenitor of the genus Homo and of the non-weeping anthropomorphous apes.
30 The fact of tears not being shed at a very early age from pain or any mental emotion is remarkable, as, later in life, no expression is more general or more strongly marked than weeping. When the habit [of weeping] has once been acquired by an infant, it expresses in the clearest manner suffering of
35 all kinds, both bodily pain and mental distress, even though accompanied by other emotions, such as fear or rage.

Passage 2

Whether you have children yourself, or just happened to get on an unlucky plane or two, you've probably been stuck at some point with the sound of a crying infant. Infamous
40 though that sound is, "crying" is a bit of a misnomer: infants don't actually shed tears for the first one to four months of life,

though after this term, tears become an essential part of an infant's response to pain and distress.

But before then, tears just don't seem to matter. It's all
45 about how crying sounds instead.

In a recent study published in the journal Nature, researchers from the New York University School of Medicine found that a baby's cries can have a direct, potent impact on maternal brain chemistry. The NYU team
50 monitored mother mice and found an intriguing link between caring instincts and the chemical oxytocin. The sharp sound of a crying infant (or at least infant mouse) causes oxytocin levels to spike, and this spike in turn causes the mother to address an infant's woes. In fact, as the NYU researchers
55 found, female mice who have simply received oxytocin injections will be highly attentive towards crying infants they have never seen before.

Of course, the research cannot be considered close to definitive until these oxytocin-related tendencies are
60 observed in humans, to say nothing of other mammals. Yet modern science is providing a confirmation of a survival mechanism that infants exhibit every day. Both developmentally and in real time, we hear infants' cries before we see their tears.

11

Which of the following is present in Passage 1 but not in Passage 2?

A) A statistical measurement related to when an infant begins to cry

B) An account of a single event witnessed by the author

C) Analysis of a commonly-used term

D) References to recent research

12

An assumption that is present in both passages is the idea that

A) crying can serve as an expression of either happiness or sadness.

B) crying is normally a response to unpleasant conditions.

C) people become ashamed to cry as they mature.

D) people find crying infants unpleasant.

CONTINUE

13

Which statement best summarizes an important difference between the discussions of crying in the two passages?

A) Only Passage 2 indicates that crying is a learned or acquired behavior.

B) Only Passage 2 records case-by-case examples of how crying functions.

C) Only Passage 2 suggests a connection between tears and screaming.

D) Only Passage 2 discusses the connection between crying and maternal instincts.

14

The research projects described in the two passages differ in that the research in Passage 1

A) involved experiments in chemistry, while the research in Passage 2 involved experiments in psychology.

B) only involved infants, while the research in Passage 2 also involved young children.

C) involved human subjects, while the research in Passage 2 involved animals.

D) imvolved a controversial approach, while the research in Passage 2 involved a famous and popular method.

15

Together, both passages indicate that infants typically begin to cry

A) within the first week of life.

B) within the first month of life.

C) within the first year of life.

D) only after the first year of life.

Questions 16-20 are based on the following passages.

Passage 1 is taken from a series of 1788 remarks to the New York Convention by Alexander Hamilton. Passage 2 is taken from the 1796 "Farewell Address" delivered by George Washington.

Passage 1

We all in equal sincerity profess to be anxious for the establishment of a republican government on a safe and solid basis. It is the object of the wishes of every honest
Line man in the United States, and I presume that I shall not be
5 disbelieved when I declare that it is an object of all others the nearest and most dear to my own heart. The means of accomplishing this great purpose become the most important study which can interest mankind. It is our duty to examine all those means with peculiar attention and to choose the best
10 and most effectual. It is our duty to draw from nature, from reason, from examples, the best principles of policy, and to pursue and apply them in the formation of our government. We should contemplate and compare the systems which in this examination come under our view; distinguish with a careful
15 eye the defects and excellencies of each, and, discarding the former, incorporate the latter, as far as circumstances will admit, into our Constitution. If we pursue a different course and neglect this duty we shall probably disappoint the expectations of our country and of the world.
20   Gentlemen indulge too many unreasonable apprehensions of danger to the State governments; they seem to suppose that the moment you put men into a national council, they become corrupt and tyrannical and lose all their affection for their fellow citizens. But can we imagine that the Senators will
25 ever be so insensible of their own advantage as to sacrifice the genuine interest of their constituents? The State governments are essentially necessary to the form and spirit of the general system. As long, therefore, as Congress has a full conviction of this necessity, they must even upon principles purely national,
30 have as firm an attachment to the one as to the other. This conviction can never leave them, unless they become madmen. While the Constitution continues to be read and its principle known the States must by every rational man be considered as essential, component parts of the Union; and therefore the idea
35 of sacrificing the former to the latter is wholly inadmissible.

Passage 2

While, then, every part of our country thus feels an immediate and particular interest in union, all the parts combined cannot fail to find in the united mass of means and efforts greater strength, greater resource, proportionably
40 greater security from external danger, a less frequent interruption of their peace by foreign nations; and, what is of inestimable value, they must derive from union an exemption

CONTINUE

from those broils and wars between themselves, which so frequently afflict neighboring countries not tied together by
45 the same governments, which their own rival ships alone would be sufficient to produce, but which opposite foreign alliances, attachments, and intrigues would stimulate and embitter. Hence, likewise, they will avoid the necessity of those overgrown military establishments which, under any
50 form of government, are inauspicious to liberty, and which are to be regarded as particularly hostile to republican liberty. In this sense it is that your union ought to be considered as a main prop of your liberty, and that the love of the one ought to endear to you the preservation of the
55 other.

These considerations speak a persuasive language to every reflecting and virtuous mind, and exhibit the continuance of the Union as a primary object of patriotic desire. Is there a doubt whether a common government can embrace so large a sphere? Let experience solve it. To listen
60 to mere speculation in such a case were criminal. We are authorized to hope that a proper organization of the whole with the auxiliary agency of governments for the respective subdivisions, will afford a happy issue to the experiment. It is well worth a fair and full experiment. With such powerful
65 and obvious motives to union, affecting all parts of our country, while experience shall not have demonstrated its impracticability, there will always be reason to distrust the patriotism of those who in any quarter may endeavor to weaken its bands.

16

Both pasages are premised on the idea that a strong and centralized "republican government" or "Union" is

A) attractive but impractical.

B) currently unpopular.

C) fundamentally beneficial.

D) potentially tyrannical.

17

An important difference between the two passages is that

A) Passage 1 describes the American government as a work in progress, while Passage 2 describes the same government as accepted and admired.

B) Passage 1 criticizes the apparent weaknesses of the American government, while Passage 2 argues that these weaknesses can be corrected.

C) Passage 1 urges a radical departure from tradition, while Passage 2 supports a return to earlier customs.

D) Passage 1 addresses state and local issues at length, while Passage 2 dismisses such issues as unimportant.

18

What point does the author of Passage 2 make about "the world" (line 19) beyond America?

A) It would respond approvingly to the creation of a strong American democracy.

B) It offers a series of useful models of government that Americans should imitate.

C) It is going through a period of chaos that has no historical precedent.

D) It contains hostile nations that would threaten a weak Union.

19

A rhetorical strategy that is used by the authors of both passages is

A) personal anecdote.

B) collective voice.

C) appeal to compassion.

D) obscure terminology.

20

Which benefit of a strong national government is discussed in Passage 2 but not at all in Passage 1?

A) Strengthening of state and local loyalties

B) The improvement of overland transportation

C) Relatively low military commitments

D) Improvements in education and manufacturing

CONTINUE

ANSWERS ON THE NEXT PAGE

ANSWERS: DOUBLE PASSAGES

1. B	11. B
2. C	12. B
3. B	13. D
4. A	14. C
5. D	15. C
6. B	16. C
7. D	17. A
8. A	18. D
9. B	19. B
10. B	20. C

PSAT
Writing & Language

GRAMMAR FUNDAMENTALS: PART 1
SUBJECT–VERB AGREEMENT

SUBJECT: The noun or pronoun that indicates what the sentence is about

VERB: The action of the noun or pronoun

REMEMBER: Subject/verb agreement is commonly tested by using: is/are, was/were, and has/have. If these words are underlined, check for subject/verb agreement.

AGREEMENT: All **subjects** and <u>verbs</u> must agree in number.

WHEN YOU SEE a verb underlined, you must ask yourself:

"Who (or what) is doing the verb, and do both subject and verb agree in number?"

SINGULAR	PLURAL
The **girl** <u>jumps</u>.	The **girls** <u>jump</u>.
He <u>is</u> happy.	**They** <u>are</u> happy.

LESSON 1.1

PREPOSITION: Any word (in, at, of, for, to, over, among, between, under…) that indicates a relationship between a noun and another part of the sentence

PREPOSITIONAL PHRASE: Any phrase (in the house, at the mall, to the store, for a jog, under the table…) that begins with a preposition and ends before the verb

Eliminate all **PREPOSITIONAL PHRASES.** The subject will never be in a prepositional phrase. Prepositional phrases contain extra details that often mislead the reader. **CROSSING THEM OUT** makes it easier to identify the subject.

EXAMPLE

The cars in the lot are clean.

The cars ~~in the lot~~ are clean. → Cross out "in the lot"

The **cars are** clean. ✓

One of the girls is visiting.

One ~~of the girls~~ is visiting. → Cross out "of the girls"

One is visiting. ✓

LESSON 1.2 **INTERRUPTER:** Any detail positioned between two commas

Eliminate all **INTERRUPTERS.** The subject will never be in an interrupter. Interrupters contain extra details that often mislead the reader. **CROSSING THEM OUT** makes it easier to identify the subject.

CONTINUE

EXAMPLE

Patrick, *in addition to Tom and Mark,* is coming to the reception.

Patrick, ~~in addition to Tom and Mark,~~ is coming to the reception. → Cross out "in addition to Tom and Mark,"

Patrick is coming to the reception. ✓

LESSON 1.3   **TRICKY SINGULAR:** A singular word that sounds plural or is commonly misused as a plural

Look out for TRICKY SINGULARS (neither, either, everyone, everybody, someone, somebody, anybody, anything, each, anyone, no one, everything, little, and much).

EXAMPLE

Neither of the twins *is* sick.

Neither ~~of the twins~~ *is* sick. → Cross out "of the twins"

Neither is sick. ✓

Either of the rooms at the hotel *is* available.

Either ~~of the rooms at the hotel~~ *is* available. → Cross out "of the rooms at the hotel"

Either is available. ✓

LESSON 1.4   **TRICKY PLURAL:** A plural word that sounds singular or is commonly misused as a singular

Look out for TRICKY PLURALS (Plural/Singular: data/datum, phenomena/phenomenon, media/medium, and criteria/criterion).

EXAMPLE

The *data* from the computer *are* on my disc.

The *data* ~~from the computer~~ *are* on my disc. → Cross out "from the computer"

The **data are** on my disc. ✓

The *criteria* for the assigned essay *are* very complex.

The *criteria* ~~for the assigned essay~~ *are* very complex. → Cross out "for the assigned essay"

The **criteria are** very complex. ✓

CONTINUE

LESSON 1.5	**NEITHER/NOR AND EITHER/OR:** Two subjects separated by a standard phrase

Look out for NEITHER/NOR and EITHER/OR phrases. Although NEITHER and EITHER are singular, when grouped with NOR/OR, the word that ends the phrase determines the verb.

FORMULA:

Either A or B → B determines the verb   Neither A nor B → B determines the verb

EXAMPLE

Either John or *Mary is* right. ✓   Neither John nor *the Parkers are* wrong. ✓

Sometimes the "B Phrase" includes a prepositional phrase. Apply the technique:

Either the Smiths or *one of the Johnsons was* expected to bring the salad.
Either the Smiths or *one of the Johnsons was* expected to bring the salad. → Cross out "of the Johnsons"
Either the Smiths or *one was* expected to bring the salad. ✓

LESSON 1.6	**INVERTED SENTENCE:** The verb comes before the subject in a sentence

Look out for anything INVERTED (VERB/SUBJECT). Sentences that start with the word "there" and compound sentences that have more than one subject/verb combination tend to be inverted.

HOW TO CHECK THE VERB:
Simply un-invert (flip) the subject and verb.

EXAMPLE

There is a **cat** in the house.

FLIPPED: *cat is* ✓

During the day, there is **ten cats** in the garage.

FLIPPED: *ten cats is* ✗

ten cats are ✓

When subject nouns are LINKED with an "AND," the subject is PLURAL.

✓ The house **and** the car *were* ruined by the storm.

✓ John **and** Mary *eat* chocolate all day.

✓ The dog **and** the cat *are* in trouble for eating the cake on the counter.

CONTINUE ➡

PARALLELISM

Making a sentence parallel simply involves making the sentence balanced. Grammar is based on parallel structure.

THE LAWS OF PARALLELISM demand that words or phrases be in the same form of speech (adjectives, verbs, nouns) and use the same structure. Often, balancing a phrase requires the removal of extraneous words.

WHEN YOU SEE lists, comparisons, standard phrases, pronouns, and conjunctions, CHECK for parallelism.

comparisons:	more than, as much as, is, like
standard phrases:	not only/but also, so/that, either/or, neither/nor, prefer/to
pronouns:	one, you
conjunctions:	and, but

LESSON 1.7   **BALANCING LISTS**

EXAMPLE

She went swimming, running, and danced all night. ✗

She went swimming, running, and *dancing* all night. ✓

This is a call for all professors, editors, and people who collaborate. ✗

This is a call for all professors, editors, and *collaborators*. ✓

LESSON 1.8   **BALANCING COMPARISONS**

EXAMPLE

Jefferson actually liked to participate in the science league more than he liked playing basketball. ✗

Jefferson actually liked *participating* in the science league more than he liked *playing* basketball. ✓

Jefferson actually liked *to participate* in the science league more than he liked *to play* basketball. ✓

CONTINUE ➡

LESSON 1.9	BALANCING TWO SIDES OF A STANDARD PHRASE
EXAMPLE	

Judging by the look on his face, Paul is either nervous or filled with excitement. ✗

Judging by the look on his face, Paul is either nervous or **excited**. ✓

I prefer eating salty foods to sweet foods. ✗

I prefer eating salty foods to **eating** sweet foods. ✓

LESSON 1.10	BALANCING PRONOUNS
EXAMPLE	

One should always do what you want. ✗

One should always do what **one** wants. ✓

You should always do what **you** want. ✓

LESSON 1.11	BALANCING TWO SIDES OF A CONJUNCTION
EXAMPLE	

To prepare for the party, we should set the table and making the pasta. ✗

To prepare for the party, we should set the table and **make** the pasta. ✓

John's book is informative but full of entertainment. ✗

John's book is informative but **entertaining**. ✓

As mentioned before, sometimes balancing a sentence merely requires the OMISSION of extraneous words.

✗   The students were happy to learn the lesson, finish the homework, and *they could* enjoy the weekend.

✓   The students were happy to learn the lesson, finish the homework, and enjoy the weekend.

CONTINUE ➡

COMPARISON

Comparison problems are often tricky to catch because the reader infers the correct comparison. Checking for comparison requires the use of visual parallelism. Be aware of what is being compared in the sentence. These comparisons must be LOGICAL.

WHEN YOU SEE these words in a sentence, check for the problems described in the following lessons.

COMPARISONS	as, than, like, to, between, among
"A" PHRASE	a student, a player, a musician
WORDS THAT DESCRIBE QUANTITY	fewer/ less, number/ amount, many/ much

---

LESSON 1.12   **ILLOGICAL COMPARISONS**

EXAMPLE   In my opinion, there is no story more intriguing than Othello. ✗

EXPLANATION   The word *than* signals that there is a comparison in this sentence. This is not a logical comparison because we must compare a "story" to a "story."

In my opinion, there is no **story** more intriguing than **the story of** Othello. ✓

EXAMPLE   Her inclination to eat a cupcake is much stronger than to go for a jog. ✗

EXPLANATION   This sentence is wrong because her "inclination [to eat a cupcake]" is being compared to "to go for a jog." You must compare *inclination* and *inclination*, not *inclination* and *to go for a jog*.

Her **inclination** to eat a cupcake is much stronger than her **inclination** to go for a jog. ✓

EXAMPLE   Napoleon Bonaparte is more famous than any leader in French history. ✗

EXPLANATION   This sentence is wrong because Napoleon Bonaparte was a leader himself, and he could not have been more famous than himself. We must compare him to *other* leaders.

Napoleon Bonaparte is more famous than any **other** leader in French history. ✓

When checking for ILLOGICAL COMPARISON, think of parallelism: *pineapples to apples*, **NOT** *pineapples to eating apples*!

77

CONTINUE ➡

LESSON 1.13   NUMBER AGREEMENT/"A" PHRASE

Things that you compare have to agree in *number*. Both are either *singular* or *plural*.

EXAMPLE   Though their parents wished otherwise, they were both struggling to be a musician. ✗

EXPLANATION   Because the word "musician" is referring to "they," we must use *musicians*.

Though their parents wished otherwise, **they** were both struggling to be **musicians**. ✓

EXAMPLE   Both Kristi and Kim are an administrator in the office. ✗

EXPLANATION   Because "administrator" is referring to "Kristi and Kim," we must use *administrators*.

Both **Kristi and Kim** are **administrators** in the office. ✓

LESSON 1.14   COUNTABLE/NOT COUNTABLE

DESCRIBES THINGS THAT ARE **COUNTABLE** (hot dogs, dollars, kisses)	DESCRIBES THINGS THAT ARE **NOT COUNTABLE** (food, money, love)
fewer / number / many	**less / amount / much**

EXAMPLE   There are much more architectural decorations on this skyscraper than I had expected. ✗

EXPLANATION   This sentence is wrong because *decorations* can be counted. We must use *many*.

There are **many** more architectural **decorations** on this skyscraper than I had expected. ✓

EXAMPLE   No one could guess the number of candy in the jar. ✗

EXPLANATION   This sentence is wrong because *candy* cannot be counted. We must use *amount*.

No one could guess the **amount** of **candy** in the jar. ✓

CONTINUE

LESSON 1.15   COMPARING EXACTLY TWO VS. THREE OR MORE

COMPARING ONLY TWO THINGS	COMPARING THREE OR MORE THINGS
between	among
more	most
-er ending words: better, faster, stronger	-est ending words: best, fastest, strongest

EXAMPLE   Of the dozens of kids in the club, Sarah was the more popular. ✗

EXPLANATION   Because there are dozens of kids (3 or more), we must use *most*.

Of the dozens of kids in the club, Sarah was the **most** popular. ✓

EXAMPLE   There was no animosity between Joe, Chris, and Patrick. ✗

EXPLANATION   Because there are three people, we must use *among*.

There was no animosity **among** Joe, Chris, and Patrick. ✓

When you see BETWEEN or AMONG, remember:

BETWEEN	AMONG
Compares exactly two things Always use "and" Always use "me", not "I"	Compares three things or more Always use "and" Always use "me", not "I"
EXAMPLE	**EXAMPLE**
The decision is between John or *I*. ✗	Among Mary, Rhonda or *I*, Mary is the prettiest. ✗
The decision is between John **and me**. ✓	Among Mary, Rhonda **and me**, Mary is the prettiest. ✓

CONTINUE

EXERCISES: GRAMMAR FUNDAMENTALS 1

DIRECTIONS: Circle the error in the sentence, and write the error type and the correct phrasing on the lines below.

1) He informed his father that there was raccoons and opossums living in the garage.

ERROR TYPE: _____ CORRECT PHRASING: _____

2) Joseph Ducreux, who painted portraits in the eighteenth century, are now the subject of a popular Internet meme.

ERROR TYPE: _____ CORRECT PHRASING: _____

3) Each of the girls are making a batch of cupcakes for Mrs. Murchison's 68th birthday.

ERROR TYPE: _____ CORRECT PHRASING: _____

4) In the novels of Ivy Comtpon Burnett, characters tell jokes, make strange remarks, and they sometimes are bickering.

ERROR TYPE: _____ CORRECT PHRASING: _____

5) Even the boss had no way of estimating the amount of employees in such a huge company.

ERROR TYPE: _____ CORRECT PHRASING: _____

6) Because there was no way to resolve the debate among my aunt and me, we simply dropped the subject.

ERROR TYPE: _____ CORRECT PHRASING: _____

7) Neither Mary nor her teacher know much about the basic principles of Buddhism.

ERROR TYPE: _____ CORRECT PHRASING: _____

8) Both the great gray whale and the humpbacked whale is species that can be found in this area of the ocean.

ERROR TYPE: _____ CORRECT PHRASING: _____

9) Steve Jobs was much more interested in leaving behind a reputation for genius than to make money.

ERROR TYPE: _____ CORRECT PHRASING: _____

10) Ultimately, there was fewer money in Bertram's bank account than anybody could have guessed.

ERROR TYPE: _____ CORRECT PHRASING: _____

CONTINUE ➡

Questions 1-10 are based on the following passage.

Geoffrey Chaucer: Inventing the English Language

Geoffrey Chaucer was born in the fourteenth century around 1343, we think: [1] there are no documents pertaining to his earliest years. However, we do know that his family members, who imported wine and resided in Cordwainers Street in London, [2] was fairly well off. Chaucer began his working life as a page in the Royal courts. His career advanced steadily; he became an ambassador for King Edward III and later for Richard II on diplomatic missions to Ireland, Flanders, France, and Italy. He married, lived in the City of London, and [3] to hold various government positions, including Controller of Customs in the Port of London and Clerk of the King's Works. He died in 1400 and was buried in Westminster Abbey, a relatively wealthy civil servant, and an ingenious poet.

During his hectic lifetime, Chaucer wrote not only a series of short poems, but also several much longer poems that can almost be regarded as stories in verse. [4] Between them was his greatest work, *The Canterbury Tales*. One might wonder when he found the time.

However, the era in which Chaucer wrote his poems was exactly the right era. Why? They were all in English, and English, until the end of the fourteenth century, [5] were almost exclusively a spoken language: if [6] you could write, then one belonged to the privileged Church and Government elites. The languages used by these prestigious groups, at least in writing,

1
A) NO CHANGE
B) there is
C) them being
D) there

2
A) NO CHANGE
B) were
C) he was
D) they were

3
A) NO CHANGE
B) holding various
C) variously holding
D) held various

4
A) NO CHANGE
B) Between they
C) Among them
D) Among they

5
A) NO CHANGE
B) was almost
C) there were almost
D) there was almost

6
A) NO CHANGE
B) one could write, then you belonged
C) you could write, then you belonged
D) DELETE the underlined portion.

CONTINUE

[7] was Latin and French. English was spoken by isolated peasants and uneducated artisans, who really did not count where matters of high culture and government interest were concerned.

Despite the views of the Norman nobility, English was rapidly developing and departing from its origins in Anglo Saxon. Speech is a living form of communication, and just as other living things adapt and [8] becomes a more advanced organism according to need and situation, forms of speech also evolve. English is the most developed spoken language in the world because it has constantly simplified its construction. Such changes were not the results of any formal decision, but the results of the essential realization that we need to communicate as directly and vividly as possible. Only [9] a small amount of languages ever achieve such sophistication.

Chaucer was the first English poet to really understand and report the essential strength, directness, and variety of English. He gloried in both [10] the subtlety and the directness of the language, and grasped the freedom it allowed its speakers and its audience.

7

A) NO CHANGE
B) were
C) to be
D) being

8

A) NO CHANGE
B) becomes more advanced organisms
C) become a more advanced organism
D) become more advanced organisms

9

A) NO CHANGE
B) a small number
C) a less amount
D) a less number

10

A) NO CHANGE
B) when it is subtle
C) to be subtle
D) subtly

CONTINUE

ANSWERS ON THE NEXT PAGE

ANSWERS: GRAMMAR 1

EXERCISES:

1) He informed his father that there **were** raccoons and opossums living in the garage. (Subject-Verb)

2) Joseph Ducreux, who painted portraits in the eighteenth century, **is** now the subject of a popular Internet meme. (Subject-Verb)

3) Each of the girls **is** making a batch of cupcakes for Mrs. Murchison's 68th birthday. (Subject-Verb, tricky singular)

4) In the novels of Ivy Comtpon Burnett, characters tell jokes, make strange remarks, and **sometimes bicker**. (Parallelism)

5) Even the boss had no way of estimating the **number** of employees in such a huge company. (Comparison)

6) Because there was no way to resolve the debate **between** my aunt and me, we simply dropped the subject. (Comparison)

7) Neither Mary nor her teacher **knows** much about the basic principles of Buddhism. (Subject-Verb, tricky singular)

8) Both the great gray whale and the humpbacked whale **are** species that can be found in this area of the ocean. (Subject-Verb)

9) Steve Jobs was much more interested in leaving behind a reputation for genius than **in making money**. (Parallelism)

10) Ultimately, there was **less** money in Bertram's bank account than anybody could have guessed. (Comparison)

PASSAGE:

1) A	6) C
2) B	7) B
3) D	8) D
4) C	9) B
5) B	10) A

CONTINUE

GRAMMAR FUNDAMENTALS: PART 2

SUBJECT–PRONOUN AGREEMENT

PRONOUN: The word that takes the place of the noun

EXAMPLES: I, you, we, us, our, me, he, she, him, her, they, their, it, its

FORMULA: *Janet* is tired because *she* studied for the SAT all day.

WHEN YOU SEE a PRONOUN underlined, you must ask yourself:

"Who (or what) is this pronoun referring to and do both (subject and pronoun) agree in number?"

SINGULAR	PLURAL
He/ She, It	They
Her/ Him, It	Them
His/ Her, Its	Their

LESSON 2.1   **DON'T MISTAKE SINGULAR SUBJECTS FOR PLURAL SUBJECTS.**

EXAMPLE

SUBJECT	PRONOUN
The University of Massachusetts (one place) = the radio station =	IT
people (more than one person) = the doctors = students =	THEY
each of the girls (Tricky Singular) =	SHE
everybody (Tricky Singular) =	HE OR SHE

LESSON 2.2   **JUST LIKE SUBJECT/VERB AGREEMENT, BE AWARE OF TRICKY SINGULARS.**

TRICKY SINGULARS
EITHER, NEITHER, EVERYONE, EVERYBODY, SOMEONE,   SOMEBODY, ANYBODY, ANYTHING, EACH, ANYONE, NO ONE,   EVERYTHING, LITTLE, MUCH

EXAMPLE   *Everyone* should brush *their* teeth three times a day. ✗

EXPLANATION   *Everyone* is a tricky singular.

Everyone should brush **his** or **her** teeth three times a day. ✓

85

CONTINUE ➡

Do NOT cross out prepositional phrases. The pronoun's subject may be in the prepositional phrase.

The quality of the *multivitamins* depends entirely on *its* ingredients. ✗

What has the ingredients? The quality or the multivitamins?

The quality of the ***multivitamins*** depends entirely on ***their*** ingredients. ✓

LESSON 2.3   **BE AWARE OF TRICKY PRONOUNS.**

What, where, when, why, who, and *how* are all interrogative pronouns that can begin a question or refer to an unknown. BUT, sometimes they refer directly to the subject.

USE **WHAT** ONLY TO REFER TO A THING.

EXAMPLE	The quality of the product is **what's** important. ✓
EXPLANATION	*What* refers to quality. Quality is important.

USE **WHERE** ONLY TO REFER TO A PLACE.

EXAMPLE	Seattle is **where** I got engaged. ✓
EXPLANATION	*Where* refers to Seattle. I got engaged in Seattle.

USE **IN WHICH** IF THE "WHERE" IS NOT LITERAL.

EXAMPLE	This is a story where the hero dies. ✗
	This is a story **in which** the hero dies. ✓
EXAMPLE	I like movies where the guy gets the girl. ✗
	I like movies **in which** the guy gets the girl. ✓

USE **WHEN** ONLY TO REFER TO A TIME.

EXAMPLE	2014 is **when** the incident happened. ✓
EXPLANATION	*When* refers to 2014. The incident happened in 2014.

CONTINUE ➤

USE **WHY** ONLY TO REFER TO A REASON.

EXAMPLE	Please tell me *why* you refuse to wear a helmet. ✓
EXPLANATION	*Why* refers to the reason you refuse to wear a helmet. (Please tell me the *reason* you refuse to wear a helmet.)

USE **WHO** TO REFER TO A PERSON. (Do not use THAT when referring to a person.)

EXAMPLE	The students that ate got sick. ✗
	The students *who* ate got sick. ✓

USE **HOW** ONLY TO REFER TO AN EXPLANATION.

EXAMPLE	Studying hard is *how* I aced my SAT. ✓
EXPLANATION	*How* refers to studying hard. (I aced my SAT by studying hard.)

LESSON 2.4	**LOOK OUT FOR AMBIGUOUS PRONOUNS.**

If the pronoun in the sentence can refer to more than one thing, it is ambiguous. The connection between the subject and the pronoun should be clear.

EXAMPLE	Austin told Joe that *he* had some spinach in his teeth. ✗
EXPLANATION	Who "had spinach in his teeth?" Austin or Joe?

EXAMPLE	Deep-sea exploration has occurred, but *they* still haven't found any new species. ✗
EXPLANATION	Who "haven't found any new species?"

CONTINUE ➡

PRONOUN CASE

WHEN YOU SEE a PRONOUN you must ask yourself:

Similar to SUBJECT/PRONOUN, **PRONOUN CASE** focuses on the correct use of a pronoun in relation to the rest of the sentence. Below are general instances in which the SAT will test PRONOUN CASE.

"Is this pronoun in the proper form?"

LESSON 2.5   **PEOPLE OR GROUPS**

You will see a pronoun combined with ANOTHER PRONOUN, PERSON, or GROUP by a conjunction.

EXAMPLE

The sports team and he...	Sally and they...

Read the following sentence:

Every Sunday at the playground, the other children and her pretended to be valiant knights.

Did you see the problem? If not, here is what you should do when you see a pronoun used in combination with another person or group:

STOP and PLACE YOUR FINGER over the other person or group and REREAD the sentence.

Every Sunday at the playground, t̶h̶e̶ ̶o̶t̶h̶e̶r̶ ̶c̶h̶i̶l̶d̶r̶e̶n̶ ̶a̶n̶d̶ her pretended to be valiant knights.

her pretended ✗	*she* pretended ✓

Every Sunday at the playground, the other children and ***she*** pretended to be valiant knights. ✓

EXAMPLE

The school presented the award to Andre and he.

The school presented the award to A̶n̶d̶r̶e̶ ̶a̶n̶d̶ he.

presented the award to he ✗

presented the award to *him* ✓

The school presented the award to Andre and ***him***. ✓

CONTINUE ➡

EXAMPLE

Us and the other parents went to the beach.

Us ~~and the other parents~~ went to the beach.

Us went ✗

We went ✓

We and the other parents went to the beach. ✓

LESSON 2.6   **THAN OR AS**

Pronoun Case may also appear in comparisons usually indicated by the words THAN or AS:

No one did better than <u>her</u>.	No one has scored as many touchdowns as <u>him</u>.

In both sentences, there is an implied verb after the pronoun. Here is what you should do: INSERT the implied verb to REVEAL the correct pronoun.

No one did better than her (did).

her did ✗

she did ✓

No one did better than *she*. ✓

No one has scored as many touchdowns as him (scored).

him scored ✗

he scored ✓

No one has scored as many touchdowns as *he*. ✓

EXAMPLE

Betty is faster than me.
Betty is faster than me (am).

me am ✗

I am ✓

Betty is faster than *I*. ✓

Chris is as noisy as her.
Chris is as noisy as her (is).

her is ✗

she is ✓

Chris is as noisy as *she*. ✓

LESSON 2.7   **REFLEXIVE PRONOUNS**

Another way that you will see PRONOUN CASE is in REFLEXIVE PRONOUNS such as *himself, herself, themselves, ourselves,* and *myself*.

To celebrate my graduation, I scheduled a party <u>for me</u> and the other graduates.

I scheduled a party for me ✗

I scheduled a party for *myself* ✓

To celebrate my graduation, I scheduled a party for *myself* and the other graduates. ✓

CONTINUE ➡

LESSON 2.8   **BETWEEN / AMONG**

Do you recall the tip from comparison about "BETWEEN" and "AMONG"? Always use "me" not "I". The same rule applies in these cases. When you see the words *between* and *among* use the **OBJECTIVE** form of the pronoun. See table below.

SUBJECTIVE	OBJECTIVE
I	Me
He	Him
She	Her
We	Us

EXAMPLE

Between Mary and I ✗	Between Mary and *me* ✓

Among Stacy, Richard, and she ✗	Among Stacy, Richard, and her ✓

DANGLING MODIFIER

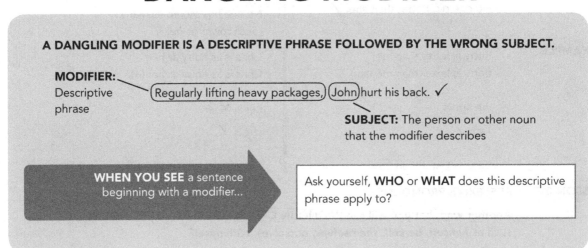

A DANGLING MODIFIER IS A DESCRIPTIVE PHRASE FOLLOWED BY THE WRONG SUBJECT.

MODIFIER:
Descriptive phrase

Regularly lifting heavy packages, John hurt his back. ✓

SUBJECT: The person or other noun that the modifier describes

WHEN YOU SEE a sentence beginning with a modifier...

Ask yourself, **WHO** or **WHAT** does this descriptive phrase apply to?

CONTINUE ➡

LESSON 2.9 **PLACING THE SUBJECT AFTER THE MODIFIER (THUS AFTER THE COMMA)**

EXAMPLE Known to be poisonous, the unsuspecting tourist was bitten by the rattlesnake. ✘

EXPLANATION *Who* is known to be poisonous—the tourist, or the rattlesnake?

Known to be poisonous, the rattlesnake bit the unsuspecting tourist. ✓

EXAMPLE Walking down the street, Jane saw a shooting star. ✓

EXPLANATION If JANE is walking down the street, then JANE must come right after the comma.

LESSON 2.10 **THE APOSTROPHE TRAP**

BE CAREFUL not to pick a subject that is a possessive noun, or a subject with an apostrophe (Picasso's paintings; Carol's legs). The apostrophe means ownership, so the word following it cannot be separated from the person. They must remain together unless the apostrophe is removed.

EXAMPLE Walking down the street, Jane's head was almost cut off by a shooting star. ✘

EXPLANATION *Jane's head* was not walking down the street.

EXCEPTION Pounding like a hammer, Jane's headache would not stop. ✓

EXPLANATION *Jane's headache* was pounding like a hammer, so there is no dangling modifier.

LESSON 2.11 **DANGLING MODIFIERS AT THE END OF THE SENTENCE**

EXAMPLE Raj swallowed his last bite of watermelon parking the truck. ✘

EXPLANATION *His last bite of watermelon* was not parking the truck.

Parking the truck, Raj swallowed his last bite of watermelon. ✓

CONTINUE

EXERCISES: GRAMMAR FUNDAMENTALS 2

DIRECTIONS: Circle the error in the sentence, and write the error type and the correct phrasing on the lines below.

1) The casual conversation between he and his teammates quickly turned into a heated dispute.

ERROR TYPE: _____ CORRECT PHRASING: _____

2) All the survivors of the plane crash found themselves in circumstances where cooperation was essential.

ERROR TYPE: _____ CORRECT PHRASING: _____

3) Rachel knows that her brother is a better pianist than her, but she still continues to practice the instrument.

ERROR TYPE: _____ CORRECT PHRASING: _____

4) New environmental hazards have arisen in the past fifteen years, but people are not sure what to do about it.

ERROR TYPE: _____ CORRECT PHRASING: _____

5) My optometrist is someone who, in every situation, thinks that they are always right.

ERROR TYPE: _____ CORRECT PHRASING: _____

6) Widely respected for his sense of form and movement, Paul Taylor's musicals are often performed at Lincoln Center.

ERROR TYPE: _____ CORRECT PHRASING: _____

7) The guide and us took a tour of Stockholm and stopped to buy souvenirs at a modern art museum.

ERROR TYPE: _____ CORRECT PHRASING: _____

8) Yesterday, Mr. Jericho saw a telephone pole covered with posters walking to the park.

ERROR TYPE: _____ CORRECT PHRASING: _____

9) One of the ideas who interests astronomers is the theory that black holes can teleport you across the universe.

ERROR TYPE: _____ CORRECT PHRASING: _____

10) Because they did not adapt to new voting patterns, the political party lost several seats in Congress.

ERROR TYPE: _____ CORRECT PHRASING: _____

CONTINUE

Questions 1-10 are based on the following passage.

Will the Real Musical Please Stand Up?

Both on Broadway and in London's West End, today's theaters offer musicals to the public, catering to **1** their tastes and their love of spectacle. For the ordinary theatergoer, the twenty-first century might seem to be a golden age for such shows. However, some of the most discerning critics disagree. Harsh words are often lavished on Andrew Lloyd Webber, **2** who is criticized for using cacophonic chords of noise and the movement of stage machinery to create spurious "emotional" effect.

So how is it possible for **3** we to tell that we are looking at a top-quality musical? A great musical has a story line that makes reference to the period in which it is written, often affectionately poking fun at contemporary politics, culture, and attitudes. The storyline, dialogue, and lyrics often wittily refer to events from **4** it. If we accept this definition, then it would seem that John Gay's "The Beggars' Opera," way back in 1728, was the very first example of this genre of entertainment. However, that seems to have been a relatively isolated piece. Writing almost a hundred years later, **5** a group of witty and popular light operas was composed by Jacques Offenbach. There is little doubt that Offenbach's success in Paris encouraged the emergence in England of the light comic operas by W. S. Gilbert and Arthur Sullivan, which mark the real beginnings of the modern musical.

1

A) NO CHANGE
B) its tastes and its love
C) his tastes and his love
D) your tastes and your love

2

A) NO CHANGE
B) where
C) which
D) how

3

A) NO CHANGE
B) they to tell
C) us to tell
D) DELETE the underlined portion.

4

A) NO CHANGE
B) they.
C) us.
D) the musical's era.

5

A) NO CHANGE
B) light operas that were witty and popular were composed in a group by Jacques Offenbach.
C) Jacques Offenbach composed a series of witty and popular light operas.
D) Jacques Offenbach's group of witty and popular light operas was composed.

CONTINUE

Gilbert and Sullivan came together from different backgrounds to foster a new and lasting form of theater. Sullivan was a proficient musician, regarded during his lifetime as one of Britain's most promising composers. Gilbert, on the other hand, began as a naval surgeon but became a writer of clever and funny short stories and verse. The collaboration **6** among them was a stroke of genius. For the first time in musical theater, composer and lyricist worked collaboratively and not separately, so that each could devote **7** him to his uinque strengths.

Gilbert and Sullivan were perhaps more influential in the United States **8** than London. The great American musicals of the early and middle twentieth century were almost exclusively hammered out, often brilliantly, by talented pairs who shared duties and created perfect harmony with **9** their audiences. (Irving Berlin and Steven Sondheim were virtual anomalies as the only creators who managed to achieve success individually in this period). Today, the mid-century musicals of Richard Rodgers and Oscar Hammerstein are regarded as among the genre's masterpieces, in part because Rodgers (who wrote the music) and Hammerstein (who wrote narratives) worked together to achieve remarkable heights of emotion. I defy anyone to listen to "As You Walk Through a Storm," one of the duo's finest **10** songs that inevitably sheds a tear. After all, powerful musicals make us feel that we have been involved in something that has helped us to accept the state of the world a little more cheerfully.

6
A) NO CHANGE
B) among they
C) between them
D) between they

7
A) NO CHANGE
B) himself
C) themself
D) theirself

8
A) NO CHANGE
B) than in London.
C) than it.
D) than in it.

9
A) NO CHANGE
B) its audiences.
C) one's audiences.
D) them.

10
A) NO CHANGE
B) songs, and it inevitably sheds a tear.
C) songs where you will inevitably shed a tear.
D) songs, which will cause you to inevitably shed a tear.

CONTINUE

ANSWERS ON THE NEXT PAGE

ANSWERS: GRAMMAR 2

EXERCISES:

1) The casual conversation between **him** and his teammates quickly turned into a heated dispute. (Pronoun Case)

2) All the survivors of the plane crash found themselves in circumstances **in which** cooperation was essential. (Subject-Pronoun, Tricky Pronouns)

3) Rachel knows that her brother is a better pianist than **she**, but she still continues to practice the instrument. (Pronoun Case)

4) New environmental hazards have arisen in the past fifteen years, but people are not sure what to do about **these hazards**. (Subject-Pronoun)

5) My optometrist is someone who, in every situation, thinks that **he is** always right. (Subject-Pronoun, Tricky Singular)

6) Widely respected for his sense of form and movement, **Paul Taylor has created musicals that** are often performed at Lincoln Center. (Dangling Modifier)

7) The guide and **we** took a tour of Stockholm and stopped to buy souvenirs at a modern art museum. (Pronoun Case)

8) Yesterday, Mr. Jericho saw a telephone pole covered with posters **while he was walking** to the park. (Dangling Modifier)

9) One of the ideas **which** interests astronomers is the theory that black holes can teleport you across the universe. (Subject-Pronoun, Tricky Pronouns)

10) Because **it** did not adapt to new voting patterns, the political party lost several seats in Congress. (Subject-Pronoun)

PASSAGE:

1) B   6) C

2) A   7) B

3) C   8) B

4) D   9) A

5) C   10) D

CONTINUE ➡

GRAMMAR FUNDAMENTALS: PART 3
ADJECTIVE VS. ADVERB

WHEN YOU SEE a descriptive word UNDERLINED – stop and ask yourself:	Lilly is **AMAZING** at baseball.
	Madison **SLOWLY** jogged on Sunday.
"What is it describing? Is it describing a noun, verb, or adjective?"	The movie was **DISTURBINGLY** horrific.

LESSON 3.1   **ADJECTIVE:** The word that describes a noun

EXAMPLE

1. Jane is *beautiful*. Beautiful describes *Jane*.

2. The beat is *constant*. Constant describes *the beat*.

3. She is a *safe* driver. Safe describes *her as a driver*.

LESSON 3.2   **ADVERB:** The word that describes a verb or an adjective

EXAMPLE   **Adverbs describing verbs**

1. Jane runs *beautifully*. Beautifully describes how Jane *runs*.

2. The beat is *constantly* playing. Constantly describes how the beat is *playing*.

3. Drive *safely*. Safely describes how to *drive*.

EXAMPLE   **Adverbs describing adjectives**

1. She is *amazingly* quick. Amazingly describes how *quick* she is.

2. She is *breathtakingly* pretty. Breathtakingly describes how *pretty* she is.

3. The casserole came out of the oven with a *horrifically* burnt top layer. Horrifically describes how *burnt* the top layer was.

ADJECTIVE VS. ADVERB seems like an easy type to detect. However, the College Board test makers are very adept at picking adjectives and adverbs that do not sound wrong even when used incorrectly.

CONTINUE

IRREGULAR VERBS

IRREGULAR VERBS: Verbs that are not conjugated by simply adding an "s" or "ed". Irregular verbs change spelling when tense changes.

WHEN YOU SEE a verb underlined, you must ask yourself:

Is there a "had/have" before it? Does this verb change spelling when the tense changes?

NORMAL VERB	
slap → slapped	step → stepped
→ had slapped	→ had stepped

IRREGULAR VERB	
break → broke	drink → drank
→ had broken	→ had drunk

LESSON 3.3   IRREGULAR VERBS

Changing "IRREGULAR VERBS" to past tense or to the "had/have" tenses is not straightforward. An easy way to spot irregular verbs on the SAT is to look for an irregular verb alone or an irregular verb paired with a *had* or *have*.

EXAMPLE

drive → drove	know → knew	creep → crept
→ had/have driven	→ had/have known	→ had/have crept

Anytime there is a **had** or **have** in front of an irregular verb, it changes its spelling to incorporate a **u, m,** or **n**. In simplest terms, if you see an irregular verb with a **u, m,** or **n** in it, it must have **had** or **have**. See below.

EXAMPLE   By the time Jeffery *had drove* to California, the rocky road ice cream stored in the trunk of his car was completely melted and inedible.

EXPLANATION   The verb *drive* is conjugated to *drove* to indicate past tense. However, because there is a *had* next to it, we must change *drove* to *driven*.

By the time Jeffery **had driven** to California, the rocky road ice cream stored in the trunk of his car was completely melted and inedible. ✓

WHENEVER YOU SEE "had" or "have" right before a verb, check that the verb is in the correct form. Refer to the list on the next page for an illustration of this principle. This list is not comprehensive, but it will give you a good foundation for checking this type of error in the future.

CONTINUE ➔

COMMON IRREGULAR VERBS ON THE SAT

INFINITIVE	PAST TENSE	"HAD" OR "HAS"/"HAVE"
To arise	Arose	Arisen
To awake	Awoke	Awoken
To beat	Beat	Beaten
To begin	Began	Begun
To bite	Bit	Bitten
To blow	Blew	Blown
To break	Broke	Broken
To choose	Chose	Chosen
To do	Did	Done
To draw	Drew	Drawn
To drink	Drank	Drunk
To drive	Drove	Driven
To eat	Ate	Eaten
To freeze	Froze	Frozen
To fly	Flew	Flown
To forsake	Forsook	Forsaken
To forget	Forgot	Forgotten
To go	Went	Gone
To know	Knew	Known
To ride	Rode	Ridden
To run	Ran	Run
To sing	Sang	Sung
To sink	Sank	Sunk
To speak	Spoke	Spoken
To spring	Sprang	Sprung
To swim	Swam	Swum
To take	Took	Taken
To tear	Tore	Torn
To write	Wrote	Written

NOTE the common change in the third column. The verbs now have a *u*, *m*, or *n*. When the helping verb is added, the main verb takes on a new form.

99

CONTINUE ➤

VERB TENSE

There are a multitude of tenses in the English language. It is not necessary for the purpose of the SAT to learn and/or memorize every single tense.

The best way to master verb tense questions is to recognize when you are being tested on tense:

WHEN YOU SEE the following references to time in a sentence, use your basic knowledge of tense to check for an error.

YEARS	1969, nineteenth century
DATES	On October 6th, 1999
TIME	2PM, 15 hours
TENSE WORDS	year, later, after, since, yesterday, tomorrow, ago, past, future

Though the SAT does not test your in-depth knowledge of tenses, it will expect you to know the basic guidelines in this chapter:

LESSON 3.4 **HAS/HAVE**

When you see HAS or HAVE before the verb, it should refer to an action or condition that began in the past, has continued to the present, and perhaps may continue into the future.

EXAMPLE

I went to see the fireworks since I was four years old. ✗

I *have been going* to see fireworks since I was four years old. ✓

LESSON 3.5 **HAD**

When you see HAD before the verb, it should refer to an event or condition that occurred prior to another event in the past.

EXAMPLE

By the time George organized his closet, his mother berated him about his filthy room. ✗

By the time George organized his closet, his mother *had berated* him about his filthy room. ✓

CONTINUE

LESSON 3.6	PAST TENSE (PART 1)

When the sentence establishes PAST TENSE, verbs describing action should not end in *ing*.

EXAMPLE

Fifty years ago, Isabella marrying a rich banker just for his money. ✗

Fifty years ago, Isabella **married** a rich banker just for his money. ✓

LESSON 3.7	PAST TENSE (PART 2)

If you see an underlined verb and you are unsure if you should change the tense, USE THE CONTEXT of the rest of the sentence to clarify the tense of the verb in question.

EXAMPLE

Megha *arrives* at the train station just when the ticket booth closed. ✗

Megha **arrived** at the train station just when the ticket booth closed. ✓

The word "being" is often wrong.

Jonathan *being remembered* because of his valiant efforts during the hurricane rescue and his legacy will endure. ✗

Jonathan **will be remembered** because of his valiant efforts during the hurricane rescue and his legacy will endure. ✓

CONTINUE ➡

IDIOM PHRASES

An **Idiom** is simply the customary way of saying a particular phrase. The idioms on the SAT should not to be confused with colloquial expressions such as "all ears" or "across the board." **Instead, an idiomatic error occurs when the preposition is used incorrectly.**

WHEN YOU SEE a preposition or a prepositional phrase underlined, STOP and CHECK:

Is this the correct preposition?

FORMULA: preposition + phrase OR preposition alone

EXAMPLES: *listen to, at the mall, from, of*

LESSON 3.8   **IDIOMATIC ERRORS**

The best way to master IDIOMATIC ERRORS on the SAT is to keep a list of the idioms, prepositions, and prepositional phrases that you come across in any SAT practice test that you might do.

EXAMPLE

She was arguing *against* her mother. ✗

She was arguing **with** her mother. ✓

When you come across an idiom that is not on your list, use the written idiom in three short and simple sentences in your head and see which preposition you use most often. If it is a different preposition than the one written, you may be looking at an idiom error. Still, remember to follow the format of the sentence. See below.

CONTINUE

LESSON 3.9	**INCORRECT PREPOSITION**

EXAMPLE	For my birthday, my parents insisted *about* taking me to dinner. ✗

EXPLANATION	To check if the preposition *about* is used correctly, quickly create three sentences in your head using the word (or phrase) before the preposition. Here, that word is *insisted*.

SENTENCE 1: They insisted *on* driving their own car.

SENTENCE 2: She insisted *on* paying me back.

SENTENCE 3: He insisted *on* opening the door for me.

For my birthday, my parents insisted **on** taking me to dinner. ✓

LESSON 3.10	**COLLOQUIAL SPEECH ERRORS**

The SAT will occasionally use COLLOQUIAL SPEECH, or slang, to hide an error.

EXAMPLE	She should of gone to the market herself if she was that hungry. ✗

EXPLANATION	Did you catch the error? The SAT selectively hides the error based on colloquial speech. In this case, *should of* sounds similar to *should've,* which is the contraction for the phrase *should have.*

She should of gone to the market herself if she was that hungry. ✗

She should'*ve* gone to the market herself is she was that hungry. ✓

She should *have* gone to the market herself if she was that hungry. ✓

Following the principle explained above, **WHEN YOU SEE** *should of, could of,* or *would of,* **these phrases are wrong**.

CONTINUE ➡

EXERCISES: GRAMMAR FUNDAMENTALS 3

DIRECTIONS: Circle the error in the sentence, and write the error type and the correct phrasing on the lines below.

1) We have wrote multiple letters to the newspaper over the past month, but we have received no replies.

ERROR TYPE: _____ CORRECT PHRASING: _____

2) There is some evidence that Emile Zola had been interested on literature from an early age.

ERROR TYPE: _____ CORRECT PHRASING: _____

3) The pop musician Prince, an incredible talented guitarist, was widely underestimated during his lifetime.

ERROR TYPE: _____ CORRECT PHRASING: _____

4) Fortunately, Mr. Wallace gets to buy a large cup of coffee right before the campus restaurant closed for the night.

ERROR TYPE: _____ CORRECT PHRASING: _____

5) Morris has waited until the bus arrived, yet he found that he was unable to find a place to sit or stand.

ERROR TYPE: _____ CORRECT PHRASING: _____

6) Though unfamiliar with the computer program, Juan worked diligent to figure out the new technology.

ERROR TYPE: _____ CORRECT PHRASING: _____

7) According from my great-grandfather, few people understand the true causes of World War I.

ERROR TYPE: _____ CORRECT PHRASING: _____

8) The children were watching the freight trains go by for the past few hours, and are still doing so right now.

ERROR TYPE: _____ CORRECT PHRASING: _____

9) My classmates are studying for the physics exam since last week and now feel increasingly confident.

ERROR TYPE: _____ CORRECT PHRASING: _____

10) The osprey being known to many as a hawk that is native to the beaches and marshlands of New Jersey.

ERROR TYPE: _____ CORRECT PHRASING: _____

CONTINUE ➡

Questions 1-10 are based on the following passage.

Temps to the Rescue!

When I graduated from college, I felt somewhat nervous about entering the job market. Of course, I **1** had worked part-time jobs in high school; I also picked up freelance writing and editing gigs to pay some of my tuition. However, the prospect of entering the full, competitive job market was daunting. In fact, I spent months applying for jobs for which I was **2** massive underqualified. I **3** would of run into greater problems, had I not found a workable solution.

It was then that I discovered the world of "temping" and, in doing so, put my job search on the right track. A "temp" is a part-time employee who works through an agency, which finds suitable and relatively low-responsibility jobs for him or her to undertake. Temps can be found in a variety **4** for fields, from accounting to programming to my own specialty, writing and editing. It is also possible to find a temp position that does not require special training of any sort. In fact, when I **5** begun my work as a temp, my first gig was as a receptionist at a small ad agency.

1
A) NO CHANGE
B) have worked
C) work
D) will work

2
A) NO CHANGE
B) massively underqualified.
C) underqualified massive.
D) underqualifiedly massive.

3
A) NO CHANGE
B) would have run
C) would of ran
D) would have ran

4
A) NO CHANGE
B) with fields
C) to fields
D) of fields

5
A) NO CHANGE
B) began my work
C) begin my work
D) beginned my work

CONTINUE

Despite the name, temp work is not temporary in a negative sense. A very good temp contract involves an hourly wage of anywhere from $15 to $25 per hour, and lasts anywhere from four months to a year. Today's most effective temp agencies also **6** takes great pride in targeting specific business sectors and building lasting relationships with **7** companies growingly. A few of my friends who majored in business and marketing, for instance, **8** finds temp jobs through an agency that works exclusively with banks and investment firms.

Especially if you are trying to build a future career, there are further advantages that have **9** drew people to temp work. Temping is a great option if you have re-located to a new area or are going through another major life change (such as leaving college). Such work can give you a respectable income even while your shift is underway. Perhaps more importantly, a temp job can help you build a strong professional network or a more permanent career. Even something that seems (by its very name) **8** purely temporarily may turn into a job that is wonderfully permanent.

6
A) NO CHANGE
B) take
C) to take
D) of taking

7
A) NO CHANGE
B) growing companies.
C) growth being companies.
D) companies growed.

8
A) NO CHANGE
B) find
C) founded
D) finding

9
A) NO CHANGE
B) drew people for
C) drawn people to
D) drawn people for

10
A) NO CHANGE
B) purely temporary
C) pure and temporarily
D) pure temporary

CONTINUE

ANSWERS ON THE NEXT PAGE

ANSWERS: GRAMMAR 3

EXERCISES:

1) We **have written** multiple letters to the newspaper over the past month, but we have received no replies. (Verb Form)

2) There is some evidence that Emile Zola had been **interested in** literature from an early age. (Idiom)

3) The pop musician Prince, an **incredibly talented** guitarist, was widely underestimated during his lifetime. (Adjective-Adverb)

4) Fortunately, Mr. Wallace **got** to buy a large cup of coffee right before the campus restaurant closed for the night. (Verb Tense)

5) Morris **had waited** until the bus arrived, yet he found that he was unable to find a place to sit or stand. (Verb Tense)

6) Though unfamiliar with the computer program, Juan **worked diligently** to figure out the new technology. (Adverb-Adjective)

7) **According to** my great-grandfather, few people understand the true causes of World War I. (Idiom)

8) The children **have been watching** the freight trains go by for the past few hours, and are still doing so right now. (Verb Tense)

9) My classmates **have been studying** for the physics exam since last week and now feel increasingly confident. (Verb Tense)

10) The osprey **is known** to many as a hawk that is native to the beaches and marshlands of New Jersey. (Verb Tense)

PASSAGE:

1) A	6) B
2) B	7) B
3) D	8) C
4) D	9) C
5) B	10) B

CONTINUE

SENTENCE STRUCTURE

ESSENTIAL CONSTRUCTIONS

SENTENCE STRUCTURE refers to the arrangement of ideas in a sentence. The arrangement should be logical and should adhere to the laws of grammar. If a sentence is illogical, it is necessary to consider the common problems below. Each problem will have a specific visual clue that will act as a guide to identifying the errors in the sentence.

LESSON 4.1	COMMA SPLICES AND RUN-ON SENTENCES

A COMMA SPLICE occurs when two full sentences (commonly called independent clauses) are combined using only a comma. To fix a comma splice problem on the SAT, you have to use a colon (:), a semi-colon (;), or a transition word (but, and, yet, or, so, for, nor).

EXAMPLE

John went to Vermont to ski, he had a really good time. ✗

John went to Vermont to ski, **and** he had a really good time. ✓

I have taken several yoga classes over the years, my favorite is Vinyasa Yoga. ✗

I have taken several yoga classes over the years, **but** my favorite is Vinyasa Yoga. ✓

BE CAREFUL when fixing comma splices. Inserting a transition word after the comma fixes the problem, but never insert a transition word *followed by* a comma. This often creates a clause that can stand alone as a sentence. This does not fix the comma splice. See below.

EXAMPLE

Cars are notoriously bad for the environment, *but,* the development of alternative fuel has mitigated the automobile's impact on emissions. ✗

Cars are notoriously bad for the environment, **but** the development of alternative fuel has mitigated the automobile's impact of emissions. ✓

CONTINUE ➤

LESSON 4.2   **THE COLON AND SEMI-COLON**

Use a SEMI-COLON (;) when joining two closely related independent clauses in a single sentence. When using a semi-colon, make sure that the two adjoining clauses can stand alone as sentences. Avoid using a semi-colon WITH a conjunction.

EXAMPLE

The film's plot was confusing; and the audience members didn't understand it. ✗

The film's plot was confusing; the audience members didn't understand it. ✓

A COLON (:) is used in basically the same way a semi-colon is used, except that a colon implies that an explanation will follow.

EXAMPLE   The house needs a serious renovation and the basement is not structurally sound. **(Clarify more)**

EXPLANATION   The sentence is grammatically correct. However, if you replace *and* with a colon, this replacement clarifies *why* the house needs a serious renovation.

The house needs a serious renovation: the basement is not structurally sound. **(Clear)** ✓

LESSON 4.3   **TRANSITION WORDS**

A TRANSITION WORD error occurs when the transition word given does not follow the logic of the sentence.

EXAMPLE   She seemed very upset at work today, and she looked happier when she left. ✗

EXPLANATION   The content of the sentence signals a CONTRAST in tone (upset to happier), but the transition word *and* implies agreement. Therefore, we must replace *and* with a word that will follow the logic of the sentence *(but, yet)*.

She seemed very upset at work, **but** she looked happier when she left. ✓

Sometimes there will be two similar conjunctions given in the same sentence. Be aware of these errors as they are often disguised. See below.

EXAMPLE   Although it rained at the family picnic, but everyone still had a good time. ✗

EXPLANATION   *Although* and *but* signify the same relationship shift (rained to good time), so including both transition words causes a redundancy error. Omit one.

Although it rained at the family picnic, everyone still had a good time. ✓
It rained at the family picnic, but everyone still had a good time. ✓

CONTINUE ➡

WHEN YOU SEE one of the following in the grammar section, check to make sure that this word is preceded by a semi-colon (;) **if it begins an independent clause.**

However • Therefore • Moreover
Consequently • Nevertheless

EXAMPLE	Many people know that eating breakfast is essential, nevertheless, most people skip this meal. ✗
EXPLANATION	In this sentence, *nevertheless* begins the independent clause *most people skip this meal*. Use a semi-colon before *nevertheless* to connect the independent clauses.
	Many people know that eating breakfast is essential; nevertheless, most people skip this meal. ✓

LESSON 4.4   STANDARD PHRASES

WHEN YOU SEE the first or second half of a standard phrase underlined, check that the other half is placed appropriately.

The SAT will test you on the correct completion of standard phrases. There are many standard phrases in the English language, but here are some common examples found on the SAT.

STANDARD PHRASE EXAMPLES

NEITHER...NOR	I was neither happy about the service or satisfied by the food at that restaurant. ✗	I was neither happy about the service *nor* satisfied by the food at that restaurant. ✓
EITHER...OR	Either we take the car into the city and hope we find parking and on the other hand we take the train in. ✗	Either we take the car into the city and hope we find parking *or* we take the train in. ✓
NOT ONLY...BUT ALSO	The dogs at the shelter were not only cramped in their cages but in addition to that they were not fed at regular intervals. ✗	The dogs at the shelter were not only cramped in their cages *but also* not fed at regular intervals. ✓
AS...AS	Janet is just as deserving of the teacher of the year award than Jeff. ✗	Janet is just as deserving of the teacher of the year award *as* Jeff. ✓
BOTH...AND	Carol is both jealous of her brother's soccer skill in addition to being mad at him for stealing her ball. ✗	Carol is both jealous of her brother's soccer skill *and* mad at him for stealing her ball. ✓

CONTINUE

LESSON 4.5	REDUNDANCY

REDUNDANCY occurs when words or phrases with the same meaning are repeated.

EXAMPLE	In the year 1912, ✗

EXPLANATION	*Year* is not needed when a specific year is given.

In 1912, ✓

EXAMPLE	Every year the college's alumni gather for the annual jamboree. ✗

EXPLANATION	*Every year* and *annual* mean the same thing.

Every year the college's alumni gather for the jamboree. ✓
The college's alumni gather for the annual jamboree. ✓

REASON/BECAUSE/SINCE/WHY
The words REASON, BECAUSE, SINCE, and WHY cannot be in the same sentence. These words all indicate explanation; therefore, it would be redundant to use them in conjunction with one another. If you see these words used in the same sentence, try replacing one of the words with *THAT*.

EXAMPLE	The *reason* I arrived late was *because* I didn't hear my alarm clock. ✗

EXPLANATION	The *explanation* for my lateness *was that I didn't hear my alarm clock.* Use the word *that* in place of *because*.

The reason I arrived late was **that** I didn't hear my alarm clock. ✓

CONTINUE ➡

HYPOTHETICAL AND SUBJUNCTIVE SENTENCES

WHEN YOU SEE *"IF"* **or** suggestions/proposals indicated by the word *"THAT"* this will indicate the SUBJUNCTIVE MOOD or simply, the HYPOTHETICAL.

he proposes that / he insists that
he asks that / he suggests that

The word *if* or *that* indicates a situation that either **HAS NOT HAPPENED YET** or **DID NOT HAPPEN AT ALL.**

LESSON 4.6	**WISH/CONDITIONAL**

FORMAT: If I were... I would... OR If I were to.... I would

EXAMPLE	If I **was** stronger, I would be able to lift that heavy box. ✘

EXPLANATION	Based on the context of the sentence, a wish or desire is indicated. Therefore, *was* must be changed to *were*.

If I ***were*** stronger, I would be able to lift that heavy box. ✓

EXAMPLE	If she **was to** own a farm, she would be self-sustaining. ✘

EXPLANATION	Based on the context of the sentence, she will be self-sustaining on the condition that she owns a farm. Therefore, *was to* must be changed to *were to*.

If she ***were to*** own a farm, she would be self-sustaining. ✓

LESSON 4.7	**PAST SUBJUNCTIVE**

FORMAT: If I had.... I would have

EXAMPLE	If he **would have** remembered earlier, he would not have missed his appointment. ✘

EXPLANATION	Notice that this sentence is in PAST TENSE, implying that this DID NOT HAPPEN AT ALL. Therefore, *would have* must be changed to *had*.

If he ***had*** remembered earlier, he would not have missed his appointment. ✓

113

CONTINUE ➡

| LESSON 4.8 | SUGGESTIONS/PROPOSALS |

If you see the word *that*, **stop and check for the following common problems:**

| EXAMPLE | The child desperately begs that his mother gives him candy. ✗ |

| EXPLANATION | Notice that his mother *has not yet* given him candy.
TO SOLVE, there are TWO steps: |

(1) Find the verb that is being suggested or proposed.

The child desperately begs that his mother **gives** him candy. ✗

He's begging for her **to give**.

(2) Insert the infinitive of the verb (to + verb) WITHOUT the preposition *to*.

The child desperately begs that his mother (~~to~~ give) him candy.

The child desperately begs that his mother **give** him candy. ✓

Remember that **is** and **are** is conjugated from the infinitive verb **to be**. See below.

| EXAMPLE | He proposed that his birthday is celebrated at the community pool. ✗ |

| EXPLANATION | Follow the TWO steps as indicated above: |

(1) Find the verb that is being suggested or proposed.

He proposed that his birthday **is** celebrated at the community pool.

He is proposing for his birthday **to be**.

(2) Insert the infinitive of the verb (to + verb) WITHOUT the preposition to.

He proposed that his birthday (~~to~~ be) celebrated at the community pool.

He proposed that his birthday **be** celebrated at the community pool. ✓

Would indicates a situation that is still possible. *Would have* indicates a situation that is a missed opportunity. *Will* indicates a definite future.

EXAMPLE	If you were to keep these tips in mind, you **would** be well-prepared.
	If you had kept these tips in mind, you **would have** been better prepared.
	If you keep these tips in mind, you **will** be well-prepared.

CONTINUE ➡

EXERCISES: SENTENCE STRUCTURE

DIRECTIONS: Circle the error in the sentence, and write the error type and the correct phrasing on the lines below.

1) Ms. Seely, who reviews movies for a living, found the director's latest effort both entertaining or educational.

ERROR TYPE: _____ CORRECT PHRASING: _____

2) You can see not only octopuses and also tiny, transparent squids at the local aquarium.

ERROR TYPE: _____ CORRECT PHRASING: _____

3) Even though the chairman urged that the proposal is put to a vote, the committee refused to take action.

ERROR TYPE: _____ CORRECT PHRASING: _____

4) While Clay Henry was a fireman who appeared in Subway commercials, yet nobody knows where he is now.

ERROR TYPE: _____ CORRECT PHRASING: _____

5) Leslie has always enjoyed rollerblading, and her mother thinks that it is a dangerous activity.

ERROR TYPE: _____ CORRECT PHRASING: _____

6) The students were fascinated by the museum exhibit, a miniature train set that was not life-size.

ERROR TYPE: _____ CORRECT PHRASING: _____

7) Monica brought a pinata to the party, however, her hosts did not seem to appreciate this gift.

ERROR TYPE: _____ CORRECT PHRASING: _____

8) Thomas was unhappy with his life because, he could not find employment as a university professor.

ERROR TYPE: _____ CORRECT PHRASING: _____

9) If I was able to travel to any country right now, I would definitely head straight to Japan.

ERROR TYPE: _____ CORRECT PHRASING: _____

10) Jasper is proud of his ability to simultaneously play the harmonica and the banjo at the same time.

ERROR TYPE: _____ CORRECT PHRASING: _____

CONTINUE

Questions 1-10 are based on the following passage.

Public Housing: Help Wanted for America's Homes

In the late 1960s, public housing was a massive failure. Initially built as a temporary measure to house the working poor, high-rise public housing units wound up housing multiple generations of low-income families. Rent money could not cover operating [1] costs, these enormous buildings became both [2] dilapidated as well as unsafe. In addition, geographic isolation from the surrounding community made it hard for residents to achieve upward mobility through social networks and employment. In effect, federal efforts to provide decent and affordable housing had merely warehoused poor [3] minorities, these are stripped of any opportunity to improve their lives.

Efforts to redress these issues began around the early 1970s. Dispersal [4] programs: aimed at deconcentrating poverty and avoiding housing discrimination, have evolved immensely since then. Planners have taken numerous approaches to tackle these problems, with varying degrees of success. At their best, dispersal programs are capable of providing low-income families with choice, individual attention, and placement assistance. They can be enormously successful in improving the quality of life for low-income Americans. At their worst, dispersal programs displace families: the burden of developing both cheap and safe housing is [5] one reason that such problems occur.

[1]
A) NO CHANGE
B) costs, and these enormous buildings became
C) costs; these enormous buildings becoming
D) costs: these enormous buildings becoming

[2]
A) NO CHANGE
B) dilapidated than unsafe.
C) dilapidated and unsafe.
D) dilapidated or unsafe.

[3]
A) NO CHANGE
B) minorities, they are stripped
C) minorities; stripping them
D) minorities, stripping them

[4]
A) NO CHANGE
B) programs; aimed at
C) programs, aimed at
D) programs, they aim at

[5]
A) NO CHANGE
B) one reason since
C) one reason because
D) one reason why

CONTINUE

In any case, dispersal programs should strive for flexibility, coordination with other programs, and a realization of their own limitations. In **6** <u>1992, which was the year it began,</u> the Housing and Community Development Act was passed. It created the Moving to Opportunity program, which creatively combined counseling and placement services with vouchers to effectively disperse poverty in some of the most poverty-stricken areas. Studies show that families who have used this program not only are generally satisfied with their new communities **7** <u>as also feeling</u> safer overall. Some have even shown gains in employment and improvement in school services.

Since the 1960s, new measures have been undertaken to aid low-income minorities. In 1965, Section 23 was **8** <u>enacted, despite allowing</u> local housing authorities to lease private homes to low-income families at strategically reduced prices. In addition, Section 23 allowed local housing authorities to build public housing in a more scattered way, across districts, and provided great potential to effectively disperse poverty. **9** <u>In addition,</u> perhaps because of the immense political backlash, scattered-site programs of this sort remain problematic. Fair share programs were also abandoned early at the federal level, and now only states whose courts have mandated them are required to incorporate a fair share of low-income housing into new developments. In effect, only one percent of African Americans have been able to move to higher-income districts. Yet there is a prevalent belief that this figure would be lowered if **10** <u>there were</u> stronger efforts to make affordable housing a major political issue.

6
A) NO CHANGE
B) 1992, when it began,
C) the year 1992,
D) 1992,

7
A) NO CHANGE
B) from also feeling
C) but also feel
D) or also feel

8
A) NO CHANGE
B) enacted, thus allowing
C) enacted; in contrast, it allowed
D) enacted; however, it allowed

9
A) NO CHANGE
B) Furthermore,
C) Fortunately,
D) However,

10
A) NO CHANGE
B) there was
C) there is
D) there are

CONTINUE

ANSWERS: SENTENCE STRUCTURE

EXERCISES:

1) Ms. Seely, who reviews movies for a living, found the director's latest effort both entertaining **and** educational. (Standard Phrase)

2) You can see not only octopuses **but also** tiny, transparent squids at the local aquarium. (Standard Phrase)

3) Even though the chairman urged that the proposal **be** put to a vote, the committee refused to take action. (Subjunctive)

4) While Clay Henry was a fireman who appeared in Subway commercials, **nobody** knows where he is now. (Transitions, could also omit "While" and leave "yet")

5) Leslie has always enjoyed rollerblading, **but** her mother thinks that it is a dangerous activity. (Transitions)

6) The students were fascinated by the museum exhibit, a miniature **train set**. (Redundancy, "miniature" and "that was not life size")

7) Monica brought a pinata to the **party; however,** her hosts did not seem to appreciate this gift. (Transitions)

8) Thomas was unhappy with his life **because** he could not find employment as a university professor. (Transitions, comma must be omitted)

9) If I **were** able to travel to any country right now, I would definitely head straight to Japan. (Subjunctive)

10) Jasper is proud of his ability to simultaneously play the harmonica **and the banjo**. (Redundancy, "simultaneously" and "at the same time")

PASSAGE:

1) B   6) D

2) C   7) C

3) D   8) B

4) C   9) D

5) A   10) A

CONTINUE

WORD USAGE, CONCISION, AND STYLE

DICTION CHOICES

Diction simply means "word choice."

WHEN YOU SEE a word that sounds similar to another word, STOP and CHECK:

"Is this the correct word?"

The SAT may use a word that appears to be the intended word, but does not make sense in context. Sometimes, a word will sound almost right, but not quite. It is usually a word that is commonly confused with another due to spelling or sound.

The best way to combat diction errors is to **KNOW YOUR VOCABULARY.** Generally, only 1 to 2 diction errors appear on any given test. On the next page is a chart of the most common diction errors on the SAT.

LESSON 5.1	DICTION

A common **DICTION** error is mixing *proceed(s)* and *precede(s)*.
Proceed(s) can function as a verb or noun depending on the context of the sentence:
Proceed(s) as a VERB means "to advance." / *Proceeds* as a NOUN refers to money.
Precede(s) as a VERB will ALWAYS mean "to come before."
Below are examples of diction errors involving the words *proceed(s)* and *precede(s)*.

EXAMPLE	We decided to precede with the business venture even though the market is volatile. ✗

EXPLANATION	*Precede* means to come before. We didn't decide *to come before* the business venture. We decided to *advance*, or *continue* with the business venture, or *proceed* with it.

We decided to **proceed** with the business venture even though the market is volatile. ✓

EXAMPLE	The precedes from the fundraiser helped to build wells in a dozen impoverished villages. ✗

EXPLANATION	Here, based on the context of the sentence, we know that we are looking for a word that means *the funds received for charitable purposes*. Therefore, *precedes* is incorrect. The correct word would be *proceeds*.

The **proceeds** from the fundraiser helped to build wells in a dozen impoverished villages. ✓

CONTINUE ➡

COMMON DICTION ERRORS ON THE PSAT

ACCEPT To agree or consent to	**EXCEPT** To exclude; to leave out
ADOPT To take in	**ADAPT** To adjust
AFFECT To influence	**EFFECT** (n) result; (v) to bring about
ALLUDE To refer to	**ELUDE** To escape from
ALLUSION An indirect reference (often to literature)	**ILLUSION** An unreal image; a false impression
ANECDOTE A short account based on real life experience	**ANTIDOTE** A remedy
ASSURE To comfort in order to dispel doubts	**ENSURE** To confirm; to make certain
COLLABORATE To work together	**CORROBORATE** To confirm
COMPLEMENT An addition that enhances or improves	**COMPLIMENT** Praise
COUNSEL To advise, to offer guidance	**COUNCIL** An advisory body that meets regularly
DEFER To put off; to comply	**REFER** To bring up; to consult
DELUDE Deceive	**DILUTE** To reduce strength
DISCRETE Separate, distinct	**DISCREET** Reserved in speech and action, circumspect
ELICIT To draw out or bring forth	**ILLICIT** Not legally allowed
FLAUNT To show off	**FLOUT** To exhibit scorn or contempt
IMMINENT Likely to occur at any moment	**EMINENT** High in rank or repute
INAPT Unsuitable	**INEPT** Unskilled
INEQUITY Inequality	**INIQUITY** Immorality
INHABIT To occupy	**INHIBIT** To constrain
PERSPECTIVE Viewpoint	**PROSPECTIVE** Potential, possible
RELUCTANT Unwilling	**RETICENT** Silent, reserved

CONTINUE →

CONCISION AND STYLE

A concision, style, or word usage error occurs when the underlined portion of a sentence does not match how the passage is written. To correct, use the sentences above and below the underlined portion.

WHEN YOU SEE an underlined portion that does not contain an explicit grammatical error:

Ask yourself:

◊ Am I using language that is consistent with the style of the passage?

◊ Am I avoiding wordiness and ambiguity?

LESSON 5.2   CONCISION

CONCISION: using as few words as possible to convey the correct meaning.

WORDINESS: expressing an idea with more words than are necessary.

Choose the shortest possible option while still conveying the original meaning of the sentence.

REDUNDANCY: repeating the same information.

Be wary of two words or phrases that seem different but mean the same thing. Here are some redundancies that the SAT will test:

"may possibly"   "initially begin"

"repeat again"   "soon quickly"

LESSON 5.3   STYLE

STYLE: the tone of the passage.

AMBIGUITY: unclear reference to ideas in the rest of the sentence, paragraph, or passage (often the word "things")

Avoid ambiguity and choose a tone that is consistent with that of the passage. Typically, the passage will be written in a "formal yet accessible" tone; the writing is scholarly but does not use unnecessarily complex vocabulary or sentence structure.

CONTINUE

General range that the PSAT will test:

CONVERSATIONAL	FORMAL YET ACCESSIBLE	ESOTERIC
"bare-bones"	"simple"	"facile"
"how-tos"	"directions"	"protocols"
"law troubles"	"legal issues"	"litigious concerns"
"hodge-podge"	"mixed"	"multifarious"
"hemmed in"	"limited"	"proscribed"
"double-dealing"	"dishonesty"	"chicanery"

EXAMPLE [**GIVEN**: the rest of the passage has a formal yet accessible tone]

The problems with genetically modified crops <u>should not be ignored.</u>
A) NO CHANGE ✓
B) oblige us to exercise meticulousness. (too esoteric)
C) are things to which we must pay attention. (too wordy; "things" is vague)
D) should not be put on the back burner. (too conversational)

REMEMBER:

These edits are CONTEXTUAL, so your job is to MATCH the prevailing tone of the passage. When the passage seems conversational, choose a conversational revision. However, highly esoteric vocabulary will rarely ever be correct.

LESSON 5.4   **WORD USAGE**

Sometimes, the answer options will present four different vocabulary words. They will typically be similar in meaning and might even be similar in tone, but these words are NOT used interchangeably.

In order to achieve correct word usage, you must be able to identify not only the meaning and tone of the word, but also the correct CONTEXT in which it is used.

Use the words in the surrounding sentence to establish the CONTEXT for your word.

CONTINUE ➡

EXERCISES: Word Usage, Concision and Style

Directions: Circle the error in the sentence, and write the error type and the correct phrasing on the lines below.

1) Convinced that her ideas were really awesome things, the young scientist prepared a PowerPoint of her findings.

Error Type: _____ Correct Phrasing: _____

2) In order to keep his children entertained during the long car ride, Mr. Charles told several humorous antidotes.

Error Type: _____ Correct Phrasing: _____

3) Meditation helps Laurel to reflect deeply and in a thoughtful manner after a hard day of work.

Error Type: _____ Correct Phrasing: _____

4) Despite the recriminatory obstreperousness of the class, the teacher proceeded to administer the pop quiz.

Error Type: _____ Correct Phrasing: _____

5) Raising taxes in the manner proposed by some politicians would have a disastrous affect on the national economy.

Error Type: _____ Correct Phrasing: _____

6) Whales, though caricatured as slow and dull, are actually intelligent animals that can adopt to new conditions.

Error Type: _____ Correct Phrasing: _____

7) My favorite drama is about a wisecracking con artist who manages to allude the authorities in every episode.

Error Type: _____ Correct Phrasing: _____

8) Because his way of talking was so superciliously grandioquent, the pediatrician was impossible to understand.

Error Type: _____ Correct Phrasing: _____

9) Unsure whether anybody still inhibited the old house, my cousins grabbed their flashlights and went to explore.

Error Type: _____ Correct Phrasing: _____

10) The sight of a man wearing an enormous wig was really not that huge of a deal in 18th-century France.

Error Type: _____ Correct Phrasing: _____

CONTINUE

Questions 1-10 are based on the following passage.

Mathematics on the High Seas

Almost from the dawn of recorded history, humanity has been fascinated by the turbulence and mystery of the world's oceans. [1] Excess to a seaport could open a budding nation to commerce and prosperity, but travel on the seas themselves could lead to sudden, catastrophic loss of life. Sailors throughout the ages have understood such uncertainties; less well understood have been the motions of the seas themselves, beyond the basic workings of the tides. A grasp of those workings could [2] ensure faster, easier, and safer travel.

Ultimately, modern mathematics and advanced software may offer a way around some of the difficulties and dangers of the oceans. In the recent past, researchers have [3] hugely gotten to the point of creating meticulously patterned computer models of perhaps the greatest of the ocean's unpredictable threats: massive, [4] sullen waves. At Stanford University, Komal Sethi and Larry Cutler have used advanced mathematics to re-create "wind-generated ocean waves" [5] in a computer application, which could accurately gauge "the amount of foam and spray generated."

1
A) NO CHANGE
B) Express
C) Assess
D) Access

2
A) NO CHANGE
B) insure
C) obscure
D) allure

3
A) NO CHANGE
B) done a lot when they are interested in
C) dedicated themselves to
D) fervently extrapolated

4
A) NO CHANGE
B) sudden
C) subtle
D) suspended

5
A) NO CHANGE
B) in a computer application which was effective, and which could accurately
C) in a computer application, which was related to waves and could accurately
D) in a computer application premised on sophisticated mathematics and which could accurately

CONTINUE

But it is [6] another recent, relatively new project—this one developed in conjunction with the University of Leeds—that may have the greatest life-saving potential. Researchers Anna Kalogirou, Vijaya Ambati, and Onno Bokhove have created a computer model that could aid in the design of "fast ships," relatively small vessels that can be used in reconnaissance and maritime law enforcement. Unfortunately, these ships are vulnerable to sudden and rapidly-growing waves. To [7] get done with this liability, the Leeds experts used [8] confusing mathematics to create "accurate simulations of linear wave-ship interactions." These simulations, along with the team's research on sea-to-ship surface pressure, could result in designs that keep fast ships more easily afloat.

According to Bokhove, the fast ships project is proof that "advanced [theoretical] mathematics can have real-world [9] argumentations that help save money and safeguard lives." Almost 2500 casualties occurred in the course of fast ship missions in 2013 alone; with any luck, Bokhove's efforts will help to reduce that number. The theoretical knowledge that civilization has [10] sequestered into a historical edifice may, indeed, be the means of fulfilling the age-old goal of keeping travelers on the high seas free from peril.

6
A) NO CHANGE
B) another relatively new project that was created
C) another relatively new project
D) another of those things

7
A) NO CHANGE
B) simply just forget about
C) disembowel
D) address

8
A) NO CHANGE
B) confining
C) complex
D) compliant

9
A) NO CHANGE
B) applications
C) editions
D) additions

10
A) NO CHANGE
B) gotten together over a really long time
C) historically made a lot about
D) accumulated over the centuries

CONTINUE

ANSWERS: WORD USAGE, CONCISION, AND STYLE

EXERCISES:

1) Convinced that her ideas were **valid**, the young scientist prepared a PowerPoint of her findings. (Style, too informal)

2) In order to keep his children entertained during the long car ride, Mr. Charles told several humorous **anecdotes**. (Diction)

3) Meditation helps Laurel to reflect deeply ~~and in a thoughtful manner~~ after a hard day of work. (Redundancy, "reflect deeply" makes the underlined portion unnecessary)

4) Despite the **loud protests** of the class, the teacher proceeded to administer the pop quiz. (Style, too elevated)

5) Raising taxes in the manner proposed by some politicians would have a disastrous **effect** on the national economy. (Diction)

6) Whales, though caricatured as slow and dull, are actually intelligent animals that can **adapt** to new conditions. (Diction)

7) My favorite drama is about a wisecracking con artist who manages to **elude** the authorities in every episode. (Diction)

8) Because his way of talking was so **showy and self-important**, the pediatrician was impossible to understand. (Style, too elevated)

9) Unsure whether anybody still **inhabited** the old house, my cousins grabbed their flashlights and went to explore. (Diction)

10) The sight of a man wearing an enormous wig was **normal** in 18th-century France. (Style, too informal)

PASSAGE:

1) D	6) C
2) A	7) D
3) C	8) C
4) B	9) B
5) A	10) D

CONTINUE

COHESION AND ORGANIZATION

Cohesion and Organization errors disrupt the logical sequence of ideas for a paragraph or for an entire passage. Corrections for these errors can include reorganizing the order of sentences or paragraphs, deleting sentences, or adding sentences.

WHEN YOU SEE questions that ask about conclusions or introductions, questions that ask where a sentence or paragraph should be placed, questions that ask whether a sentence should be added or deleted, and questions that ask which choice most effectively accomplishes a goal:

Ask yourself:

◊   Am I following the exact wording of the question?

◊   Do the sentences or paragraphs form a logical transition with those before and after?

LESSON 6.1   **COHESION AND ORGANIZATION**

COHESION: the continuity from sentence to sentence, with regards to style and content.

ORGANIZATION: the logical presentation of ideas in the passage, especially with regards to sentence order.

BREAKDOWN   **LOGICAL SEQUENCE OF IDEAS**

Sentences should be positioned so that they flow seamlessly from a given sentence to the following sentence. As a general rule, ideas in a paragraph should go from general to specific and back to general:

FIRST SENTENCE OF THE PARAGRAPH: States the general topic and central point of the paragraph.

MIDDLE SENTENCES OF THE PARAGRAPH: Provide specific details and analyses that are relevant to the topic and that support the central point of the paragraph.

LAST SENTENCE OF THE PARAGRAPH: Restates the general topic and central point of the paragraph.

CONTINUE

NOTE: Sometimes the question asks where an existing sentence should be placed, and sometimes the question states that the writer plans to add a sentence and asks you where it should be placed. In both cases, the standards by which you make your choice are the same:

1

To make this paragraph most logical, sentence 4 should be placed

A) where it is now.
B) after sentence 1.
C) after sentence 2.
D) after sentence 5.

2

The writer wants to add the following sentence to the paragraph.

> The courtiers were too busy constructing a nonsense image of Camelot.

The best placement for the sentence is immediately

A) before sentence 1.
B) after sentence 1.
C) after sentence 2.
D) after sentence 3.

Place the sentence so that it does not abruptly change the topic of the paragraph, and so that it enhances and clarifies the meaning of the previous and the following sentences

EXAMPLE

[1] Jocelyn was a generally well-behaved girl. [2] She did her homework promptly, played nicely with her friends, and was respectful to her parents. [3] However, sometimes she acted out of character, breaking the rules. [4] On these nights, she simply could not resist the temptation that the sweet night air and beckoning tree posed.

The writer plans to add the following sentence.

> For instance, sometimes Jocelyn would sneak out after dark, without her parents' permission, to climb the tree that she so dearly loved.

To make this paragraph most logical, the sentence should be placed

A) after sentence 1.
B) after sentence 2.
C) after sentence 3. ✓
D) after sentence 4.

EXPLANATION

A) (the new sentence is NOT an instance of Jocelyn being "well-behaved.")
B) (the new sentence is NOT an instance of Jocelyn being "respectful to her parents.")
C) (the new sentence IS an instance of "her breaking the rules.")
D) (sentence 4 would be unclear without the appropriate introduction to "these nights" and the "tree.")

CONTINUE ➤

NOTE: Sometimes the question will ask where to place a certain paragraph in the context of the passage as a whole. In these cases, the same standards apply as those involving sentence placement:

EXAMPLE   When you read a paragraph, keep in mind what each paragraph does (see below). This will help you answer the questions about paragraph placement more aptly.

[GIVEN THAT...]

[Paragraph 1 introduces a museum.]

[Paragraph 2 describes the details of a specific exhibit.]

[Paragraph 3 introduces a specific exhibit within that museum.]

[Paragraph 4 expands on the details of that specific exhibit.]

[Paragraph 5 mentions how museum visitors respond to that specific exhibit.]

To make the passage most logical, paragraph 2 should be placed

A)   where it is now.
B)   after paragraph 3. ✓
C)   after paragraph 4.
D)   after paragraph 5.

EXPLANATION

A)   (details may confuse the reader without an introduction to the exhibit)
B)   (describing details of the exhibit should be placed BEFORE *expanding* on those details)
C)   (expanding on details should come after the details)
D)   (describing details at the end would interrupt the flow between the paragraphs about the details of the exhibit.)

CONTINUE

| LESSON 6.2 | USING YOUR UNDERSTANDING OF THE PASSAGE |

Over the course of the passage, you must:

◊ Identify the main focus of the passage.

◊ Identify the more specific topics of the paragraphs.

◊ Understand the writer's stance on the topic he or she has written about.

Ensure that content that is RETAINED IN or ADDED TO the passage clarifies or supports the writer's point. Make sure to DELETE content that is irrelevant to the topic of the paragraph or passage, DELETE content that is redundant, and DELETE content that directly contradicts the writer's point.

 NOTE: Some questions ask whether an underlined portion should be deleted, and some ask whether a given sentence should be added to the passage. In order to answer these questions, you must apply your understanding of the passage as a whole:

EXAMPLE

Green energy sources represent a valuable opportunity to improve the environment and maintain our current standard of living in a sustainable way. Wind power, solar power, and even wave power—<u>an emerging field that harnesses the kinetic energy of waves in the ocean</u>—are growing sectors of the energy economy and should not be ignored....

[GIVEN THAT THE FOLLOWING PARAGRAPH IS ABOUT WAVE POWER.]

The writer is considering deleting the underlined portion. Should the writer make this deletion?

A) Yes, because the underlined portion detracts from the paragraph's focus on green energy.

B) Yes, because the information in the underlined portion is provided in the previous sentence.

C) No, because the underlined portion defines a term that is important to the passage. ✓

D) No, because the underlined portion gives an example of a particular ocean that can efficiently provide wave power.

 In the answer choices for these types of questions:

The BECAUSE is just as important as the YES or NO. Carefully read all answer options before selecting one. If you use your knowledge of the entire passage, it is possible to PREDICT the answer to be YES or NO prior to process of elimination.

CONTINUE

LESSON 15.3   **FOLLOWING INSTRUCTIONS IN THE QUESTION**

Often, questions will be worded as follows:

◊   The writer wants to do X. Which choice best accomplishes this goal?

◊   Which choice does X?

Choose the option that fulfills the instructions given as X. Some options will satisfy one part of X but not all. These are incorrect.

EXAMPLE

Reading every day has many benefits.

The writer wants to *provide a specific example of a positive effect of reading every day.* Which choice best accomplishes this goal?

A) NO CHANGE
B) Those who read often find that their eyesight is significantly improved.
C) Reading every day can mean that you have less time for other activities.
D) Reading daily has improved my IQ score by 10 percentage points. ✓

EXPLANATION

A) (does not give "a specific example")
B) (does not specify "reading every day")
C) (does not give a "positive effect")
D) (provides a "specific positive effect")

 NOTE: Sometimes, more than one answer option will make sense. If this is the case, pick the one that is most concise:

EXAMPLE

Typically, the forest begins to show evidence of browsing in early autumn. This follows several weeks of deer population growth.

Which choice most effectively combines the two sentences at the underlined portion?

A) autumn, following ✓
B) autumn, and this browsing follows
C) autumn, and such browsing follows
D) autumn, and this evidence follows

CONTINUE ➤

EXERCISES: COHESION AND ORGANIZATION

DIRECTIONS: WORK THROUGH EACH QUESTION TYPE AS INDICATED BELOW.

1) Place the following sentences in the correct order

A.   You can start by opening an online brokerage account.
B.   Then, figure out the kinds of stocks and bonds that suit your financial needs.
C.   Investing in the stock market is easier than most people believe.

First: _____ Second: _____ Third: _____

2) Place the following sentences in the correct order

A.   Physicist Brian Greene believes that even difficult theories can be explained using simple metaphors.
B.   According to many readers, it is impossible to understand theoretical physics without a physics degree.
C.   However, physicists themselves to not see the situation in this manner.

First: _____ Second: _____ Third: _____

3) Place the following sentences in the correct order

A.   I had never seen such a remarkable tree in my entire life.
B.   Even more amazingly, one of roots looked almost exactly like an elephant's foot.
C.   Its bark had the color and texture of the skin of an elephant.

First: _____ Second: _____ Third: _____

4) Which sentence does not belong?

A.   The giant anteater is native to Africa and tends to avoid human settlements.
B.   Typically, young anteaters will be raised by their mothers, while adult male anteaters strike out on their own.
C.   To me, the giant anteater, with is impressive gray and white coloration, seems oddly intelligent.

Choice: _____ Reasoning: _____

5) Which sentence does not belong?

A.   In the 1990s, Bill Clinton won the presidency by appealing to African Americans and suburban women.
B.   By 2050, African Americans may account for over 25% of all Americans casting presidential ballots.
C.   Barack Obama built on Clinton's successes to become the first African-American president.

Choice: _____ Reasoning: _____

CONTINUE

Questions 1-10 are based on the following passage.

Much Ado about Waterloo

— 1 —

[1] No one perhaps could be more certain of the truth of this statement than the Duke himself. [2] When asked to reveal the details of the battle of Waterloo in 1815, the Duke of Wellington replied, "The history of a battle is not unlike the history of a ball... no individual can recollect the order in which [the individual events] occurred." [3] On the fifteenth evening of June 1815, **1** which is a date that historians remember, he was the guest of honor at the Duchess of Richmond's **2** ball. [4] This ball took place just a short distance from the fields that witnessed the final overthrow of Napoleon Bonaparte. [5] The juxtaposition of that evening of revelry and the ensuing days of bloody maneuvers and relentless battle has fascinated historians. [6] Later, scenes of the ball were used in several historical novels, **3** not the least of which were Tolstoy's *War and Peace* and Thackeray's *Vanity Fair*. [7] The apparent sangfroid displayed by the Duke at the ball is both thrilling history and the stuff of legend. **4**

1

The writer wishes to explain why the fifteenth of June is historically significant. Which choice best accomplishes this goal?
A) NO CHANGE
B) the night before the battle of Waterloo,
C) when the night was starry and serene,
D) a date that meant little to the Duke,

2

Which choice best combines the two sentences at the underlined portion?
A) ball, and in fact the ball was taking place just
B) ball, it was also taking place just
C) ball and where it was just
D) ball, just

3

The writer wishes to give specific examples of historical novels that respond to Waterloo. Which choice best accomplishes this goal?
A) NO CHANGE
B) including several that are still taught in college literature courses today.
C) along with plays and poems that appeared well after the battle took place.
D) although the battle may be most famous for inspiring a poem by Lord Byron.

4

For the logic and coherence of the paragraph, sentence 2 should be placed
A) where it is.
B) before sentence 1.
C) before sentence 6.
D) after sentence 7.

CONTINUE

— 2 —

[1] Actually, much of what the general public accepts as the truth about Waterloo is little more than legend or hearsay. [2] On learning of this maneuver during the Duchess's ball, Wellington admitted, "Napoleon has humbugged me, by God, and has gained twenty four hours' march on me." [3] Or so it is alleged. [4] Famously, the Duke scanned a map of the area and pointed at the small **5** village of Quatre Bras. [5] At this village, the Duke had intended to halt Napoleon's advance. [6] He then remarked, "We shall not stop him here, and so, I must fight him here," as his finger stabbed the name "Waterloo." However, after the battle, Wellington claimed that he had always intended to meet the French on the fields of Waterloo: **6** he had supposedly made that decision two days before the ball. **7**

5

Which choice most effectively combines sentence 4 and sentence 5 into a single sentence?

A) village of Quatre Bras, and at this village, the Duke
B) village of Quatre Bras, and this was the village where the Duke
C) village of Quatre Bras, where the Duke
D) village of Quatre Bras, the Duke

6

Should the writer delete the underlined content (ending with a period after "Waterloo" and adjusting any other punctuation as needed)?

A) Yes, because the sentence shifts the emphasis of the passage to Napoleon.
B) Yes, because it is not clear why the Duke was attending the ball.
C) No, because the sentence demonstrates that the Duke was generous and easygoing.
D) No, because the sentence adds relevant detail about the Duke's strategies.

7

The writer wishes to add the following sentence to the paragraph.

> Napoleon's approach caught the Grand Alliance off guard, separating the Russian and Austrian forces.

To make the order of ideas in the paragraph most logical, this new sentence should be placed

A) before sentence 1.
B) before sentence 2.
C) before sentence 3.
D) before sentence 4.

CONTINUE

— 3 —

Whatever the true details may be, the events of the Duchess of Richmond's ball and the battle of Waterloo are inextricably linked in the public's conception of that turning point in European history. The central figures now seem legendary. **8** Oddly enough, none of the American war heroes of the era figured prominently in the campaign against Napoleon. The attitude of Wellington defined a very stoic approach to serious events: it is not foolishness to dance in the face of death, but an awareness of the joy of life.

— 4 —

Even the details of the ball have become romanticized over the years. Instead of an elegant affair in the spacious rooms of a splendid townhouse on one of those tree-lined avenues we associate with European cities, the event was actually held in a small coach house behind the Duke of Richmond's rented mansion in Brussels. The site, in fact, was an outlying structure with a low-lying, insignificant entrance. This building with, one may assume, few windows, had been papered for the occasion with a pattern of roses climbing a trellis. Some younger attendees attempted to dance **9** despite the impending battle, but many of those invited hurried away to watch the troops marching through the streets.

Question 10 asks about the previous passage as a whole.

8

The writer is considering deleting the underlined sentence. Should the writer delete the sentence?

A) Yes, because it introduces a topic that is not discussed at any other point.

B) Yes, because it creates a negative image of the Duke of Wellington.

C) No, because it introduces a topic discussed earlier in the passage.

D) No, because it supports the writer's positive ideas about the Duke of Wellington.

9

The writer wishes to add a description that returns to the points made earlier about the "small coach house". Which choice best accomplishes this goal?

A) NO CHANGE

B) in these close quarters,

C) with their new acquaintances,

D) in a lively manner,

Think about the previous passage as a whole as you answer question 10.

10

To make the order of ideas in the passage most logical, paragraph 4 should be placed

A) where it is now.

B) before paragaph 1.

C) before paragraph 2.

D) before paragraph 3.

CONTINUE

ANSWERS: COHESION AND ORGANIZATION

EXERCISES:

1) C (general instructional topic); A (first piece of advice); B (second piece of advice)

2) B (topic and a position); C (contrasting position); A (evidence for contrasting position)

3) A (topic and a position); C (first supporting detail); B (second supporting detail)

4) C (records opinions and impressions, while A and B both state only facts)

5) B (predicts a future occurrence, while A and C both describe past events)

PASSAGE:

1) B	6) D
2) D	7) B
3) A	8) A
4) B	9) B
5) C	10) D

CONTINUE ➡

PUNCTUATION

Punctuation errors occur when a punctuation is misused according to the standards of conventional English. Much like the rules of Sentence Structure, the rules of punctuation logically arrange and present the ideas in a sentence.

WHEN YOU SEE answer options that have semicolons, colons, em dashes, apostrophes, or quotations:

;	semicolon
:	colon
—	em dash
'	apostrophe
" "	quotation

Ask yourself:

◊ Am I following the semicolon rule?

◊ Am I avoiding creating or retaining a comma splice?

◊ Am I avoiding unnecessary punctuation?

◊ Am I using possessive nouns appropriately?

◊ Am I avoiding redundancy?

◊ Am I setting off modifiers from the rest of the sentence?

LESSON 7.1   **SEMICOLONS, COMMA SPLICES, AND REDUNDANCY**

The semicolon rule and comma splice rules should be familiar to you from lesson 11 (sentence structure):

SEMICOLON RULE: a semicolon must separate two independent clauses that CAN STAND ALONE AS 2 SEPARATE SENTENCES.

Make sure that on both sides of the semicolon you have two distinct, independent clauses.

COMMA SPLICE: in layman's terms, a comma splice is a type of error in which TWO FULL SENTENCES are combined using only a comma.

Make sure that you do not choose an option that creates or retains a comma splice.

REDUNDANCY: in punctuation questions, generally a "subject, subject verb"

CONTINUE

Redundancy in punctuation questions will look something like this:

...Shirley, she is... ✗	...Shirley is... ✓	OR ...she is... ✓
...my car, it is... ✗	...my car is... ✓	OR ...it is... ✓
...happiness, this feeling is... ✗	...happiness is... ✓	OR ...this feeing is... ✓

EXAMPLE

I tend to bite my nails when I am <u>nervous; this feeling is</u> usually because I have a presentation to make in school.
A) NO CHANGE (creates redundancy)
B) nervous, ✓
C) nervous, this is (creates a comma splice; redundant)
D) nervous; (violates semicolon rule)

My school has just ratified a new set of rules, some <u>of them</u> are exceedingly strict.
A) NO CHANGE (retains a comma splice)
B) rules (retains comma splice)
C) of which ✓
D) DELETE the underlined portion (retains comma splice)

| **LESSON 7.2** | **COMMONLY CONFUSED POSSESSIVES AND CONTRACTIONS** |

POSSESSIVES: words that indicate ownership.

CONTRACTIONS: words that combine two words.

| **EXAMPLES** | **Its versus It's versus Its'** |

Its is the possessive version of a singular noun.

<u>The car's</u> air conditioning is broken. = <u>Its</u> air conditioning is broken.

It's is a contraction, the combined form of "it is" or "it has"

<u>The car has</u> been painted green. = <u>It's</u> been painted green.

<u>The car is</u> green. = <u>It's</u> green.

Its' is NEVER CORRECT, and actually does not exist in English.

| **EXAMPLES** | **There versus Their versus They're** |

There describes a place that is not here. *There* is neither a contraction nor a possessive.

I am parking the car in <u>the garage.</u> = I am parking the car in <u>there.</u>

Their is the possessive version of a plural noun.

<u>The kids'</u> toys are blue. = <u>Their</u> toys are blue.

They're is a contraction, the combined form of "they are"

<u>They are</u> well-behaved. = <u>They're</u> well-behaved.

CONTINUE ➡

EXAMPLES   **Noun's versus Nouns' versus Nouns's versus Nouns**

Using "Insect" as the noun:

Insect's is the possessive form of a singular noun.

The wings of that insect are green = The insect's wings are green.

Insects' is the possessive form of a plural noun.

The wings of those insects are green = The insects' wings are green.

Insects is plural, not possessive.

More than one insect = Insects

Insects's is NEVER CORRECT.

For words ending with y, use these examples when indicating ownership:

The laws of the country = The country's laws, NOT the countries' laws

The skin of the body = The body's skin, NOT the bodies' skin.

LESSON 7.3   **PUNCTUATION FOR MODIFIERS**

MODIFIERS: descriptive phrases that provide extra information AND are not central to the structure of the sentence.

EXPLANATION   The lawnmower is old and broken. NOT A MODIFIER.

The lawnmower, old and broken, is going to be replaced soon. A MODIFIER.

To set off modifiers from the rest of the sentence, make sure that you use the SAME punctuation on either side of the modifier.

EXAMPLE

The lawnmower, old and broken, is going to be replaced soon.
A) NO CHANGE ✓
B) broken is
C) broken; is
D) broken—is

My sister—or, at least, the closest thing to a sister that I have just got married.
A) NO CHANGE
B) have, just
C) have—just ✓
D) have: just

CONTINUE

LESSON 7.4   **UNNECESSARY PUNCTUATION**

<u>Dogs, love</u> to please their owners.
A) NO CHANGE
B) Dogs: love
C) Dogs; love
D) Dogs love ✓

I couldn't stop poking fun at my <u>professor, Mr. Green's,</u> bright orange bifocals.
A) NO CHANGE
B) professor, Mr. Green's
C) professor Mr. Green's,
D) professor Mr. Green's ✓

EXPLANATION

There is no punctuation needed between the subject (Dogs) and their verb (love).

Commas inappropriately separate parts of the noun phrase ("my professor Mr. Green's bright orange bifocals").

LESSON 7.5   **ITEMS IN A LIST**

Use commas or the word *and* to separate items in a list, and use a colon to introduce a list.

EXAMPLES

Alexander's pets, <u>plants; and</u> peaches are all downstairs.
A) NO CHANGE (violates semicolon rule; fails to recognize that items are part of a list)
B) plants, and ✓
C) plants: and (fails to recognize that items are part of a list)
D) plants, and, (adds unnecessary comma)

Alexander has moved his <u>belongings:</u> his pets, plants, and peaches.
A) NO CHANGE (appropriately uses a colon to introduce a list) ✓
B) belongings; (violates semicolon rule)
C) belongings, (incorrectly positions "belongings" as a member of the list)
D) belongings (needs a colon to introduce the list)

CONTINUE

EXERCISES: Punctuation

Directions: Circle the error in the sentence, and write the error type and the correct phrasing on the lines below.

1) Because there going to see a long movie, they will not be back for at least two more hours.

Error Type: _____   Correct Phrasing: _____

2) Jenny and Barbara had never been skydiving before last April, they now enjoy skydiving immensely.

Error Type: _____   Correct Phrasing: _____

3) Her roommate, who is a ballerina: intends to spend at least one year in a study abroad program.

Error Type: _____   Correct Phrasing: _____

4) Although I am confident that its' going to snow, the weather forecast is only predicting light rain.

Error Type: _____   Correct Phrasing: _____

5) My whole family gathered around the television, eagerly awaiting the candidates closing statements.

Error Type: _____   Correct Phrasing: _____

6) The villains's plan was quickly foiled; in fact, their odds of success had always been quite slim.

Error Type: _____   Correct Phrasing: _____

7) A chameleon changes the colors of it's skin using special cells that contain different pigments.

Error Type: _____   Correct Phrasing: _____

8) Knowing that his hosts liked healthy food, Cliff brought tofu; hummus, and pita chips to the party.

Error Type: _____   Correct Phrasing: _____

9) The store sells computers made by three companies Apple, Lenovo, and Hewlett-Packard.

Error Type: _____   Correct Phrasing: _____

10) In Las Vegas, you will come across many Elvis impersonators, some of them are actually quite clever.

Error Type: _____   Correct Phrasing: _____

CONTINUE

2 Writing and Language 2

Questions 1-10 are based on the following passage.

Geologists: Keeping Science Down-to-Earth

Geology is a branch of earth science that is devoted to the earth's composition and the processes by which it changes. Within this field, **[1]** they're are many subspecialties, and careers range from academic inquiry to applied science. Geology research can reveal what the earth was like hundreds of millions of **[2]** years ago, its can indicate what kinds of changes the earth will undergo far into the future. And geologists themselves can help architects and builders to understand where it is safe to build, and plan for what kinds of natural events (such as earthquakes and sinkholes) may occur in a region.

Sometimes, researchers stumble upon unexpected phenomena while pursuing **[3]** there scientific goals. Recently, scientists at NASA's Earth Observatory—which gleaned data from the satellite-based Operational Land **[4]** Imager, noticed a strange feature in a section of the Caspian Sea. The sea is especially shallow, about three meters deep, in this region. Across this area, the sea floor was covered in **[5]** scrape mark's that remained static over several months. While the researchers had hypotheses about the cause of the marks, they turned to the public, via Twitter, to investigate. Many suggested human causes, like boat propellers, but the answer came from a geological scientist at Lomonosov Moscow State University, Stanislav Ogorodov. This perceptive **[6]** researchers explanation was that ice fragments, called hummocks, pushed around

1
A) NO CHANGE
B) there are
C) its
D) its'

2
A) NO CHANGE
B) years ago, it can
C) years ago; its can
D) years ago; it can

3
A) NO CHANGE
B) their
C) they're
D) there's

4
A) NO CHANGE
B) Imager—noticed
C) Imager: noticed
D) Imager noticed

5
A) NO CHANGE
B) scrape marks that
C) scrape mark's, they
D) scrape marks, they

6
A) NO CHANGE
B) researchers'
C) researcher's
D) researchers's

142

CONTINUE

©Integrated Educational Services, 2020 **www.iestestprep.com** | Unauthorized copying or reuse of any part of this page is illegal.

by wind and water currents, routinely scrape the sea floor. Like other scientists, geologists benefit from collaborative problem-solving approaches.

Within the geological community, possibilities for specialization abound. Two related subfields of geology are seismology and volcanology, the **7** studies of earthquakes and volcanoes, respectively. Discoveries in these fields can keep humanity safe. Today, new research by a team from the Volcanological and Seismological Observatory of Costa Rica may be able to **8** predict when: where, and how a deadly form of seismic explosion, the phreatic or hydrothermal eruption, will occur. Dr. Maarten de Moor, the team lead, said that these explosions "usually occur with no appreciable precursors" or precedents. However, the team discovered that a spike in sulfur dioxide **9** gas, occurs immediately before an explosion. If scientists can overcome the current barriers to regular detection of phreatic **10** explosions, including the acidic post-explosion environment this discovery could save lives.

7
A) NO CHANGE
B) studies'
C) studie's
D) studies's

8
A) NO CHANGE
B) predict when; where, and how
C) predict when, where, and how
D) predict when, where: and how

9
A) NO CHANGE
B) gas—occurs immediately
C) gas; occurs immediately
D) gas occurs immediately

10
A) NO CHANGE
B) explosions including, the acidic post-explosion environment this
C) explosions including the acidic, post-explosion environment this
D) explosions, including the acidic post-explosion environment, this

CONTINUE

ANSWERS: PUNCTUATION

EXERCISES:

1) Because **they're** going to see a long movie, they will not be back for at least two more hours. (Commonly Confused Forms)

2) Jenny and Barbara had never been skydiving before last **April; they** now enjoy skydiving immensely. (Comma Splice)

3) Her roommate, who is a **ballerina, intends** to spend at least one year in a study abroad program. (Sentence Fragment/Coordinating Ideas)

4) Although I am confident that **it's** going to snow, the weather forecast is only predicting light rain. (Commonly Confused Forms)

5) My whole family gathered around the television, eagerly awaiting the **candidates'** closing statements. (Possessive)

6) The **villains'** plan was quickly foiled; in fact, their odds of success had always been quite slim. (Possessive)

7) A chameleon changes the colors of **its** skin using special cells that contain different pigments. (Commonly Confused Forms)

8) Knowing that his hosts liked healthy food, Cliff brought **tofu, hummus,** and pita chips to the party. (Coordinating Ideas)

9) The store sells computers made by three **companies: Apple,** Lenovo, and Hewlett-Packard. (Coordinating Ideas/Introducing Lists)

10) In Las Vegas, you will come across many Elvis **impersonators; some** of them are actually quite clever. (Coordinating Ideas/Comma Splice)

PASSAGE:

1) B	6) C
2) D	7) A
3) B	8) C
4) B	9) D
5) B	10) D

CONTINUE

GRAMMAR TECHNIQUE

On the PSAT, you will encounter four main question types.

Grammar

◊ Includes 13 types of grammar and punctuation rules

Tone/ Style

◊ Revising words, thesis, topic sentences; adding and omitting content

◊ Understanding main idea, tone, and supporting claims

◊ Precision, conclusion, style, and syntax revisions

Placement

◊ Adding, omitting, organizing; logical sequences and conclusions

Graphs

◊ Applying quantitative information from a graph to the passage

GRAMMAR TECHNIQUE STEPS (S.E.E.)

SAT Grammar is not difficult, though it is very easy to make a mistake. Often, these mistakes come from colloquial speech and things that we "hear" in acceptable daily conversation. However, for SAT Grammar, DO NOT use your ears.

Use your EYES and S.E.E. (Skim, Edit, Eliminate)

. . . .

CONTINUE ➡

(1) SKIM

Skim from the beginning of the passage and into Question #1.

Option: Some test-takers are fine with only reading a couple of sentences before the question and will go back and read extensively only as needed. Your GOAL is always to assess the author's overall point and tone.

 NOTE: If you see a paragraph in which every sentence is numbered with brackets [#], you should read the entire paragraph because this indicates that a placement question will be imminent:

[1] _____

[2] _____

_____

_____ [3] _____

_____

 The writer plans to add the following sentence to this paragraph.

_____

_____

_____

_____

_____

(2) EDIT

Make an initial edit ON THE PASSAGE (yes, write on the passage!) before looking at answer choices. An EDIT is a change made to the underlined portion of the passage that adheres to the question types and grammar rules.

 NOTE: This EDIT may seem daunting at first. Yet the more you get used to the question types and grammar rules, the easier it will be to make precise edits.

EXAMPLE 1

A practiced test-taker will see the following sentence and know to EDIT for **parallelism** list and **punctuation** rules.

These ideas are known to water filter manufacturers, food scientists; and elected officials.

A) NO CHANGE
B) scientists—and
● scientists, and
D) scientists, but

CONTINUE ➡

EXAMPLE 2

A practiced test-taker will see the following sentence and know to EDIT for **subject/pronoun agreement** and the **difference between it/its/it's.**

its

Scientists have long known that dirt particles hasten melting by darkening snow and obstructing <u>it's</u> ability to absorb the sun's rays efficiently.

S   *P*

A) NO CHANGE
B) its
C) its'
D) it

EXAMPLE 3

A practiced test-taker will see the following sentence and know to EDIT for aptness of word choice while keeping style in mind. Remember, when you are dealing with concision, style, and word usage, your EDIT may be notes that help you choose the best answer.

Given these solutions as well as the many health benefits of clean air, the advantages of air filters <u>outdo</u> the drawbacks of their expensive production.

to be better than

Advantages are <u>more important</u> than drawbacks. They are NOT competing with each other.

A) NO CHANGE
B) outmaneuver ———— *to move better than*
C) outperform ———— *to do better than*
D) outweigh

to be more important than

NOTE: If the EDIT seems difficult, you may require a greater area of reading in order to understand important context clues. Broaden your reading area while keeping in mind the exact question.

EXAMPLE

A practiced test-taker will see context clues in the paragraph and know to EDIT for aptness of word choice while keeping style in mind.

personal pronoun

While you may not realize this at first, calories in a fruit or vegetable are actually forms of solar energy. Your fruits and vegetables undergo a chemical reaction known as photosynthesis, which converts air, water, and other nutrients by using the sun's rays. Because calories measure energy, one can say that eating fruits and vegetables is indeed inherently solar.

personal pronoun

not a personal pronoun

A) NO CHANGE
B) you can say
C) it can be stated
D) DELETE the underlined portion.

147

CONTINUE

2 | Writing and Language | 2

③ ELIMINATE

Now, use your EDIT to perform a Process of Elimination (**POE**). This process involves eliminating any choice that does not fall within your initial edit.

EXAMPLE

If your edit for the underlined portion indicates a change from THEY to IT, go through and cross out THEY and any plural pronouns in the answer choices.

(they) will be remembered.
it

A) NO CHANGE
B) ~~their~~ memories will live on.
C) ~~them~~ remembering.
D) it will not be forgotten.

. . . .

◊   Do not substitute all choices into the sentence. Trust your edit!

◊   Control the test by using your edit to eliminate.

◊   Cross out the wrong answer choices for quick and accurate POE.

BEWARE (PITFALLS AND COMMON MISTAKES)

1. STYLE CHANGES

Changing an answer to what YOU think sounds better WITHOUT using grammar and rules of logic.

2. NOT USING A CONTEXTUAL EDIT

Editing a sentence for style but NOT using surrounding sentences and context to determine this edit. REMEMBER: your answer may be correct for the line, but NOT correct when read in context.

3. "IT SOUNDS FINE"

Choosing an answer because you trust your ear. Always apply the rules of grammar and context by looking at both the rest of the sentence and the surrounding sentences. **Remember S.E.E. !**

PSAT
Graphics

READING AND WRITING GRAPHICS

On the PSAT, some passages will have a graphic or visual representation of a concept or idea that the writer is discussing. On the Reading section, you will be asked to analyze the graphic or relate it to the passage; on the Writing section, you will be asked to respond to the graphic in an accurate sentence.

WHEN YOU SEE questions that ask you to respond to or make a revision to a passage based on the information provided in a graph, table, chart, map, or other visual that supplements the passage...

Ask yourself:

◊ Do I know how the information in the graphic relates to the information in the passage?

◊ Do I know how to accurately interpret the information in the graphic?

LESSON	ACCURATE INTERPRETATION

ACCURATE: directly supported by the information presented in the graphic

INTERPRETATION: translating the visual information from the graphic into words.

EXAMPLE	UNDERSTANDING KEY COMPONENTS

Before reading the answer options, circle or underline any key components of the graphic—the title, the legend, the units, and any other labels or captions. Make sure you understand how these components interact.

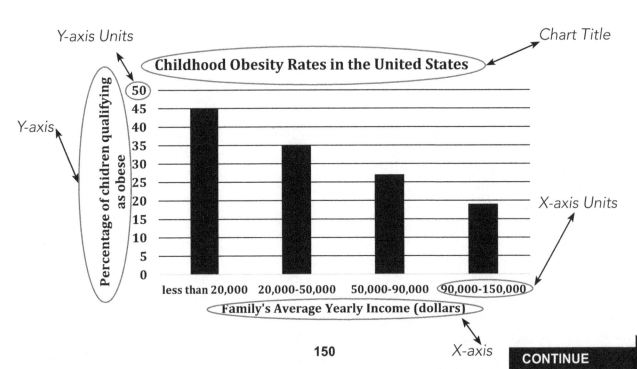

CONTINUE

PSAT Graphics

To briefly test your understanding of the graphic, randomly choose one point on the graphic and put it into words. To maintain accuracy, keep the words you use close to the words used in the graphic.

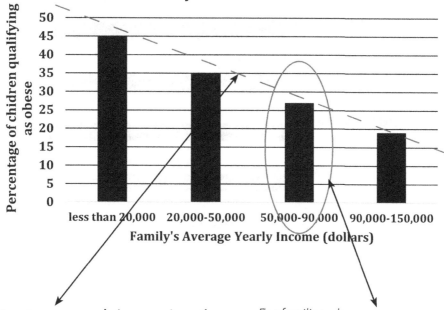

Childhood Obesity Rates in the United States

*It appears that as **average yearly income rises**, the percent of children qualifying as **obese decreases**.*

*For families whose **average yearly income** is between **50,000 and 90,000 dollars**, slightly over 25 percent of children qualify as obese.*

Make a mental note of any obvious correlation between variables.

LESSON   ANSWERING THE QUESTION

Once you understand the graphic, you are ready to respond to the passage.

Be careful about the units used in the answer options. For instance, when percentages are involved, take note of the PERCENTAGE OF *WHAT (is being measured)*! There will most likely be a trap answer that uses the wrong units according to the graph.

CONTINUE

PSAT Graphics

[**GIVEN**: the passage claims that students who eat breakfast succeed in school.]

Perceived Effect of Breakfast on Student Behavior

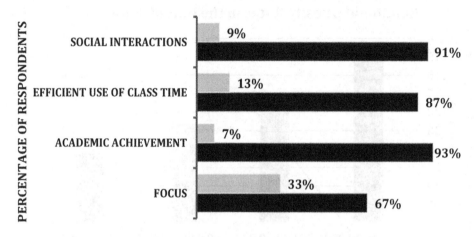

Which choice most effectively provides relevant and accurate information based on the graph above?

A) 93 percent of respondents noted that eating breakfast hindered their academic achievement. (Graph indicates that 93 percent of respondents noted a positive impact on their academic achievement.) ✗

B) Respondents credited eating breakfast with 67 percent of their focus. (Graph measures the percentage of respondents, not the percentage of focus.) ✗

C) 87 percent of respondents indicated that eating breakfast increased their efficient use of class time. ✓

D) Respondents reported that their social interactions improved by 9 percent after eating breakfast. (Graph measures percentage of respondents, not the percentage of improvement; in addition, 9 percent is associated with a negative impact.) ✗

When you are fixing an <u>underlined portion of a sentence</u>, the non-underlined portion will often tell you where to look in the graphic. Be sure to look in the right spot, as dictated by the sentence. There will frequently be a trap answer for those test-takers who are simply looking in the wrong spot for their answers.

DO NOT make any assumptions beyond the graphic.

Especially in the PSAT Reading section, trap answers will ask you about factors that are not explicitly considered in a graphic, or time periods that occur either BEFORE or AFTER the time period for a graphic. These are false answers: broad assumptions that a graphic does not support MUST be eliminated.

CONTINUE

PSAT Graphics

As the graph shows, patients *who follow a low-cholesterol diet but do not exercise daily* experience <u>roughly 30% fewer cases of atherosclerosis than</u> patients *who do not follow a low-cholesterol diet and do not exercise daily.*

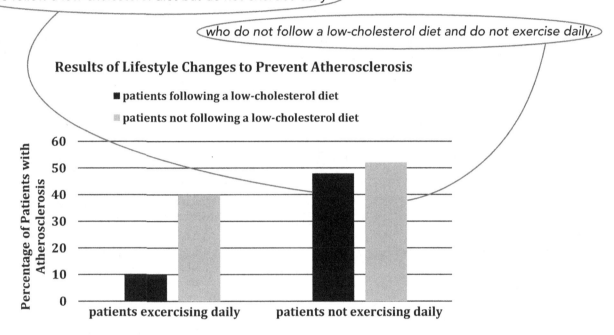

Which choice offers an accurate interpretation of the data in the chart?

A) NO CHANGE

B) a substantially lower rate of atherosclerosis than

C) four times as many cases of atherosclerosis as

D) a slightly lower rate of atherosclerosis than ✓

BE CAREFUL of key words and phrases like:.

◊   "roughly" (means about, not precisely)

◊   "slightly" (means a little bit)

◊   "substantially" (means a lot)

◊   "completely" (means entirely, absolutely)

◊   "as low as" and "at least" (implies no lower than)

CONTINUE

Reading Graphics

While you have probably learned how to graph shapes and lines in your algebra classes, chances are that you have not learned anything about what is called "graph theory" in
Line modern mathematics. In fact, you probably wouldn't call
5 the diagrams studied by this theory "graphs" at all! These interconnected dots and lines, while mysterious to most secondary mathematics students, are extremely useful for mapping delivery routes, managing interpersonal connections in an organization, and efficiently scheduling business
10 meetings. Despite a few applications in chemistry, the fact that graph theory has little connection to traditional secondary science education seems to keep it out of the high school curriculum.

Presence of Graph Theory in United States Math Curricula, Dec. 2015-Jan. 2016 Survey

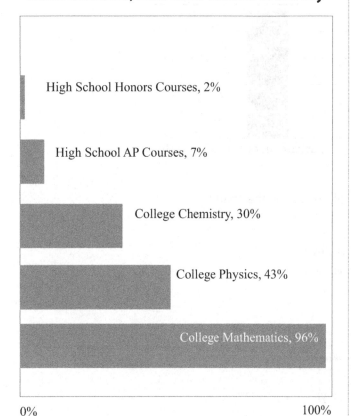

High School Honors Courses, 2%

High School AP Courses, 7%

College Chemistry, 30%

College Physics, 43%

College Mathematics, 96%

0%   100%

What are the KEY COMPONENTS?

What are some RELATIONSHIPS?

1

Which of the following statements can be reasonably inferred from the graph?

A) The percentage of college chemistry departments that feature graph theory is greater than the number of college physics departments that feature graph theory.

B) The percentage of college chemistry departments that feature graph theory is less than the number of college physics departments that feature graph theory.

C) Most college chemistry courses involve some form of graph theory.

D) Most college physics courses involve some form of graph theory.

2

Does the graph support the ideas put forward by the author of the passage?

A) Yes, because it indicates that graph theory is rarely taught at the high school level.

B) Yes, because it indicates that graph theory is enormously popular at the college level.

C) No, because the author is most concerned with the origins of graph theory.

D) No, because the author never discusses AP courses.

CONTINUE

Reading Graphics

In 2013, the public was graced with the first ever YouTube Music Awards, where the judges aggregated posts and hashtags and clicks galore to determine which artist had the most popular music videos. The South Korean pop group Girls'
Line
5 Generation won Video of the Year, earning nearly ten times as many "votes" as a few other, primarily English-language, artists (the nine members of the group perform in Korean, Japanese, and English in sold-out concerts around the world). Many North American fans complained that their favorites had
10 lost (again, by a factor of ten) to "unknowns."

Votes for the Best Band Finalists for the 2016 YouTube Music Awards, by Percentage

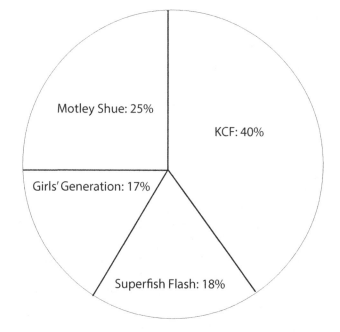

What are the KEY COMPONENTS?

What are some RELATIONSHIPS?

3

The winner of the Best Band award is determined by which individual band gets the most votes. Based on the pie chart, the winner for 2016 would be

A) Girls' Generation
B) Motley Shue
C) Superfish Flash
D) KCF

4

A student claims that the pie chart directly supports the ideas put forward in the passage. Why is the student's claim problematic?

A) The pie chart and the passage consider different genres of music.
B) The pie chart and the passage consider different voting methods.
C) The pie chart and the passage consider different years.
D) The pie chart and the passage do not consider any of the same bands.

CONTINUE

Reading Graphics

Before plants, most of the oxygen on Earth was bound up in compounds such as water and carbon dioxide. As part of photosynthesis, plants take in carbon dioxide and release *Line* oxygen into the air, which animals can then breathe in. This
5 complex system of life has kept the atmospheric concentration of oxygen around 21%, up from basically zero before life. Some scientists postulate that methane gas, produced by certain bacteria, combines with excess oxygen gas to create more carbon dioxide, keeping oxygen concentration where it
10 needs to be in order to maintain favorable conditions for life to continue.

What are the KEY COMPONENTS?

What are some RELATIONSHIPS?

5

According to the table, which of the following accounts for the greatest percentage of the atmosphere?

A) Carbon dioxide before plant life emerged

B) Oxygen after plant life emerged

C) Nitrogen before plant life emerged

D) Nitrogen after plant life emerged

6

Data from the table most directly supports the idea from the passage that

A) the emergence of plant life increased the amount of nitrogen in the atmosphere.

B) the emergence of plant life increased the amount of carbon dioxide in the atmosphere.

C) the emergence of plant life increased the amount of oxygen in the atmosphere.

D) the emergence of plant life decreased the amount of oxygen in the atmosphere.

Composition of the Earth's Atmosphere, by Percentage

Period of Natural History	Carbon Dioxide	Oxygen	Nitrogen
Before Plant Life Emerged	27%	Less than 1%	53%
After Plant Life Emerged	Less than 1%	21%	78%

CONTINUE

Reading Graphics

Toys represent more than a plaything to their child owners, which results in the child's infuriation at the flippant attitudes most adults have towards toys. Just the other day I
Line was cleaning my son's Lego blocks and he responded with
5   such ardent venom that I forgot we were arguing over toys! It hadn't occurred to me—all the worlds he had built, the friendships he had made amongst his tiny people. Now I let my son decide when to tear down his worlds, when to end his friendships. In the indelible words of the prominent child
10   psychologist Albert Emmington, "Give the children toys. What are all things that matter most to us in life but toys?"

What are the KEY COMPONENTS?

What are some RELATIONSHIPS?

7

Which toy company saw its stock price rise by the greatest amount per share between 2012 and 2016?

A) Marmaluke Toys
B) PeopleTown
C) Rojack
D) Fandana

8

The author would see the information in the graph as

A) irrelevant, because he is concerned mostly with how individual children react to toys.
B) enlightening, because most people assume that children are most interested in toys from large companies.
C) problematic, because it contadicts the ideas of Albert Emmington.
D) useful, because it proves his point that adults should take toys more seriously.

Stock Prices for Four Small Toy Companies in Dollars per Share, 2012-2016

Fandana: ——————

Rojack: — — — —

Marmaluke Toys: · · · · · · · · · · ·

PeopleTown: ∞∞∞∞∞∞∞∞∞∞∞

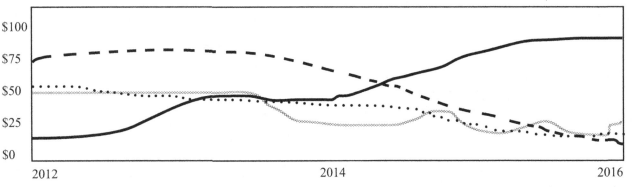

CONTINUE

Reading Graphics

Although the Humboldt squid isn't nearly as giant as the giant squid, it still grows to the length of an adult human—instead of legs, though, it has tentacles with razor-sharp teeth
Line on its suckers, which can flay flesh from bone in seconds! The
5 Humboldt squid, which normally lives in deep water off the western coast of Central and South America, has recently been seen close to the shore as far north as Canada. Some people blame overfishing of its predators, while others blame climate change for this spread; either way, this ruthless killer is getting
10 farther from its own habitat—and closer to ours.

What are the KEY COMPONENTS?

What are some RELATIONSHIPS?

9

During which of the following years did the observed range of the Humboldt squid cover the smallest area?

A) 2010
B) 2011
C) 2012
D) 2013

10

According to the passage, the overall trend recorded in the graph might be explained by

A) tourism.
B) polluted waterways.
C) squid migrations.
D) climate change.

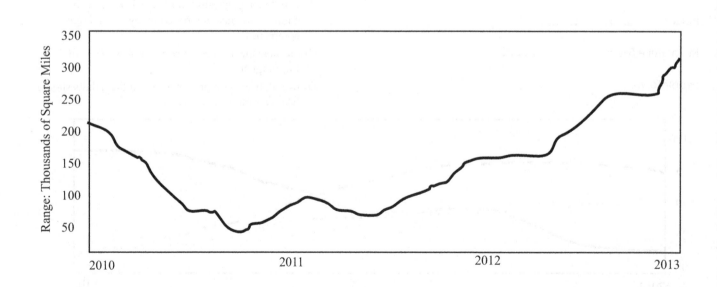

CONTINUE

Writing Graphics

Questions 11-20 are based on the following passage.

Keeping Education "Centered" on Science

It is often argued, and argued loudly, that science education in America is in a state of crisis. Yet the crisis-mongers may have a valid point: by popularly-accepted international standards such as the PISA Scores, America ranks **11** significantly above nations such as Korea, Finland, and Japan. For instance, on the 2006 PISA, **12** Japan ranked sixth in Math and ninth in Science; in those same PISA categories, the United States placed 24th and 25th, respectively. **13** Nor have the numbers for American math and science education improved in the years since.

11

Which choice most effectively reflects the information contained in the table?
A) NO CHANGE
B) a few places above
C) significantly behind
D) only a few places behind

12

The author wishes to add relevant information that reflects the data in the table. Which choice accomplishes this goal?
A) NO CHANGE
B) Japan ranked ninth in Math and sixth in Science
C) Japan ranked second in Math and first in Science
D) Japan ranked first in Math and second in Science

13

At this point, the writer wishes to insert an additional example that accurately reflects the contents of the table. Which of the following would be the best choice?
A) Indeed, all of these countries invest more in both their teachers and their students.
B) In terms of ranking, America was much more comparable to countries such as Spain and Italy.
C) Even a near neighbor, Canada, outranked the United States by a considerable margin.
D) Scandinavian countries such as Norway and Denmark also performed remarkably well compared to the United States.

2006 PISA Rankings for Selected Countries

Country	Finland	Korea	Canada	Japan	United States
Math	1	2	5	6	24
Science	2	1	3	9	25

CONTINUE

Writing Graphics

While already distressing in and of themselves, these deficiencies in American science education at the primary and secondary levels could cause problems for America down the road. It is expected that, **[14]** over the next couple of years, wages in professions such as biomedical engineering, software development, and college mathematics teaching will rise. Naturally, some increases will be greater: the expected percentage increase for software developers, for instance, **[15]** is half as great as that for math professors. To fill these essential and high-powered careers, is radical change necessary?

14

Which choice offers an accurate interpretation of the factors considered in the chart?

A) NO CHANGE
B) over the next decade and a half, wages in
C) over the next couple of years, demand for employees in
D) over the next decade and a half, demand for employees in

15

Which choice accurately responds to the percentages listed in the chart?

A) NO CHANGE
B) is just under twice as great as that for math professors.
C) is just over twice as great as that for math professors.
D) is three times as great as that for math professors.

Expected Increases in Demand for Select Science Professions, 2016-2031

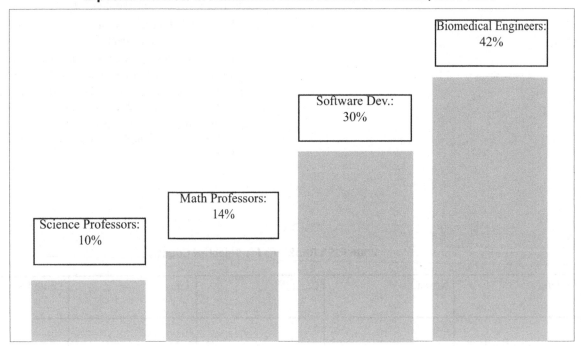

Science Professors: 10%
Math Professors: 14%
Software Dev.: 30%
Biomedical Engineers: 42%

CONTINUE

Writing Graphics

Perhaps not. After all, some of the most valuable science education can occur well outside a formal classroom. As valuable as rigorous training are the experiences that inspire students towards scientific excellence: in providing such experiences, the United States may be uniquely well equipped. Among the country's great resources are science museums: perhaps the two most famous of these are the Liberty Science Center (LSC) and the Boston Science Museum. The LSC, for instance, devotes **16** all of its space to topics in applied physics and engineering and to topics in biology and the health sciences: the wonders of astronomy take up **17** a rapidly growing portion of the LSC floorplan. **18** Even students interested in such intricate topics as theoretical mathematics may find something to enjoy. Each floor of the Center uses a hands-on approach to effortlessly teach students the fundamentals of scientific analysis.

16

Which choice most effectively interprets the pie chart?
A) NO CHANGE
B) an undisclosed amount of its
C) roughly equal
D) exactly equal

17

Which choice most effectively interprets the pie chart?
A) NO CHANGE
B) a smaller but still sizable
C) an excessive
D) a negligible

18

The writer wants the underlined sentence to reflect information from the pie chart. In light of this intention, should the sentence be kept or deleted?
A) Kept, because it is clear from the chart that students interested in theoretical mathematics would also enjoy applied physics.
B) Kept, because it is clear from the chart that students interested in theoretical mathematics do not visit the Liberty Science Center.
C) Deleted, because the chart does not specify theoretical mathematics as a concern of the Liberty Science Center.
D) Deleted, because the chart implies that astronomy and mathematics are related topics.

Exhibit Floor Space at the Liberty Science Center

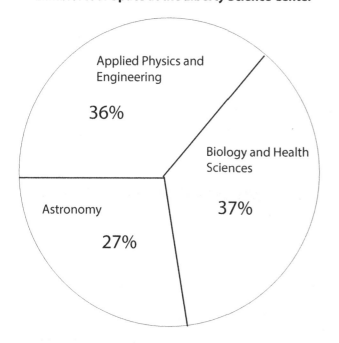

Applied Physics and Engineering
36%

Biology and Health Sciences
37%

Astronomy
27%

CONTINUE

Writing Graphics

In fact, science centers such as these have been central to American success stories in the past. Multibillionaire Michael Bloomberg, for instance, credits much of his success to [19] his childhood visits to the Liberty Science Center: "I loved science—still do—and there was nowhere else I'd rather be." Today, Bloomberg is convinced that "how things work—and how they can work better —is what led me to become an engineer, a technology entrepreneur, a philanthropist [20] and a novelist." If more and more students take the time to "figure out how things work" in the same way, America can take confidence in a bright future of scientific inquiry.

19

Which choice continues the writer's argument by accurately responding to the details of the timeline below?
A) NO CHANGE
B) his childhood visits to the Boston Museum of Science
C) his company's investment in the Liberty Science Center
D) his company's investment in the Boston Museum of Science

20

Which choice accurately interprets the timeline?
A) NO CHANGE
B) and a college president.
C) and a presidential candidate.
D) and a mayor.

Timeline for Michael Bloomberg (b. 1942)

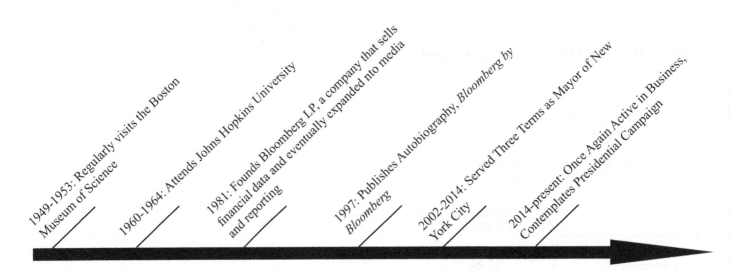

CONTINUE

ANSWERS ON THE NEXT PAGE

ANSWERS: PSAT GRAPHICS

1. B	11. C
2. A	12. A
3. D	13. C
4. C	14. D
5. D	15. C
6. C	16. C
7. D	17. B
8. A	18. C
9. A	19. B
10. D	20. D

PSAT
Timed Practice

Note: the following timed sections are structured based on the PSAT 8/9 format. However, the passages, question-types, and time per question will all be similar to that of the PSAT 10/N format. **Complete the following sections within the given time limits** to practice the skills and strategies that you have learned earlier in this book. Good luck!

Practice Test
ONE

Reading Test
55 MINUTES, 42 QUESTIONS

Turn to Section 1 of your answer sheet to answer the questions in this section.

Each passage or pair of passages below is followed by a number of questions. After reading each passage or pair, choose the best answer to each question based on what is stated or implied in the passage or passages and in any accompanying graphics (such as a table or graph).

Questions 1-8 are based on the following passage.

Adapted from the short story "Life in the Iron-Mills" by Rebecca Harding Davis. Originally published in 1861.

A cloudy day: do you know what that is in a town of iron-works? The sky sank down before dawn, muddy, flat, immovable. The air is thick, clammy with the breath of
Line crowded human beings. It stifles me. I open the window, and,
5 looking out, can scarcely see through the rain the grocer's shop opposite, where a crowd of drunken Irishmen are puffing Lynchburg tobacco in their pipes. I can detect the scent through all the foul smells ranging loose in the air.
The idiosyncrasy of this town is smoke. It rolls sullenly
10 in slow folds from the great chimneys of the iron-foundries, and settles down in black, slimy pools on the muddy streets. Smoke on the wharves, smoke on the dingy boats, on the yellow river,—clinging in a coating of greasy soot to the house-front, the two faded poplars, the faces of the passers-by.
15 The long train of mules, dragging masses of pig-iron through the narrow street, have a foul vapor hanging to their reeking sides. Here, inside, is a little broken figure of an angel pointing upward from the mantel-shelf; but even its wings are covered with smoke, clotted and black. Smoke everywhere! A dirty
20 canary chirps desolately in a cage beside me. Its dream of green fields and sunshine is a very old dream,—almost worn out, I think.
From the back-window I can see a narrow brick-yard sloping down to the river-side, strewed with rain-butts and
25 tubs. The river, dull and tawny-colored (the beautiful river!), drags itself sluggishly along, tired of the heavy weight of boats and coal-barges. What wonder? When I was a child, I used to fancy a look of weary, dumb appeal upon the face of the river slavishly bearing its burden day after day. Something of the
30 same idle notion comes to me to-day, when from the street-window I look on the slow stream of human life creeping

past, night and morning, to the great mills. Masses of men, with dull, besotted faces bent to the ground, sharpened here and there by pain or cunning; skin and muscle and
35 flesh begrimed with smoke and ashes; stooping all night over boiling caldrons of metal, laired by day in dens of drunkenness and infamy; breathing from infancy to death an air saturated with fog and grease and soot, vileness for soul and body. . .
40 Can you see how foggy the day is? As I stand here, idly tapping the windowpane, and looking out through the rain at the dirty back-yard and the coalboats below, fragments of an old story float up before me,—a story of this house into which I happened to come to-day. You may think it a
45 tiresome story enough, as foggy as the day, sharpened by no sudden flashes of pain or pleasure.—I know: only the outline of a dull life, that long since, with thousands of dull lives like its own, was vainly lived and lost: thousands of them, massed, vile, slimy lives, like those of the torpid lizards in
50 yonder stagnant water-butt.—Lost? There is a curious point for you to settle, my friend, who study psychology in a lazy, dilettante way. Stop a moment. I am going to be honest. This is what I want you to do. I want you to hide your disgust, take no heed to your clean clothes, and come right down
55 with me,—here, into the thickest of the fog and mud and foul effluvia. I want you to hear this story.

CONTINUE

1

Which of the following best describes the passage as a whole?

A) A cautionary narrative about the consequences of excessive greed

B) An examination of the day-to-day routines of a downtrodden segment of society

C) A recollection of a uniquely distressing event in the life of the narrator

D) A detailed description of thoroughly unpleasant surroundings

2

It can be reasonably inferred that the narrator of the passage is

A) a detached commentator assessing the economy of an impoverished area.

B) a nostalgic artist attempting to re-create childhood scenes.

C) a social reformer who wishes to move the reader of the passage to action.

D) a firsthand observer of the community that the passage describes.

3

Which choice provides the best evidence for the answer to the previous question?

A) Lines 15-17 ("The long train . . . sides")

B) Lines 27-29 ("When I was . . . day")

C) Lines 40-43 ("As I stand . . . before me")

D) Lines 50-53 ("There is a . . . to do")

4

As used in line 26, "heavy" most nearly means

A) cumbersome.

B) important.

C) undisciplined.

D) immobile.

5

As used in line 53, "hide" most nearly means

A) secure.

B) stifle.

C) smuggle.

D) isolate.

6

The narrator indicates how oppressive the "town of iron-works" (lines 1-2) is by describing

A) how the town looks in the aftermath of a calamity.

B) the personalities of individual town residents who are desperate to change their lives.

C) the town's crippling effects on even its non-human inhabitants.

D) opportunities for social advancement that are only available in other communities.

7

Which choice provides the best evidence for the answer to the previous question?

A) Lines 2-4 ("The sky . . . beings")

B) Lines 9-13 ("The idiosyncrasy . . . river")

C) Lines 19-22 ("Smoke . . . I think")

D) Lines 32-35 ("Masses of men . . . ashes")

8

The narrator's reference to the "beautiful river" (line 25) can best be understood as

A) delusional.

B) sarcastic.

C) tearful.

D) optimistic.

169

CONTINUE

Questions 9-17 are based on the following passage and supplementary material.

This reading is from an article that addresses recent assessment measures in education, and the debates that have centered on these measures.

2G

With the "No Child Left Behind Act," recent concerns have arisen amongst educators about the role that exams play in determining a school's federal funding. With this
Line act, teachers must adjust their lessons plans to prepare
5 their students for standardized exams. Consequently, some question whether this act is merely a superficial quick fix since its aim is to ensure a school's pecuniary stability and not necessarily improve its educational approach. This act forces educators to focus on their school's Adequate
10 Yearly Progress, or AYP. Since AYP has become a "hot button" issue, factious quarrels have pervaded even the most common conversations among educators: tiny measures of annual advancement have, arguably, replaced the larger and longer-term goals that may be better indications of a school's
15 academic and institutional health.

However, meeting or exceeding AYP objectives is a significant step toward educational reform. AYP sets reasonable goals for each school and is a relatively reliable method for keeping educators accountable: an emphasis on "long-term
20 progress" can too often lapse into an excuse for short-term leniency. And these goals are actually quite reasonable because each AYP plan is specified to an individual school's target areas. Experienced educators, commissioned via the "No Child Left Behind Act," compile data based on the median student of
25 their home states. The AYP criteria are then utilized to set the troubled school's progress plan for the next year. Ultimately, those critical of the standardized examination tend to forget that the word "adequate," within the acronym AYP, is not tantamount to nuclear fission or organic chemistry. "Adequate" simply
30 means satisfactory. No one is proposing that the school become an International Baccalaureate overnight. Such hyperbole is often used, however, to refute the necessity of examination.

Because public schools rely on federal funding to operate, it is imperative that they provide the necessary proof (in particular,
35 sufficient AYP results) to secure that money. However, some disagree. "This type of 'education' only works to gloss over the crux of a systematic problem detailed by the almighty dollar," said Anna Thompson, a high school teacher for more than twenty years. She believes that there are possible correlations
40 between a school's socioeconomic background and AYP results. Thus, she asks, "how can a school acquire the much needed funding to succeed in AYP objectives, if it relies on that same funding to reform its teaching staff? It's a Catch-22 in which teachers who are needed in failing districts are instead hired
45 in more affluent towns because these districts can offer higher

salaries. 'Bubbling up' the answer key, taking the cash, and cashing the check—this is not education."

Yet Thompson and her supporters tend to overlook a very important detail. Schools in need of AYP are operating below
50 the standards that are set in place by their respective states. Thus, while some teachers may feel the pressure to tailor their lessons plans to a particular standardized test, at least the concepts that they are preparing their students to address are not abstract, obscure theories. Rather, they are basic practices
55 with real-life applications that any school should be able to sustain. Sometimes both students *and* teachers need to be reined in. Otherwise, what can we reasonably expect from our students if our educational system doesn't look out for them?

9

The main purpose of this passage is to

A) assess a controversial standard that is used in contemporary education.

B) criticize a legislative measure that has completely undermined the quality of American schools.

C) demonstrate why the "No Child Left Behind Act" is superior to AYP criteria.

D) portray the ideas of Anna Thompson and other educators as destructive.

10

As used in line 4, "adjust" most nearly means

A) move.

B) modify.

C) repair.

D) camouflage.

11

Overall, the author of the passage would argue that "Adequate Yearly Progress" measures (lines 9-10) are

A) flawless.

B) incomprehensible.

C) outdated.

D) constructive.

CONTINUE ▶

Percentage of U.S. Federal Education Funding Based on AYP Benchmarks (2012)

% of Benchmarks Met	50%-60%	61%-70%	71%-80%	81%-90%	91%-100%
% of Funding Received	7%	9%	10%	19%	25%

12

Which choice provides the best evidence for the answer to the previous question?

A) Lines 10-12 ("Since . . . educators")

B) Lines 16-17 ("However . . . reform")

C) Lines 29-31 ("Adequate . . . overnight")

D) Lines 41-43 ("Thus . . . staff?")

13

The author most clearly indicates that which of the following should be prioritized by modern education?

A) Information that prepares students for government jobs

B) Difficult subjects in math and science

C) Understandable ideas and practical skills

D) Only those topics that appear on standardized tests

14

Which choice provides the best evidence for the answer to the previous question?

A) Lines 5-8 ("teachers must . . . approach)

B) Lines 26-29 ("Ultimately . . . chemistry")

C) Lines 33-36 ("Because . . . disagree")

D) Lines 52-56 ("the concepts . . . sustain")

15

As used in line 34, "proof" most nearly means

A) mathematical demonstration.

B) legal argument.

C) documented results.

D) essential clue.

16

The author of the passage would see the information in the table as evidence that

A) AYP benchmarks are extremely subjective.

B) AYP benchmarks will soon be abolished.

C) AYP benchmarks are used to determine federal funding.

D) AYP benchmarks do not normally determine federal funding.

17

A student notices that the percentages in the table for "Funding Received" do not sum to 100%. Which of the following would be the best explanation for this aspect of the table?

A) Schools that met below 50% of the benchmarks account for the remaining percentage points.

B) Schools that met above 50% of the benchmarks account for the remaining percentage points.

C) Schools located in different countries account for the remaining percentage points.

D) Schools that had been closed several years before account for the remaining percentage points.

CONTINUE

Questions 18-26 are based on the following passage.

Adapted from Danielle Barkley, "The Known Unknowns of Our Solar System: All Eyes on Planet 9."

The search for discoveries hidden in the depths of outer space has usually focused on the hunt for other life forms. Now, new evidence suggests that something much bigger
Line might be lurking at the far reaches of our own solar system:
5 an entire planet. Dubbed "Planet Nine," this hypothetical planet is estimated to be giant, with a mass approximately ten times greater than that of Earth, and a diameter ranging from two to four times Earth's. Its location is so distant that Planet Nine may well need about 15,000 years to complete one orbit
10 around the sun.

The hunt for Planet Nine began in the Kuiper Belt, a ring-shaped collection of small bodies of matter such as asteroids, dwarf planets, and fragments of rock and ice left behind after collisions (or after the genesis of new stars). Located
15 beyond the orbit of Neptune, the Kuiper Belt is home to Pluto, previously considered a planet but reclassified as a dwarf planet in 2006. Studies of the region have revealed that the belt consists of thousands of bodies of matter, known as Kuiper Belt Objects or KBOs, each with a circumference of 60 miles
20 or greater, as well as trillions of smaller fragments. Evidence of the existence of Planet Nine relies on the observation of the orbits of these objects. Six Kuiper Belt Objects have been observed to share remarkably similar orbits. Although the objects are all moving at different speeds, their elliptical
25 paths are tilted in the same direction, and at roughly the same angle. The odds of this occurring by chance are predicted to be approximately 0.007 percent.

Increasingly, researchers have hypothesized that the presence of a large and distant planet—Planet Nine—could
30 be the cause of this irregularity. If it exists, Planet Nine would exert a gravitational pull that would shape the orbit of nearby objects in the very pattern that has been observed. Additionally, the predicted gravitational pull would force a second set of objects into a different, roughly perpendicular
35 pattern of orbit. The orbits of five other KBOs have been charted and demonstrate this type of movement, lending further credibility to the Planet Nine hypothesis. "We plotted up the positions of those objects and their orbits, and they matched the simulations exactly. When we found
40 that, my jaw sort of hit the floor," astronomer Mike Brown comments.

While its very existence remains unconfirmed, there has already been speculation about possible characteristics and origins of Planet Nine. It is possible that Planet Nine
45 actually formed much nearer to the sun, but at some point, an encounter with the gravitational pull of either Jupiter or Saturn knocked it out of its initial position and propelled it towards its current location at the far reaches of the solar system. It has been suggested that Planet Nine could
50 resemble Uranus and Neptune, having been formed out of a mixture of rock and ice with a small envelope of gas surrounding it. If this new planet exists, it should be possible to observe Planet Nine with high-power telescopes, such as the Subaru Telescope, which have already been used
55 to confirm other distant objects. The abiding challenge is that, while the orbit of Planet Nine has been mapped, its exact location remains unknown. Curious eyes, however, are already trained on the predicted range, as astronomers worldwide hope to get a glimpse.

Size Estimates for Planet 9 (All Figures Drawn to Scale)

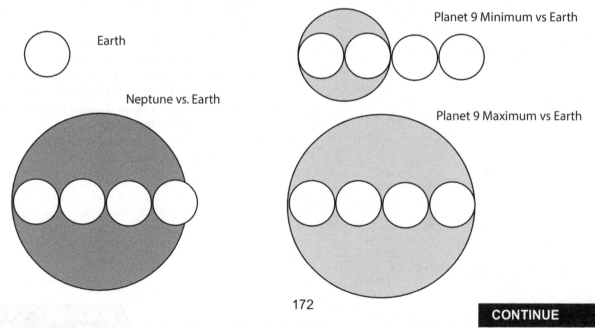

Earth

Planet 9 Minimum vs Earth

Neptune vs. Earth

Planet 9 Maximum vs Earth

CONTINUE

18

The main purpose of the passage is to

A) explain why astronomers so often have trouble proving the existence of new planets.

B) demonstrate that life is unlikely to exist on other planets.

C) settle a controversy in the development of new telescope technology.

D) record the efforts that have surrounded a recent speculation by astronomers.

19

As used in line 12, "bodies" most nearly means

A) masses.

B) organisms.

C) anatomies.

D) organizations.

20

As used in line 37, "credibility" most nearly means

A) honesty.

B) plausibility.

C) morality.

D) dependability.

21

The author of the passage would agree that Planet 9

A) has not been confirmed, but should be detectable using existing telescope technology.

B) has been confirmed, and resembles Uranus and Neptune in appearance.

C) has not been confirmed, but has emitted sound waves that are definitive proof of its presence.

D) has been confirmed, and is much too far from the sun to harbor any form of life.

22

Which choice provides the best evidence for the answer to the previous question?

A) Lines 8-10 ("Its location . . . sun")

B) Lines 49-52 ("Planet . . . surrounding it")

C) Lines 52-55 ("If this . . . objects")

D) Lines 57-59 ("Curious . . . glimpse")

23

Which of the following, according to the passage, could indicate the presence of Planet 9?

A) Abnormalities in the movements of other objects in the solar system

B) An increase in the number of asteroids and large ice fragments in the Kuiper Belt

C) A change in the orbit path followed by a known planet

D) The discovery of another previously unknown planet much closer to the sun

24

Which choice provides the best evidence for the answer to the previous question?

A) Lines 11-14 ("The hunt . . . stars")

B) Lines 28-30 ("Increasingly . . . irregularity")

C) Lines 42-44 ("While . . . Nine")

D) Lines 46-49 ("an encounter . . . system")

25

According to the information in the graphic, Planet 9 at its maximum size would be

A) almost the same size as Neptune.

B) almost the same size as Earth.

C) almost the same mass as Neptune.

D) almost the same mass as Earth.

26

The information in the passage and in the graphic indicates which of the following about Planet 9?

A) It is the same size as Neptune.

B) It is much smaller than Neptune.

C) Its actual size has not yet been determined.

D) Its actual size will probably never be determined.

CONTINUE

Questions 27-34 are based on the following passage.

Passage 1 is adapted from the *Narrative of the Life of Frederick Douglass* by Douglass himself, a former slave (1845); Passage 2 is adapted from a fragmentary essay written by Abraham Lincoln (1851).

Passage 1

In the early part of the year 1838, I became quite restless. I could see no reason why I should, at the end of each week, pour the reward of my toil into the purse of my master. When
Line I carried to him my weekly wages, he would, after counting
5 the money, look me in the face with a robber-like fierceness, and ask, "Is this all?" He was satisfied with nothing less than the last cent. He would, however, when I made him six dollars, sometimes give me six cents, to encourage me. It had the opposite effect. I regarded it as a sort of admission of my
10 right to the whole. The fact that he gave me any part of my wages was proof, to my mind, that he believed me entitled to the whole of them. I always felt worse for having received any thing; for I feared that the giving me a few cents would ease his conscience, and make him feel himself to be a pretty
15 honorable sort of robber. My discontent grew upon me. I was ever on the look-out for means of escape; and, finding no direct means, I determined to try to hire my time, with a view of getting money with which to make my escape. In the spring of 1838, when Master Thomas came to Baltimore to
20 purchase his spring goods, I got an opportunity, and applied to him to allow me to hire my time. He unhesitatingly refused my request, and told me this was another stratagem by which to escape. He told me I could go nowhere but that he could get me; and that, in the event of my running away, he should spare
25 no pains in his efforts to catch me. He exhorted me to content myself, and be obedient. He told me, if I would be happy, I must lay out no plans for the future. He said, if I behaved myself properly, he would take care of me. Indeed, he advised me to complete thoughtlessness of the future, and taught me to
30 depend solely upon him for happiness. He seemed to see fully the pressing necessity of setting aside my intellectual nature, in order to contentment in slavery. But in spite of him, and even in spite of myself, I continued to think, and to think about the injustice of my enslavement, and the means of escape.

Passage 2

35 We know Southern men declare that their slaves are better off than hired labourers amongst us. How little they know whereof they speak! There is no permanent class of hired labourers amongst us. Twenty-five years ago I was a hired labourer. The hired labourer of yesterday labours on his
40 own account to-day, and will hire others to labour for him tomorrow.

Advancement—improvement in condition—is the order of things in a society of equals. As labour is the common burden of our race, so the effort of some to shift their share
45 of the burden on to the shoulders of others is the great durable curse of the race. Originally a curse for transgression upon the whole race, when, as by slavery, it is concentrated on a part only, it becomes the double-refined curse of God upon his creatures.
50 Free labour has the inspiration of hope; pure slavery has no hope. The power of hope upon human exertion and happiness is wonderful. The slave-master himself has a conception of it, and hence the system of tasks among slaves. The slave whom you cannot drive with the lash to
55 break seventy-five pounds of hemp in a day, if you will task him to break a hundred, and promise him pay for all he does over, he will break you a hundred and fifty. You have substituted hope for the rod.

27

As used in line 1, "restless" most nearly means
A) ambitious.
B) nervous.
C) exhausted.
D) dissatisfied.

28

Both passages discuss which of the following topics?
A) The payments that slaves may receive for their work
B) The preparations that slaves make before trying to escape
C) The senseless violence promoted by slave owners
D) The founding American principles that are in clear conflict with slavery

29

As used in line 23, "get" must nearly means
A) purchase.
B) apprehend.
C) rescue.
D) understand.

CONTINUE

30

In Passage 1, what can be reasonably inferred about the advice offered by "Master Thomas" (line 19)?

A) It did not have the impact that Master Thomas had desired.

B) It was offered in order to encourage Douglass to acquire new skills.

C) It was never intended as a long-term solution.

D) It revealed his hateful and irresponsible personality.

31

Which choice provides the best evidence for the answer to the previous question?

A) Lines 21-23 ("He unhesitatingly . . . escape")

B) Lines 25-37 ("He exhorted . . . future")

C) Lines 27-30 ("He said . . . happiness")

D) Lines 32-34 ("But in . . . escape")

32

The author of Passage 2 would most likely argue which of the following about Douglass's "master" (line 3) in Passage 1?

A) Douglass's master valued Douglass much more highly than he would have valued a hired laborer.

B) Douglass's master followed a method of compensation that few other slave masters would have endorsed.

C) Douglass's master was aware of Douglass's natural desires and was determined to stifle them.

D) Douglass's master enjoyed a lifestyle that was not in any way stressful or challenging.

33

Which choice provides the best evidence for the answer to the previous question?

A) Lines 35-36 ("We know . . . us")

B) Lines 38-41 ("Twenty-five . . . tomorrow")

C) Lines 43-46 ("As labour . . . race")

D) Lines 51-54 ("The power . . . slaves")

34

Which of the following writing strategies is present in both passages?

A) Personal testimony

B) Extended analogy

C) Rhetorical questions

D) Intentional caricature

175

CONTINUE

Questions 35-42 are based on the following passage.

Adapted from Nathaniel Hunt, "Born to Run? A New Perspective on Human Evolutionary History."

Human beings are often described as "natural-born
runners," believed to be blessed with a plethora of evolutionary
adaptations designed to help us run long distances. These
Line adaptations make us uniquely suited to hunt down prey
5 animals until they're exhausted or overheated. In other words,
we don't need to run faster than our prey, just farther. Yet
runners have among the highest injury rates of all athletes. In
fact, it's estimated that between 30% and 75% of all runners
are injured every season. How can something that humans are
10 so uniquely adapted to do cause us so much injury?

The human body has been shaped by the activity of
running. On the African Savannah—and without weapons,
claws, or armor—humans developed a unique hunting strategy
that eventually helped them gain the top slot in the food chain.
15 The top two traits that helped our ancestors eat seem rather
odd: obstinacy and sweat. These two traits were first cited
by Harvard Anthropology Professor Daniel Lieberman, who
sought to explain why human beings would voluntarily run
vastly long distances—similar to those of today's Marathons.
20 Lieberman's findings were astonishing. In many ways,
humans are the best runners in the animal kingdom. Other
animals known for running long-distance, such as horses and
dogs, will generally only run if forced to do so. Humans, on
the other hand, will run just for sport. In addition, Lieberman's
25 research indicates that humans are even better long-distance
runners than horses or dogs.

"Humans are terrible athletes in terms of power and
speed, but we're phenomenal at slow and steady." Lieberman
said. Physiological adaptations that help humans dump heat
30 (including relative sparsity of body hair, abundant sweat
glands, and the ability to breathe through the mouth) are
enormously advantageous when it comes to running. Other
physical adaptations include our large gluteus muscles, our
springy tendons, and the way in which we counterbalance
35 each stride with arm movements. These adaptations all add up
to a severely decreased energy expenditure for humans when
maintaining a running pace. Other animals, by contrast, have
to expend a huge amount of energy to speed up, particularly
when switching to full gallop.
40 So if human beings are such natural-born runners, with
millions of years of adaptations to make us running hunters,
why are modern humans injured so frequently while running?
The answer lies largely in how individual runners land during
each stride. In one 2012 Harvard study, it was found that where
45 a runner lands on his or her foot was highly correlated with
injury likelihood. For runners that land on their heels, injury
rates were higher than for runners who land on their forefeet.

In a 2016 study that looked at runners, researchers
decided to study runners who had never been injured and
50 to compare this group to runners with a history of injury.
The findings indicate that the manner of landing each stride
has an enormous effect on injury rate. The runners who had
never been injured completed each stride much less abruptly.
The lead researcher, Irene Davis, noted that the difference in
55 running styles is analogous to the difference between landing
from a jump with bent knees (and thus allowing the legs to
flex) and landing stiff-legged (which doesn't disperse any of
the impact).

Perhaps the most surprising finding, however, was
60 that the weight of the runner was not correlated with the
suddenness of the stride force. The good news is that anyone
can learn how to run with a lighter touch, leading to lower
rates of injury and helping us reclaim our biological heritage
as runners.

35

The information in lines 6-9 ("Yet runners . . . season")
serves to

A) highlight an apparent oddity.
B) introduce a famous experiment.
C) predict a future event.
D) paraphrase a controversial idea.

36

The primary purpose of the second paragraph
(lines 11-19) is to

A) directly answer the question posed at the end of the
first paragraph.
B) suggest that Lieberman's findings were a source of
debate among scientists.
C) demonstrate why humans no longer find running
useful.
D) explain the role of running in human efforts to adapt
and survive.

37

The author of the passage develops his thesis about why
humans suffer so many running injuries by

A) asking unanswerable questions.
B) describing a newly-discovered culture.
C) citing recent research.
D) criticizing an authority.

CONTINUE

38

Which choice provides the best evidence for the answer to the previous question?

A) Lines 9-10 ("How can . . . injury?")

B) Lines 12-14 ("On the African . . . chain")

C) Lines 27-29 ("Humans are . . . said")

D) Lines 48-50 ("In a 2016 . . . injury")

39

According to the author, how can a human runner best avoid injury while running?

A) By landing each stride in a specific manner

B) By losing weight and maintaining a healthy diet

C) By running long distances to stay in shape

D) By running over hilly terrain instead of over flat terrain

40

Which choice provides the best evidence for the answer to the previous question?

A) Lines 18-19 ("human beings . . . Marathons")

B) Lines 35-37 ("These . . . pace")

C) Lines 59-61 ("Perhaps . . . force")

D) Lines 61-64 ("The good . . . runners")

41

As used in line 36, "decreased" most nearly means

A) diminished.

B) shortened.

C) humbled.

D) cheapened.

42

As used in line 58, "impact" most nearly means

A) final meaning.

B) personal influence.

C) physical force.

D) historical consequence.

STOP

177

Writing Test
30 MINUTES, 40 QUESTIONS

Turn to Section 2 of your answer sheet to answer the questions in this section.

DIRECTIONS

Each passage below is accompanied by a number of questions. For some questions, you will consider how the passage might be revised to improve the expression of ideas. For other questions, you will consider how the passage might be edited to correct errors in sentence structure, usage, or punctuation. A passage or a question may be accompanied by one or more graphics (such as a table or graph) that you will consider as you make revising and editing decisions.

Some questions will direct you to an underlined portion of a passage. Other questions will direct you to a location in a passage or ask you to think about the passage as a whole.

After reading each passage, choose the answer to each question that most effectively improves the quality of writing in the passage or that makes the passage conform to the conventions of standard written English. Many questions include a "NO CHANGE" option. Choose that option if you think the best choice is to leave the relevant portion of the passage as it is.

Questions 1-10 are based on the following passage.

A New Dimension of Pharmaceuticals

Pharmacists have long acknowledged the limitations of drugs that are **1** swallowed, they are tablets and capsules. Delivering accurate dosage is difficult when tablets and capsules usually come in just a few sizes. Sometimes, doctors will resort to pill-cutters, asking their patients to cut their pills in half **2** to achieve a more nuanced prescription dosage. Yet these devices are faulty, and at-home use can lead to mistakes and **3** inconsistent dosage. This lack of flexibility is especially problematic for children and older patients. For children, dosage is based almost entirely on weight, so doctors and pharmacists should be able to produce minutely adjusted individual doses;

1

A) NO CHANGE
B) swallowed, those are
C) swallowed, like
D) swallowed by

2

The writer is considering deleting the underlined portion in order to improve the paragraph. Should the writer do so?

A) Yes, because this information contradicts the passage's main argument.
B) Yes, because pill-cutters are not discussed elsewhere.
C) No, because this information explains why pill-cutters offer the most effective dosage method.
D) No, because this information clarifies the motives for using pill-cutters.

3

A) NO CHANGE
B) dosed inconsistency
C) the dosage is inconsistent
D) the dosage which is inconsistent

CONTINUE

for their part, **4** people that are old must often juggle tiny, precise doses of many different medications. In addition, controlled-release oral dosages require specific internal structures that are difficult to customize.

Fortunately, there is a solution. The relatively new measuring and modeling technology known as 3-Dimensional Printing (or 3DP) offers unprecedented flexibility in terms of material, microstructure, surface texture, and scalability. Now, both the very young and the very old **5** has a cost-effective solution to their pharmaceutical issues.

6 Controversial manufacturing methods in the field of pharmacy are labor-intensive and involve separate stages. The first step includes creating the form or shape of the dosage. **7** Prior to the development of 3DP, the release characteristics of a dosage relied on the chemical and physical properties of "excipients" (or inactive ingredients) within the drug. These factors limit flexibility in terms of dosage ingredients and industrial processes. Compared to these standard methods, 3DP is a simple, one-step process that can be customized digitally and reproduced endlessly. 3DP increases precision of dosage to the nanogram (one billionth of a gram). Moreover, 3DP can

4
A) NO CHANGE
B) more elder people
C) patients which are older
D) older patients

5
A) NO CHANGE
B) have
C) had
D) had had

6
A) NO CHANGE
B) Coveted
C) Conventional
D) Convened

7
The writer wishes to add meaningful information that maintains the focus of this portion of the paragraph. Which of the following sentences would best be inserted here?
A) After that, this form is coated with a liquid substance that dries to create a release barrier for the active ingredients.
B) Attempts to explain 3DP without resorting to technical and specialized terminology have tended to fail.
C) Although cost-effective, 3DP is not always compatible with the technologies that are entrenched in older companies.
D) This generation of a specific shape is one of the separate stages involved in the different methods that preceded 3DP.

CONTINUE

increase the complexity of a pill's internal structure, freeing pharmaceutical manufacturers from heavy reliance on excipient properties. Perhaps best of all for the most sensitive medications, 3DP is operable at [8] room temperature. Therefore, 3DP provides an advantage over competing technologies that tend to require high temperatures in the early stages of production and naturally distort the properties of a pill's ingredients.

For pharmaceutical companies determined to save time and money, 3DP is faster and cheaper than much of the widespread [9] technology, which is much more costly. According to the *Journal of Pharmaceutical Sciences*, commercially available 3DP machines produce about twenty thousand tablets per hour. Another advantage of 3DPs devices is [10] that it is office-friendly and thus trim the time between design adjustment and production.

[8]

Which of the following best combines the two sentences at the underlined portion?
A) room temperature, where it provides
B) room temperature, when it provides
C) room temperature, thus providing
D) room temperature, it provides

[9]

A) NO CHANGE
B) technology, which operates much more slowly.
C) technology which is now prevalent.
D) technology.

[10]

A) NO CHANGE
B) that they are
C) as
D) DELETE the underlined portion.

CONTINUE

Questions 11-20 are based on the following passage.

The Good, the Bad, and the Owls

Through the ages, owls have been regarded as symbols of wisdom; **11** they have also been seen as harbingers of death and ill fortune. In many African and Arab countries, owls are regarded as messengers of bad luck, ill health, and death. **12** However, in Europe, they are associated with sorcery and dark ideas. Even Shakespeare, in *Julius Caesar*, refers to the legend that an owl perched in the Forum of Rome was a sign that Caesar would be assassinated.

Owls are one of the few nocturnal birds of prey. **13** Nonetheless, it is possible that Shakespeare exaggerated the ominous, menacing qualities of owls. Because of this association with stealthy aggression, some Kenyans and Native Americans believe that an owl will perch outside the home of a shaman or magician. They **14** maintain that the owl carries messages back and forth from the spirit world, a source of baneful power. In the African nation of Cameroon, the owl has no official name: it is simply referred to as "the bird that makes you afraid." In some regions of the Malaysian islands, owls are believed to eat new-born babies and to bring sickness to children.

11

Which of the following is the best replacement for the underlined portion?
A) NO CHANGE
B) owls have
C) symbols have
D) certain nations have

12

A) NO CHANGE
B) As a result, in Europe,
C) In Europe as well,
D) In Europe, shockingly,

13

Which choice provides relevant information that directly supports the writer's ideas about owls in this paragraph?
A) NO CHANGE
B) Silent and deadly, they glide along, hunting small rodents and birds.
C) Few people are aware of this fact, and some believe that eagles are also nocturnal.
D) They dwell in the upper branches of dark forests, serenely surveying the world below.

14

A) NO CHANGE
B) prove that
C) desire that
D) are really sure that

CONTINUE

To skeptics, these cultural myths may seem to be only that—myths. But there is some substance to these sociocultural beliefs, [15] owls do not truly possess mystical or fanciful properties. (After all, such associations were usually birthed from uncertainties [16] against the natural world.) Like owls, snakes have been symbolically significant in many cultures both as omens of death and [17] symbolic of power.

15

A) NO CHANGE
B) where owls
C) why owls
D) even if owls

16

A) NO CHANGE
B) to the natural
C) for the natural
D) about the natural

17

A) NO CHANGE
B) as symbols of
C) symbolizing
D) to symbolize

CONTINUE

What does this ambivalence about specific predators suggest about humans and [18] their fear of the unknown? Consider for a moment that you are confronted by an owl's mysterious presence in the middle of the night. It can be [19] neurological: the steady, unmoving gaze of the owl's glaucous eyes and the turning of its head almost in a full circle, like the head of a clockwork toy. The owl's eyes are fixed, [20] calling to mind those of a vindictive judge: a stare so steady as to haunt its victims, who are often unaware of an imminent demise. Like those of a judge on his high bench, or of a teacher surveying a group of wary students, those eyes consider and condemn the owl's prey. Imagine that penetrating, yellow gaze upon you.

[18]

A) NO CHANGE
B) your fear
C) one's fear
D) his or her fear

[19]

A) NO CHANGE
B) strong-nerved
C) annoying
D) unnerving

[20]

The writer wishes to add information that explains a practical benefit of the owl's fixed eyes. Which of the following is the best choice?

A) NO CHANGE
B) making it a figure of fear for many writers and poets
C) ensuring precision before the owl makes its strike
D) giving the owl an eerily human-like anatomy

CONTINUE

Questions 21-30 are based on the following passage.

Jane Austen: The Sensibility of a Novelist

Until the nineteenth century, only a few women were prominent in the world of novel-writing. [21] Scandalously, Aphra Behn was a popular playwright and did produce a few novels. Yet after Behn was buried in Westminster Abbey in 1689, the popularity of both her novels and her plays declined very quickly. There is also the marginally better-known Fanny Burney, [22] who wrote the novels *Camilla* and *Cecilia* at the end of the eighteenth century. Today, literary scholars have a tendency to neglect her novels, while the general public remains in complete ignorance of these books. Indeed, if Burney is remembered at all, it is for her more famous Diary.

21
A) NO CHANGE
B) Astonishingly,
C) In addition,
D) For instance,

22
A) NO CHANGE
B) who writes
C) she wrote
D) she writes

CONTINUE

There are reasons for this dearth of female novelists before 1800, the first being that the novel was a relatively new genre of writing. The [23] early recognized novelist in England is Samuel Richardson, who produced *Pamela, or Virtue Rewarded* in 1740. Richardson's success prompted Henry Fielding to write *Joseph Andrews* and *Tom Jones*, which in turn encouraged Smollett, Sterne, and Goldsmith to [24] see what they had at the new literary genre. The narration of their novels can be overbearing, the satire unrestrained: one may well understand why a demure lady of the eighteenth century [25] might not be, encouraged, to participate in this imperious form of writing.

Then, in the last year of the eighteenth century, a sharp-witted young lady named Jane Austen amused her family [26] by writing a small book that punctured the posturing absurdity of her era's popular novels with a hard dose of common sense. That book, *Northanger Abbey*, transformed Jane Austen into the leader of the women [27] writers, they so often dominated the literature of the nineteenth century.

[23]
A) NO CHANGE
B) earlier
C) more early
D) earliest

[24]
A) NO CHANGE
B) try their hands
C) test it out
D) determine their attributes

[25]
A) NO CHANGE
B) might not be encouraged to participate in this imperious form, of, writing.
C) might not, be encouraged to participate in this imperious form of writing.
D) might not be encouraged to participate in this imperious form of writing.

[26]
A) NO CHANGE
B) as writing
C) until writing
D) writing

[27]
A) NO CHANGE
B) writers, this group so often
C) writers who so often
D) writers so often

185

CONTINUE

[1] In her fiction, Austen never patronizes her reader. [2] The action is mostly domestic: with her down-to-earth material, **28** it is laced with common sense and a distinct awareness of irony, Jane Austen gave the novel a new psychological intensity. [3] To read *Sense and Sensibility*, or *Persuasion*, or any other of the six major novels she wrote, is to see precisely what life was really like for the women of Austen's era. **29**

The nineteenth century is rightly deemed the period when the novel came to fruition: **30** you were Mary Ann Evans ("George Eliot"), Elizabeth Gaskell, and the Brontë sisters. They are all heirs of Jane Austen. Their great-great-great grand-daughters should be proud.

28
A) NO CHANGE
B) she laced it with
C) it is with
D) laced with

29
The writer wishes to add the following sentence to this paragraph

She speaks for them all, quietly but clearly.

The best placement for this new sentence would be
A) before sentence 1.
B) after sentence 1.
C) after sentence 2.
D) after sentence 3.

30
A) NO CHANGE
B) its novels were
C) the era of
D) DELETE the underlined portion.

CONTINUE

Questions 31-40 are based on the following passage.

Marketing Day

Do you have high attention to detail, and a high-level ability to determine the few details that really matter? Do you have the ability to evaluate a product critically and honestly, and make the most of its strengths? If you answered "yes" to these questions, you may be [31] perfect suited to a career in marketing, the art of strategically presenting goods and services in the most favorable light possible.

31

A) NO CHANGE
B) perfectly suited
C) suited from perfection
D) perfect suitedly

CONTINUE

The attractions of a job in marketing can be numerous. Even when other professions face hiring cuts, demand for marketing and advertising professionals can remain robust: both big-name **32** to small-name companies will always crave advice that could maximize their appeal. And these companies will pay handsomely, whether **33** they use an independent marketing firm or **34** using an in-house marketing department. The average salary for a marketing employee who has just left college is **35** $68,500, well above the United States average salary for employees at *all* levels, $45,800. Moreover, thanks to the television show *Mad Men*—which takes place in **36** an outlandish 1960s advertising agency—marketing and related fields have taken on new aura of elegance and excitement in recent years.

Job Statistics in the United States

Category	Average Yearly Salary
Marketing Entry Level	$53,400
Marketing Mid Level	$68,500
All U.S. Jobs	$45,800

32
A) NO CHANGE
B) or small-name
C) and small-name
D) in addition to small-name

33
A) NO CHANGE
B) it uses
C) you use
D) one uses

34
A) NO CHANGE
B) an in-house marketing department.
C) doing the marketing in-house.
D) the marketing is done in-house.

35
Which choice provides the most accurate interpretation of the information in the table?
A) NO CHANGE
B) $53,000, well above the United States average salary for employees at *all* levels, $45,800.
C) $68,500, well above the United States average salary for employees at *all* levels, $53,400.
D) $45,800, slightly below the United States average salary for employees at *all* levels, $53,400.

36
Which choice most effectively captures the writer's argument about the appeal of the show *Mad Men*?
A) NO CHANGE
B) a glamorous
C) an old-timey
D) a tragicomic

CONTINUE

Yet perhaps the greatest draw of becoming a marketer is the ability to shape the fates of companies and consumers in ways that few other professionals can. Not even the world's most powerful brand, Coca-Cola, is immune. In 1975, Pepsi marketers [37] from having as a leader executive John Sculley created the Pepsi Challenge, a blind taste test: consumers would sip small quantities of Coke and Pepsi and then state a preference. When consumers opted overwhelmingly for Pepsi, Coke was sent into a tailspin. [38] Pepsi was the clear choice of those who took the Pepsi Challenge and Coke's market share declined, prompting Coke executives to try a variety of new [39] maneuvers. It included the introduction of the sweet-tasting New Coke, which consumers loathed, in 1985.

The Pepsi Challenge was really a clever bit of manipulation, since Pepsi is sweeter [40] then Coke and thus more satisfying in short sips (yet not in large portions). Although they simply made the most of a single product difference, Sculley's marketing tactics worked. Today, marketing continues to offer similar possibilities for creativity. No other profession is so uniquely dedicated to reading the minds and speaking to the desires of modern consumers.

37
A) NO CHANGE
B) and their leading one was executive
C) and their leader was executive
D) led by executive

38
The writer is considering deleting the underlined information (beginning the sentence with the word "Coke's"). Should the writer delete this part of the sentence?
A) Yes, because it simply reformulates a thought expressed slightly earlier.
B) Yes, because the writer never explains why participants in the Pepsi Challenge preferred Pepsi.
C) No, because the writer has not sufficiently established that the Pepsi Challenge caused problems for Coke.
D) No, because this phrase introduces a specific and important detail.

39
A) NO CHANGE
B) maneuvers. Including
C) maneuvers, including
D) maneuvers, these include

40
A) NO CHANGE
B) than Coke
C) then those of Coke
D) than those of Coke

STOP

Answer Key: TEST 1

SECTION 1—READING

1. D	9. A	18. D	27. D	35. A
2. D	10. B	19. A	28. A	36. D
3. C	11. D	20. B	29. B	37. C
4. A	12. B	21. A	30. A	38. D
5. B	13. C	22. C	31. D	39. A
6. C	14. D	23. A	32. C	40. D
7. C	15. C	24. B	33. D	41. A
8. B	16. C	25. A	34. A	42. C
	17. A	26. C		

SECTION 2—WRITING

1. C	11. B	21. D	31. B
2. D	12. C	22. A	32. C
3. A	13. B	23. D	33. A
4. D	14. A	24. B	34. B
5. B	15. D	25. D	35. B
6. C	16. D	26. A	36. B
7. A	17. B	27. C	37. D
8. C	18. A	28. D	38. A
9. D	19. D	29. D	39. C
10. B	20. C	30. C	40. B

Practice Test

TWO

Reading Test
55 MINUTES, 42 QUESTIONS

Turn to Section 1 of your answer sheet to answer the questions in this section.

DIRECTIONS

Each passage or pair of passages below is followed by a number of questions. After reading each passage or pair, choose the best answer to each question based on what is stated or implied in the passage or passages and in any accompanying graphics (such as a table or graph).

Questions 1-8 are based on the following passage.

Adapted from H.G. Wells, *War of the Worlds* (1898).

Then came the night of the first falling star. It was seen early in the morning, rushing over Winchester eastward, a line of flame high in the atmosphere. Hundreds must have seen
Line it, and taken it for an ordinary falling star. Albin described it
5 as leaving a greenish streak behind it that glowed for some seconds. Denning, our greatest authority on meteorites, stated that the height of its first appearance was about ninety or one hundred miles. It seemed to him that it fell to earth about one hundred miles east of him.
10   I was at home at that hour and writing in my study; and although my French windows face towards Ottershaw and the blind was up (for I loved in those days to look up at the night sky), I saw nothing of it. Yet this strangest of all things that ever came to earth from outer space must have fallen
15 while I was sitting there, visible to me had I only looked up as it passed. Some of those who saw its flight say it travelled with a hissing sound. I myself heard nothing of that. Many people in Berkshire, Surrey, and Middlesex must have seen the fall of it, and, at most, have thought that another meteorite
20 had descended. No one seems to have troubled to look for the fallen mass that night.
   But very early in the morning poor Ogilvy, who had seen the shooting star and who was persuaded that a meteorite lay somewhere on the common between Horsell, Ottershaw, and
25 Woking, rose early with the idea of finding it. Find it he did, soon after dawn, and not far from the sand pits. An enormous hole had been made by the impact of the projectile, and the sand and gravel had been flung violently in every direction over the heath, forming heaps visible a mile and a half away.
30 The heather was on fire eastward, and a thin blue smoke rose against the dawn.
   The Thing itself lay almost entirely buried in sand, amidst the scattered splinters of a fir tree it had shivered to fragments in its descent. The uncovered part had the appearance of a
35 huge cylinder, caked over and its outline softened by a thick scaly dun-coloured incrustation. It had a diameter of about thirty yards. He approached the mass, surprised at the size and more so at the shape, since most meteorites are rounded more or less completely. It was, however, still so hot from
40 its flight through the air as to forbid his near approach. A stirring noise within its cylinder he ascribed to the unequal cooling of its surface; for at that time it had not occurred to him that it might be hollow. . .
   And then he perceived that, very slowly, the circular
45 top of the cylinder was rotating on its body. It was such a gradual movement that he discovered it only through noticing that a black mark that had been near him five minutes ago was now at the other side of the circumference. Even then he scarcely understood what this indicated, until
50 he heard a muffled grating sound and saw the black mark jerk forward an inch or so. Then the thing came upon him in a flash. The cylinder was artificial—hollow—with an end that screwed out! Something within the cylinder was unscrewing the top!
55   "Good heavens!" said Ogilvy. "There's a man in it— men in it! Half roasted to death! Trying to escape!"
   At once, with a quick mental leap, he linked the Thing with the flash upon Mars.

CONTINUE ➡

1

The passage as a whole is notable for its use of

A) complex analogies.

B) scientific terminology.

C) incidental dialogue.

D) visual description.

2

As used in line 27, "impact" most nearly means

A) subtle influence.

B) physical force.

C) ideological importance.

D) accepted role.

3

In the course of the passage, the narrator does which of the following?

A) Indulges in sarcastic humor when describing Ogilvy

B) Presents a precise record of Ogilvy's thoughts

C) Defends his reserved and studious personality from criticism

D) Provides a sympathetic account of Ogilvy's demise

4

Which choice provides the best evidence for the answer to the previous question?

A) Lines 3-4 ("Hundreds must . . . star")

B) Lines 10-13 ("I was at . . . of it")

C) Lines 25-26 ("Find it . . . pits")

D) Lines 57-58 ("At once . . . Mars")

5

As used in line 35, "outline" most nearly means

A) summary.

B) contour.

C) boundary.

D) diagram.

6

According to the passage, the observation attributed to Ogilvy in lines 40-42 ("A stirring . . . surface") is

A) scientifically rigorous.

B) remarkably clever.

C) childishly imaginative.

D) ultimately inaccurate.

7

The narrator of the passage would most agree with which of the following statements about "The Thing" (line 32)?

A) It did not cause a particularly great commotion when it first appeared.

B) It has been studied at length by a large number of authoritative scientists.

C) It did not resemble any other falling star that had been observed.

D) It caused widespread destruction and was regarded as a threat by the people who first saw it.

8

Which choice provides the best evidence for the answer to the previous question?

A) Lines 1-3 ("Then came . . . atmosphere")

B) Lines 4-8 ("Albin described . . . miles")

C) Lines 17-21 ("Many people . . . night")

D) Lines 26-29 ("An enormous . . . away")

CONTINUE

Questions 9-17 are based on the following passage and supplementary material.

Adapted from Christopher Holliday, "The Culture Business: Entertainment in the Private and Public Sectors."

Whether we admit it or not, many of us tend to think of national identity as a static set of myths, symbols, and slogans—a simple understanding, but a pervasive one. But
Line the true sign of a vital national identity, or a vital national
5 institution, is the ability to adapt to the times. This is true of relatively new economic powers (China, India) that find their institutions in flux: it is also true of some of the oldest players on the world stage. . . Great Britain, for instance, may be poised for an economic renaissance in the decades ahead,
10 but its musical culture has always been healthy. Consider the famed Promenade Concerts, a throwback to the Victorian era that has had no trouble finding a place in the twenty-first century.

Originally, the Promenade Concerts were open-air
15 events. People strolled through one of the many pleasure gardens of London while an orchestra played music in the background. Then in 1895, Robert Newman, wishing to establish a larger audience for classical music, created a different kind of "Prom": the Proms moved indoors, with
20 both areas of seating and galleries where people could stand to listen. Newman was an entrepreneur, not a musician, and he put the choice of program in the hands of Sir Henry Wood, a visionary conductor who promoted the work of then-groundbreaking composers such as Delius, Richard Strauss,
25 and Ralph Vaughan Williams.

The Newman Proms were a quietly radical institution from the beginning, and proved adept at responding to dramatic turns of events. When Newman went bankrupt, the patronage of what had become known as the "Sir Henry
30 Wood Promenade Concerts" at the Queen's Hall was taken over by others until, eventually, these events were put in the financial care of the state-sanctioned and publicly-funded British Broadcasting Corporation (or BBC). After the Queen's Hall was destroyed in the Blitz of 1941, the
35 Proms were moved to the Royal Albert Hall. Yet thanks to the BBC, you can enjoy today's Proms for nothing. Every performance is broadcast on the radio and many of them are televised, sometimes live but often recorded for airing at a later date. Under this network's guidance, the Proms have
40 grown and evolved. In addition to the great orchestral events in the Albert Hall, Proms in the Park take place in many different cities across the country. The scope of the music that is performed each season has gradually widened, until now the concerts range from full performances of six-hour-long
45 operas by Wagner to nights devoted to the theme songs of British and American films. . .

Naturally, some musical purists have scoffed at this inclusiveness, presuming that melodies designed to accompany westerns or a love stories have nothing to do
50 with classical music. These elitists forget that Tchaikovsky, Verdi, Puccini, and Mozart—though not able to pen film scores for quite obvious reasons—actually did for the popular entertainments of their times what the composers of film scores do for today's movies. Music snobs should
55 also remember Robert Newman's original intentions when he started the Proms back in 1895. Although some may have qualms about an afternoon performance devoted to the music of *Doctor Who*, today's children can only benefit from the realization that a real orchestra making music can
60 be just as exciting as the electric throbbing of an iTunes playlist. . .

The Proms are now part of the UK's national heritage: nowhere is this more evident than in the Royal Albert Hall on the last night of the Proms every year. Flags are
65 waved furiously by the Promenaders, balloons are let loose, streamers are thrown into the orchestra. Behind the orchestra, on a pedestal, is the laurel-wreathed bust of Sir Henry Wood, smiling benignly over a part of British life that is remarkable precisely because it attests to the value of
70 change.

9

The author focuses primarily on which aspect of the Proms?

A) Their adaptability to new historical conditions
B) Their emphasis on conservative and well-known music
C) Their continuing financial problems
D) Their exclusive and aristocratic status

10

Which choice provides the best evidence for the answer to the previous question?

A) Lines 10-13 ("Consider . . . century")
B) Lines 14-17 ("Originally . . . background")
C) Lines 21-25 ("Newman . . . Williams")
D) Lines 28-31 ("When Newman . . . others")

CONTINUE

Genre of Music at the Promenade Concerts
Two Different Performance Years

1956

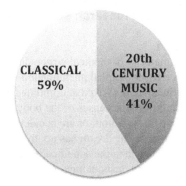

CLASSICAL 59%

20th CENTURY MUSIC 41%

2016

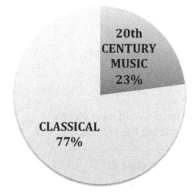

20th CENTURY MUSIC 23%

CLASSICAL 77%

11

As used in lines 30-31, "was taken over by" most nearly means

A) was conquered by.

B) was made the responsibility of.

C) was made obedient by.

D) was a special privilege of.

12

Which of the following best describes the developmental pattern of the passage as a whole?

A) A single country is criticized for supporting a needless form of entertainment.

B) A traditional style of music is compared to other forms of art and expression.

C) A position that promotes diversity is supported despite its many flaws.

D) An idea about culture is supported through the use of an extended example.

13

As used in line 62, "part of" most nearly means

A) an ally of

B) a position of.

C) a region of.

D) an element of.

14

It can be inferred that some of the new musical selections featured in the Proms

A) are seen as unacceptable by certain listeners.

B) will one day be featured in films and television programs.

C) were created exclusively for the BBC.

D) are in fact the re-discovered compositions of Sir Henry Wood.

15

Which choice provides the best evidence for the answer to the previous question?

A) Lines 35-36 ("Yet thanks . . . nothing")

B) Lines 47-50 ("Naturally . . . music")

C) Lines 58-61 ("today's children . . . playlist")

D) Lines 66-70 ("Behind . . . change")

CONTINUE ➡

16

The two pie charts indicate that the percentage of classical music performed at the Proms

A) has increased over time.

B) has decreased over time.

C) has remained the same over time.

D) explains the popularity of the Proms.

17

Which group or individual would most clearly find the tendency recorded in the pie charts to be a positive development?

A) "new economic powers" (line 6)

B) "Robert Newman" (line 17)

C) "musical purists" (line 47)

D) "today's children" (line 58)

Questions 18-25 are based on the following passages.

Passage 1 is adapted from *Dream Psychology* **(translated 1920) by Sigmund Freud; Passage 2 is adapted from an essay on recent medical and psychological research surrounding dreams.**

Passage 1

The majority of medical writers hardly admit that the dream is a psychological phenomenon at all. According to them dreams are provoked and initiated exclusively by stimuli
Line proceeding from the senses or the body, which either reach
5 the sleeper from without or are accidental disturbances of his internal organs. The dream has no greater claim to meaning and importance than the sound called forth by the ten fingers of a person quite unacquainted with music running his fingers over the keys of an instrument. The dream is to be regarded,
10 says Binz, "as a physical process always useless, frequently morbid." All the peculiarities of dream life are explicable as the incoherent effort, due to some physiological stimulus, of certain organs, or of the cortical elements of a brain otherwise asleep.
15 But slightly affected by scientific opinion and untroubled as to the origin of dreams, the popular view holds firmly to the belief that dreams really have got a meaning, in some way they do foretell the future, whilst the meaning can be unravelled in some way or other from its oft bizarre and enigmatical content.
20 The reading of dreams consists in replacing the events of the dream, so far as remembered, by other events. This is done either scene by scene, *according to some rigid key*, or the dream as a whole is replaced by something else of which it was a *symbol*. Serious-minded persons laugh at these efforts—
25 "Dreams are but sea-foam!"

One day I discovered to my amazement that the popular view grounded in superstition, and not the medical one, comes nearer to the truth about dreams. I arrived at new conclusions about dreams by the use of a new method of psychological
30 investigation, one which had rendered me good service in the investigation of phobias, obsessions, illusions, and the like, and which, under the name "psycho-analysis," had found acceptance by a whole school of investigators.

Passage 2

Once dismissed by respectable scientists as beneath
35 serious study, dreams are now among the indispensable materials of psychologists and anthropologists. (Whether they are the indispensable materials of everyday human beings is another matter: surely you have had a dream that was 100% nonsense. I know I have.) In fact, researchers now classify
40 dreams, much as critics classify different types of art and literature. . . While some of these schemes can be much too convoluted for popular use, dream researcher Kelly Bulkeley

CONTINUE ➡️

recently developed one that is simple on the surface but, deeper down, potentially complex.

45   Bulkeley simply divides dreams into "small dreams" and "big dreams": the first are reactions to "relatively everyday, mundane kinds of things", the second are concerned with "deeper life issues with powerful emotions attached" and tend to be "most celebrated in spiritual and

50 religious contexts." Small dreams may proceed from the events of a single, ultimately significant day; big dreams manifest the essentials of the dreamer's personality or the dreamer's broad interaction with his or her culture. . . Yet don't assume that "small" means "insignificant." Bulkeley's

55 small dreams aren't throwbacks to the days when scientists disregarded these, since even these "lesser" dreams can help us understand the "nexus of the body and the mind and the spirit."

18

How would the author of Passage 2 respond to the statements about dreams in lines 6-11 ("The dream . . . morbid") of Passage 1?

A) By noting that dreams have gradually gained acceptance as a valuable research topic

B) By agreeing that dreams should never be taken as a subject of scientific study

C) By arguing that dream research still has not produced any meaningful or definite results

D) By demonstrating why Binz's ideas about dreams are clearly superior to Kelly Bulkeley's

19

Which choice provides the best evidence for the answer to the previous question?

A) Lines 34-36 ("Once . . . anthropologists")

B) Lines 36-39 ("Whether . . . I have")

C) Lines 41-44 ("While some . . . complex")

D) Lines 54-58 ("Bulkeley's . . . spirit")

20

Both Passage 1 and Passage 2 include references to

A) the impossibility of dreams ever being seriously considered by scientists.

B) a specific frame of reference for understanding dreams.

C) the strong resemblance between dreams and various psychological abnormalities.

D) specific dreams that can change a dreamer's life.

21

As used in line 27, "grounded in" most nearly means

A) punished with.

B) premised on.

C) immobilized by.

D) buried under.

22

With which of the following statements would the author of Passage 1 most likely agree?

A) Dreams are much easier to understand than are other aspects of medicine and psychology.

B) Those who construe dreams as unimportant are both uneducated and dishonest.

C) Dreams of any sort are a sign of poor mental health and should be addressed through therapy.

D) Those who possess scientific expertise do not always draw the right conclusions about dreams.

23

Which choice provides the best evidence for the answer to the previous question?

A) Lines 2-6 ("According to . . . organs")

B) Lines 20-21 ("The reading . . . events")

C) Lines 26-28 ("One day . . . dreams")

D) Lines 28-31 ("I arrived . . . the like")

24

Which of the following best explains the function of the second paragraph (lines 45-58) of Passage 2?

A) A listing of the qualifications of an authority on dreams

B) An explanation of a recent controversy surrounding dreams

C) A description of an experiment that is now famous

D) An extended analysis of concepts in dream research

25

As used in line 50, "proceed" most nearly means

A) profit.

B) result.

C) make progress.

D) move away.

CONTINUE

Questions 26-33 are based on the following passage.

Adapted from Charles William Eliot, "Five American Contributions to Civilization" (1895). Eliot served as President of Harvard from 1869 to 1909.

Looking back over forty centuries of history, we observe that many nations have made characteristic contributions to the progress of civilization, the beneficent effects of which
Line have been permanent, although the races that made them may
5 have lost their national form and organization, or their relative standing among the nations of the earth. Thus, the Hebrew race, during many centuries, made supreme contributions to religious thought; and the Greek, during the brief climax of the race, to speculative philosophy, architecture, sculpture, and the
10 drama. The Roman people developed military colonization, aqueducts, roads and bridges, and a great body of public law, large parts of which still survive; and the Italians of the middle ages and the Renaissance developed ecclesiastical organization and the fine arts, as tributary to the splendor
15 of the church and to municipal luxury. England, for several centuries, has contributed to the institutional development of representative government and public justice; the Dutch, in the sixteenth century, made a superb struggle for free thought and free government; France, in the eighteenth century, taught the
20 doctrine of individual freedom and the theory of human rights; and Germany, at two periods within the nineteenth century, fifty years apart, proved the vital force of the sentiment of nationality. I ask you to consider with me what characteristic and durable contributions the American people have been
25 making to the enrichment of civilization.

The first and principal contribution to which I shall ask your attention is the advance made in the United States, not in theory only, but in practice, toward the abandonment of war as the means of settling disputes between nations, the substitution
30 of discussion and arbitration, and the avoidance of armaments. If the intermittent Indian fighting and the brief contest with the Barbary corsairs be disregarded, the United States have had only four years and a quarter of international war in the one hundred and seven years since the adoption of the Constitution.
35 Within the same period the United States have been a party to forty-seven arbitrations—being more than half of all that have taken place in the modern world. . . Confident in their strength, and relying on their ability to adjust international differences, the United States have habitually maintained, by voluntary
40 enlistment for short terms, a standing army and a fleet which, in proportion to the population, are insignificant.

The beneficent effects of this American contribution to civilization are of two sorts: in the first place, the direct evils of war and of preparations for war have been diminished;
45 and secondly, the influence of the war spirit on the perennial conflict between the rights of the single personal unit and

the powers of the multitude that constitute organized society—or, in other words, between individual freedom and collective authority—has been reduced to the lowest terms.
50 War has been, and still is, the school of collectivism, the warrant of tyranny. Century after century, tribes, clans, and nations have sacrificed the liberty of the individual to the fundamental necessity of being strong for combined defense or attack in war. Individual freedom is crushed in war, for
55 the nature of war is inevitably despotic. It says to the private person: "Obey without a question, even unto death; die in this ditch, without knowing why; walk into that deadly thicket; mount this embankment, behind which are men who will try to kill you, lest you should kill them; make part of an
60 immense machine for blind destruction, cruelty, rapine, and killing." At this moment every young man in Continental Europe learns the lesson of absolute military obedience, and feels himself subject to this crushing power of militant society, against which no rights of the individual to life,
65 liberty, and the pursuit of happiness avail anything. This pernicious influence, inherent in the social organization of all Continental Europe during many centuries, the American people have for generations escaped, and they show other nations how to escape it.

26

In the first paragraph (lines 1-25), Eliot lists a large number of

A) reasons why America is superior to other nations.
B) exceptional achievements by various cultures.
C) technological breakthroughs that advanced civilization.
D) ideas that should be rescued from unpopularity.

27

As used in line 27, "advance" most nearly means
A) preparation.
B) aggression.
C) maneuver.
D) progress.

CONTINUE

28

As used in line 31, "contest" most nearly means

A) competition.
B) conflict.
C) entertainment.
D) debate.

29

The main purpose of the passage as a whole is to

A) encourage Americans to contribute more to the "enrichment of civilization" (line 25).
B) warn that the "abandonment of war" (line 28) may be short-lived.
C) describe the context and importance of an American "contribution to civilization" (lines 42-43).
D) criticize the leaders who caused a disastrous "moment" (line 61) in history.

30

Eliot believes that the armed forces of the United States are

A) likely to be reduced and then abolished as the United States becomes more influential.
B) completely similar to the armed forces of less advanced countries.
C) advanced in their strategies and technology, but widely criticized.
D) not overwhelmingly large, but still sufficient and effective.

31

Which choice provides the best evidence for the answer to the previous question?

A) Lines 26-29 ("The first . . . nations")
B) Lines 37-41 ("Confident . . . insignificant")
C) Lines 51-54 ("Century . . . attack in war")
D) Lines 61-65 ("At this . . . anything")

32

Eliot argues that a lifestyle thoroughly based on warfare is

A) necessary to the progress of civilization.
B) one of the main features of American life.
C) morally and psychologically oppressive.
D) uncommon in the modern world.

33

Which choice provides the best evidence for the answer to the previous question?

A) Lines 10-12 ("The Roman . . . survive")
B) Lines 23-25 ("I ask . . . civilization")
C) Lines 35-37 ("Within the . . . world")
D) Lines 54-55 ("Individual . . . despotic")

CONTINUE

Questions 34-42 are based on the following passage and supplementary material.

Adapted from a recent journal article on newly-developed medical procedures.

Organ transplants stand as one of the greatest achievements of modern medicine, offering the possibility to both extend life and improve its quality. However, transplant
Line procedures have always been fraught with challenges, ranging
5 from a shortage of available organs to difficulties with finding a suitable match between donor and recipient. At present, there are about 100 000 individuals in the United States on the wait list for a kidney donation. Of those, an estimated 50% face an additional hurdle: their bodies could easily attack
10 a transplanted organ, significantly increasing the odds of rejection. Of those 50%, about a fifth are so sensitive that it is virtually impossible to find a compatible match.

A new medical procedure known as desensitization may change these grim odds. A study of 1025 patients has
15 shown that doctors were successfully able to alter patients' immune systems so as to allow for kidney transplants between previously incompatible donors and recipients.

Desensitization, as the name implies, works to suppress the immune system's response to a foreign substance. It does
20 so by targeting antibodies, the proteins produced by the white blood cells which are a key part of the body's normal defense mechanism. When a bacterium or virus, for example, enters the body, antibodies work to detect and neutralize it. While everyone's blood contains antibodies, some individuals are
25 more sensitized than others. For kidney transplant patients, a key problem is posed by antibodies that respond to a protein known as human leukocyte antigen (HLA). HLA is found in most cells and is used as a kind of "matching" mechanism to detect whether cells are foreign or not. If a patient has
30 previously been exposed to foreign HLA (most commonly through pregnancy, a blood transfusion, or a previous organ transplant), his or her antibodies continue to exist on a kind of "high alert." When a new organ is introduced, it will most likely be rejected.
35 Desensitization involves filtering these problematic antibodies out of a patient's blood prior to surgery. Then, new antibodies are introduced to both replace the sensitized ones and prevent their return. This process effectively replaces a patient's previous, highly sensitive immune system with one
40 that is much less reactive and therefore more receptive to a donated organ. The procedure is initiated several days prior to surgery, and repeated several times both before and after the transplant takes place. Patients treated with desensitization require only the usual regiment of anti-rejection drugs after the
45 transplant.

Desensitization may mean that patients who previously waited years for a compatible donor will now have access to a donated organ in a much shorter time frame. It can also benefit the unknown number of individuals who remove
50 themselves from the donor list in the belief that a suitable transplant will never be available and resign themselves instead to a lifetime of dialysis treatments. Likely to increase quality of life, a kidney transplant also proves cost-effective over time, since dialysis treatments can easily cost up to
55 $70 000 per year and must continue for the duration of the patient's life. While to date desensitization has only been explored in relation to kidney transplants, it may also prove to be an asset in other transplant procedures involving living donors, such as liver and lung transplants. Yet because the
60 desensitization procedure must be commenced up to a week prior to the surgery, it is not an option for transplants from deceased donors, which occur with only a few hours' notice.

Procedure	Cost	One Time or Annual
Dialysis	$70,000	Annual
Kidney Transplant (No Desensitization)	$250,000	One Time
Kidney Transplant (Desensitization)	$300,000	One Time

34

As used in line 1, "stand as" most nearly means

A) assert themselves as.

B) are widely considered.

C) are commemorated as.

D) are positioned alongside.

35

According to the passage, the medical technique known as "desensitization" was created in order to

A) help scientists understand how the immune system functions.

B) increase the success rate of organ transplants.

C) deal with a temporary organ donor shortage.

D) combat allergies to common pharmaceuticals.

CONTINUE

36

Which choice provides the best evidence for the answer to the previous question?

A) Lines 13-17 ("A new . . . recipients")

B) Lines 23-25 ("While . . . others")

C) Lines 35-38 ("Desensitization . . . return")

D) Lines 43-45 ("Patients . . . transplant")

37

In the final paragraph (lines 46-62), the author

A) expresses the belief that desensitization will never become a popular technique.

B) criticizes dialysis treatments as completely useless.

C) proposes an increase in medical research funding.

D) lists a few of the current limits that desensitization procedures face.

38

Which of the following, according to the passage, would be a result of successful desensitization procedures?

A) The complete elimination of kidney-related diseases

B) Reduced waiting periods for organ donations

C) The disappearance of fatal viruses and bacteria

D) Reduced costs for dialysis and similar procedures

39

Which choice provides the best evidence for the answer to the previous question?

A) Lines 22-23 ("When a . . . neutralize it")

B) Lines 29-33 ("If a . . . alert")

C) Lines 46-48 ("Desensitization . . . frame")

D) Lines 52-56 ("Likely to . . . life")

40

As used in line 49, "unknown" most nearly means

A) undetermined.

B) unimportant.

C) intriguing.

D) obscure.

41

Which of the following would be the most costly way to deal with a kidney problem, according to the table?

A) Kidney transplant without desensitization

B) Kidney transplant with desensitization

C) Five years of dialysis

D) Ten years of dialysis

42

According to the table, kidney transplants with desensitization are more costly than kidney transplants without desensitization. Why, on the basis of the passage, might desensitization involve additional costs?

A) It is riskier than traditional procedures and decreases the chance of a successful transplant.

B) It is in some cases illegal but often increases the chance of a successful transplant.

C) It is quicker than traditional procedures but decreases the chance of a successful transplant.

D) It involves additional procedures that increase the chance of a successful transplant.

STOP

Writing Test

30 MINUTES, 40 QUESTIONS

Turn to Section 2 of your answer sheet to answer the questions in this section.

DIRECTIONS

Each passage below is accompanied by a number of questions. For some questions, you will consider how the passage might be revised to improve the expression of ideas. For other questions, you will consider how the passage might be edited to correct errors in sentence structure, usage, or punctuation. A passage or a question may be accompanied by one or more graphics (such as a table or graph) that you will consider as you make revising and editing decisions.

Some questions will direct you to an underlined portion of a passage. Other questions will direct you to a location in a passage or ask you to think about the passage as a whole.

After reading each passage, choose the answer to each question that most effectively improves the quality of writing in the passage or that makes the passage conform to the conventions of standard written English. Many questions include a "NO CHANGE" option. Choose that option if you think the best choice is to leave the relevant portion of the passage as it is.

Questions 1-10 are based on the following passage.

More Money, More Athleticism

I've heard that those who grow up to become successful sportsmen were born rich. There are equipment fees, training fees, **1** club fees, tournament fees, and there are traveling fees: over the years, the total payment must be enormous. For someone born into a wealthy family, this sacrifice may be manageable. **2** And for you raised without considerable wealth, becoming an athlete may seem like the impossible dream.

When I was eleven, my parents sent me to a specialized school in China for table tennis, **3** where I'd train for four hours a day, six days a week. After the first few days, my temporary allure as the "American girl" wore off. I was then promptly disregarded by the coaches and all the other students:

1

A) NO CHANGE
B) club fees, there are tournament fees and traveling fees
C) club fees; and tournament fees, and traveling fees
D) club fees, tournament fees, and traveling fees

2

A) NO CHANGE
B) And for those
C) But for you
D) But for those

3

Which of the following most effectively maintains the focus of the passage?
A) NO CHANGE
B) even though my mother had initially raised objections to this plan.
C) despite their own fascination with completely different sports.
D) since they thought that I needed to cultivate a much greater sense of self-reliance.

CONTINUE

4 shockingly enough, I ranked among the worst players, and soon the only words I exchanged with the coach were translations for the other, *better* foreign students. I slogged my way 5 against the next few weeks there as an invisible girl, the girl without the potential of the other kids.

The last week of my stay, my dad came to visit and watch my training session. Without warning or reason, I was promoted to the better group and allowed to train with the kids who were 6 regarded as better tennis players than I was. For the next four hours, the coach came to me every few minutes to point out and adjust my weaknesses. When I won a match, I was lavishly praised. When I lost, the coach 7 has shrugged and patted me on the back. When my father left, I was sent back to the lowest group.

[1] It turns out that the school was courting my father's money. [2] I later found that, in many sports clubs, having good connections and bribing the coaches is a common way to guarantee better training for your children. [3] Instead of giving each child equal attention and focus, such coaches pick and choose based on the openness of the parents' wallets. 8

4
A) NO CHANGE
B) however,
C) after all,
D) in the end,

5
A) NO CHANGE
B) through the next
C) of the next
D) as the next

6
A) NO CHANGE
B) assigned to that particular group.
C) prepping for professional table tennis.
D) DELETE the underlined portion and end the sentence with a period.

7
A) NO CHANGE
B) shrugged and patted
C) shrugs and pats
D) will shrug and pat

8
The writer wishes to add the following sentence to the paragraph.

Why not, if it's a better deal for them?

To make the order of ideas in the paragraph most logical, this sentence should be placed
A) before sentence 1.
B) after sentence 1.
C) after sentence 2.
D) after sentence 3.

CONTINUE

Becoming an athlete is neither easy nor cheap. Even those [9] blundering with talent will find it difficult without certain means. Especially in the more obscure sports, where scouting rarely occurs, motivation and [10] raw talented are only as good as the money to back them up.

9

A) NO CHANGE
B) burdened
C) bursting
D) burst

10

A) NO CHANGE
B) raw talent
C) rawly talented
D) talented rawness

CONTINUE

Questions 11-20 are based on the following passage and supplementary material.

Can Landfills Save the Environment?

In the post-industrial world, greenhouse gas emissions have warmed the globe, impacting sea level and weather patterns. Curbing the human impact on climate change by capturing emissions and shifting away from fossil fuel use is among the environmental goals of world governments today: simply put, humans must <u>[11] be exhausted by</u> the CO_2-producing fuels that are warming the planet. <u>[12] Indeed, the situation seems hopeless.</u> A potent and short-lived greenhouse gas, methane (CH_4) is a useful fuel source, and some CH_4 emissions can be captured and substituted for fossil fuels. But where can substantial CH_4 emissions be found? Landfills, it turns out, <u>[13] are rich in CH_4, compared to other gases.</u> By putting these presumed "wasted spaces" to new uses, humanity can make progress in a variety of realms—environmental, economic, and medical.

COMPOSTION OF LANDFILL GAS

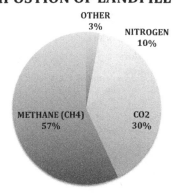

[11]
A) NO CHANGE
B) cut back on
C) get sick of
D) be over and done with

[12]
Which of the following choices offers the most appropriate and effective transition?
A) NO CHANGE
B) Is such government intervention appropriate?
C) Are consumers aware of the problems that they are causing?
D) Fortunately, there may be a solution.

[13]
Which of the following provides the most accurate interpretation of the information contained in the graphic?
A) NO CHANGE
B) emit little CH_4, compared to other gases.
C) emit more CO_2 than CH_4.
D) emit more nitrogen than CH_4.

CONTINUE

Indeed, there are multiple indirect benefits to avoiding fossil fuel and **14** one uses CH_4 and various other landfill-produced "biogases." Biogas burns cleaner than fossil fuel, preventing pollutants like sulfur dioxide (a cause of acid rain), particulate matter (a threat to respiratory health), and nitrogen oxides from entering the atmosphere. **15** The potential, benefits are immense: nitrogen oxides, for example, help form smog and ozone, which can damage vegetation and harm animals' respiratory systems. Though equipment that burns landfill gas does emit some nitrogen oxides, **16** yet the overall mitigation of environmental pollution makes up for this one liability.

Capturing landfill gas also prevents harmful compounds that are produced with the gas *itself* from entering the atmosphere. Trace compounds in landfill gas include non-CH_4 compounds that can be toxic. Hazardous air pollutants found in landfill gas include benzene, toluene, ethyl benzene, and vinyl chloride. These substances can cause **17** cancerous illness, central nervous system damage, and respiratory problems. Other compounds in landfill gas afflict humans with unpleasant odors. Inorganic compounds like hydrogen sulfide are particularly pungent and are eliminated when landfill gas is used. Capturing landfill **18** gas, it reduces odors that threaten to lower property values and reduce air quality in areas near landfills.

14
A) NO CHANGE
B) you use
C) using
D) use

15
A) NO CHANGE
B) The potential benefits are, immense
C) The potential benefits, are immense
D) The potential benefits are immense

16
A) NO CHANGE
B) however the overall
C) and the overall
D) the overall

17
Which choice provides the most relevant and meaningful details at this point in the passage?
A) NO CHANGE
B) problems that are not typically associated with CH_4.
C) problems for a large number of the people who are exposed to them.
D) illnesses and other problems that have been well-documented by researchers.

18
A) NO CHANGE
B) gas, which reduces odors
C) gas reducing odors
D) gas reduces odors

CONTINUE

Moreover, capturing landfill gas reduces the risk of accidents involving [19] unstable, unpredictable substances. Lateral, subsurface migration of landfill gas frequently occurs in older landfills that lack protective linings. Since landfill gas is about 50 percent CH_4, a potentially explosive gas, landfill gas accumulated in subsurface pockets may ignite. Fires and explosions caused by subsurface migration [20] happen in the past, but will not—with the right processes in place—be future threats.

[19]

A) NO CHANGE
B) unstable and unpredictable substances.
C) unstably volatile substances.
D) volatile substances.

[20]

A) NO CHANGE
B) have happened
C) are happening
D) will happen

CONTINUE

Questions 21-30 are based on the following passage.

Isaac Mizrahi: Jack of All Trades, Master of Fashion

Even a versatile, respected artist needs to cut loose on occasion—or, in the case of Isaac Mizrahi, on quite a few occasions. Best known as a designer of women's clothing, Mizrahi has worked in a variety of other fields, from costume design to puppetry to popular television. [21] With his chatty and whimsical sense of humor, he may not fit the stereotype of a solemn "Renaissance Man." Yet it is impossible to deny Mizrahi's [22] devotion for his art, in all its fanciful forms.

21
A) NO CHANGE
B) He possesses a chatty and whimsical sense of humor,
C) His sense of humor is chatty and whimsical,
D) He is humorous, chatty, and whimsical,

22
A) NO CHANGE
B) devotion with
C) devotion as
D) devotion to

CONTINUE

Born into a Jewish family in Brooklyn in 1961, Mizrahi began his education at a local Yeshiva school. Over time, his talent for the visual arts [23] become apparent, and he completed his studies at New York City's High School for the Performing Arts and the Parsons School of Design. By the late 1980s, he was well-established in the New York fashion scene. Mizrahi's name is now synonymous with bold shades of red, orange, and green: unlike a designer such as Calvin Klein, [24] who is a less visible celebrity but has a much greater retail presence, Mizrahi lives for exuberance.

The same lively energy is apparent in Mizrahi's other pursuits. [25] Television is one of the designer's favorite media. Mizrahi hosted his own daytime talk show, which ran for five seasons, and has served as a judge on *Project Runway All Stars* and as a contestant on *Celebrity Jeopardy!* Yet a few of his other projects are [26] most specific to New York and Manhattan. He has created costumes for Manhattan dance impresarios Mark Morris and Twyla Tharp, and presents his own annual rendition of "Peter and the Wolf" [27] every year at the Guggenheim Museum.

23

A) NO CHANGE
B) becomes
C) became
D) will become

24

Which choice most effectively draws a contrast between the design approaches favored by Calvin Klein and Isaac Mizrahi?

A) NO CHANGE
B) who thrives on limited color choices and minimalistic designs,
C) who was active in the world of fashion several decades before Mizrahi was,
D) who has branched out to produce several popular colognes,

25

Which sentence provides the most effective transition to the discussion that follows?

A) NO CHANGE
B) Most of Mizrahi's endeavors can be accurately classified as outlandish.
C) In this regard, Mizrahi truly does resemble older designers such as Ralph Lauren and Calvin Klein.
D) Such versatility can be traced to the designer's education.

26

A) NO CHANGE
B) more
C) least
D) less

27

A) NO CHANGE
B) at the Guggenheim Museum on a yearly basis.
C) at the Guggenheim Museum in order to showcase his unique version of the performance.
D) at the Guggenheim Museum.

CONTINUE →

However, fashion and design [28] they remain Mizrahi's first and foundational inspirations. His approach is wonderfully hands-on: even as computer programs open new possibilities for clothing designers, Mizrahi stays committed to the art of the hand-drawn sketch. He also prefers [29] when he works with live models to working with mannequins, in part because much of his approach is based on how garments move—how they react to the human body. [30] As Mizrahi himself puts it, "This is what I like about being a designer. You can't really get it until you see it."

[28]
A) NO CHANGE
B) that remain
C) remaining
D) remain

[29]
A) NO CHANGE
B) to work with live
C) working with live
D) live

[30]
A) NO CHANGE
B) Despite what Mizrahi himself thinks,
C) In contrast to Mizrahi's normal ideas,
D) If you want to go ahead and take it from Mizrahi himself,

CONTINUE

Questions 31-40 are based on the following passage.

I See England, I See France, I See—Politics

I live in an area of northern France that is quite close to England, right on the British Channel. As a result, I can watch not only all the TV channels available in France, [31] as well as those in the United Kingdom. Every night, I am reminded of how completely the two countries differ in [32] their approaches to political life.

[33] In the UK, the broadcasting organizations constantly examine and criticize the British government. Politicians are scrutinized, interrogated, confronted with their failures, made to defend the reasons for their policies, and [34] they ought to give answers that the general public can weigh. There is a constant interaction between those who govern and those who are governed: this interaction does not always work to the advantage of those who govern. According to recent polls, the British trust their politicians only a bit [35] less as another widely-criticized group, bankers.

31
A) NO CHANGE
B) not to mention
C) and also
D) but also

32
A) NO CHANGE
B) there approaches
C) its approach
D) its' approach

33
The writer is considering deleting the underlined sentence from the paragraph. Should the writer do so?
A) Yes, because it repeats a sentence structure used elsewhere in the passage.
B) Yes, because presents the UK in a negative fashion and thus contradicts the author's main argument.
C) No, because this sentence makes it immediately clear which country the author is analyzing.
D) No, because this sentence summarizes the main difference between France and the United Kingdom.

34
A) NO CHANGE
B) they had better give
C) to give necessary
D) required to give

35
A) NO CHANGE
B) less than
C) least as
D) least than

211

CONTINUE

In France, [36] however, politicians are rarely questioned. To a large extent, their private lives and activities are neither reported nor examined in the press: there are French rules of [37] etiquette, when they cannot be broached. This does not mean that the population of France believes that their politicians are impeccable. They simply pardon the excesses and vices of their politicians, who are at times treated more like minor celebrities than like public servants.

[36]
A) NO CHANGE
B) moreover,
C) for instance,
D) consequently,

[37]
A) NO CHANGE
B) etiquette, where they
C) etiquette which
D) etiquette, they

CONTINUE

After watching these dueling approaches year in and year out, [38] I am convinced that there are strong ideological reasons for these differences. The British have a deeply rooted belief that those in power have a duty to set a moral example. Yet the French, who are much more pragmatic as a nation, have no such expectations: they merely shrug their shoulders and murmur, "That's just how it is." The British believe that all problems can be resolved if [39] one discards them and lets society run its course, while the French believe that if one leaves a problem alone for long enough, it will eventually diminish and disappear, or become irrelevant. [40] Indeed, the French are somewhat set in their ways: the hereditary head of state from before the Revolution (the King) has been replaced by a head of state who is elected every five years (the President). As my French neighbors would say, "that's just how it is."

38

A) NO CHANGE
B) my conviction is that there are strong ideological reasons for these differences.
C) there are strong ideological reasons for these differences.
D) strong ideological reasons exist for these differences.

39

Which of the following choices effectively supports the writer's characterization of the British as contrasted with the author's characterization of the French?

A) NO CHANGE
B) one pays greater attention to national newscasts
C) one works long enough and hard enough,
D) one relies entirely on tradition,

40

At this point, the writer is considering adding the following sentence.

There have, of course, been departures from this complacent attitude, such as the infamous political violence of the French Revolution.

Should the write make this addition here?

A) Yes, because it offers a new example of a difference between the British and the French.
B) Yes, because it explains the writer's motives for criticizing the French so harshly.
C) No, because the writer establishes earlier that the French have been the same since ancient times.
D) No, because it distracts from the writer's analysis of French life in the present day.

STOP

Answer Key: TEST 2

SECTION 1—READING

1. A	9. A	18. A	26. B	34. B
2. B	10. A	19. A	27. D	35. B
3. B	11. B	20. B	28. B	36. A
4. D	12. D	21. B	29. C	37. D
5. B	13. D	22. D	30. D	38. B
6. D	14. A	23. C	31. B	39. C
7. A	15. B	24. D	32. C	40. A
8. C	16. A	25. B	33. D	41. D
	17. C			42. D

SECTION 2—WRITING

1. D	11. B	21. A	31. D
2. D	12. D	22. D	32. A
3. A	13. A	23. C	33. C
4. C	14. C	24. B	34. D
5. B	15. D	25. A	35. B
6. C	16. D	26. B	36. A
7. B	17. A	27. D	37. C
8. D	18. D	28. D	38. A
9. C	19. D	29. C	39. C
10. B	20. B	30. A	40. D

Practice Test
THREE

Reading Test
55 MINUTES, 42 QUESTIONS

Turn to Section 1 of your answer sheet to answer the questions in this section.

Each passage or pair of passages below is followed by a number of questions. After reading each passage or pair, choose the best answer to each question based on what is stated or implied in the passage or passages and in any accompanying graphics (such as a table or graph).

Questions 1-8 are based on the following passage.

Adapted from Willa Cather, O Pioneers! (1913). The scene that follows depicts Carl, a young man who as left his rural community to live in the city, and Alexandra, who has remained in the community. Emil, Alexandra's brother, is often mentioned.

Carl had changed, Alexandra felt, much less than one might have expected. He had not become a trim, self-satisfied city man. There was still something homely and wayward and
Line definitely personal about him. Even his clothes, his Norfolk
5 coat and his very high collars, were a little unconventional. He seemed to shrink into himself as he used to do; to hold himself away from things, as if he were afraid of being hurt. In short, he was more self-conscious than a man of thirty-five is expected to be. He looked older than his years and not very
10 strong. His black hair, which still hung in a triangle over his pale forehead, was thin at the crown, and there were fine, relentless lines about his eyes. His back, with its high, sharp shoulders, looked like the back of an over-worked German professor off on his holiday. His face was intelligent, sensitive,
15 unhappy.
That evening after supper, Carl and Alexandra were sitting by the clump of castor beans in the middle of the flower garden. The gravel paths glittered in the moonlight, and below them the fields lay white and still.
20 "Do you know, Alexandra," he was saying, "I've been thinking how strangely things work out. I've been away engraving other men's pictures, and you've stayed at home and made your own." He pointed with his cigar toward the sleeping landscape. "How in the world have you done it? How
25 have your neighbors done it?"
"We hadn't any of us much to do with it, Carl. The land did it. It had its little joke. It pretended to be poor because nobody knew how to work it right; and then, all at once, it worked itself. It woke up out of its sleep and stretched itself,
30 and it was so big, so rich, that we suddenly found we were

rich, just from sitting still. As for me, you remember when I began to buy land. For years after that I was always squeezing and borrowing until I was ashamed to show my face in the banks. And then, all at once, men began to come
35 to me offering to lend me money—and I didn't need it! Then I went ahead and built this house. I really built it for Emil. I want you to see Emil, Carl. He is so different from the rest of us!"
"How different?"
40 "Oh, you'll see! I'm sure it was to have sons like Emil, and to give them a chance, that father left the old country. It's curious, too; on the outside Emil is just like an American boy,—he graduated from the State University in June, you know,—but underneath he is more Swedish than any of us.
45 Sometimes he is so like father that he frightens me; he is so violent in his feelings like that."
"Is he going to farm here with you?"
"He shall do whatever he wants to," Alexandra declared warmly. "He is going to have a chance, a whole chance;
50 that's what I've worked for. Sometimes he talks about studying law, and sometimes, just lately, he's been talking about going out into the sand hills and taking up more land. He has his sad times, like father. But I hope he won't do that. We have land enough, at last!" Alexandra laughed.

CONTINUE

1

The first paragraph (lines 1-15) serves primarily to provide

A) a series of indications that Carl has suffered during his time in the city.

B) a subtle argument that sensitive individuals should not leave familiar surroundings.

C) a balanced assessment of Carl's appearance and mannerisms.

D) a systematic criticism of Carl's quirks and pretensions.

2

As used in line 10, "strong" most nearly means

A) vigorous.

B) coherent.

C) valid.

D) interesting.

3

As used in line 30, "rich" most nearly means

A) luxurious.

B) overdone.

C) fertile.

D) moneyed.

4

It can be reasonably inferred from the passage that Alexandra

A) can find hidden beauty in settings that other people would view with disdain.

B) resents Carl for adopting new trends and habits.

C) has forgiven her neighbors for their harsh and demeaning treatment of her.

D) sees her good fortune as the result not of talent but of circumstance.

5

Which choice provides the best evidence for the answer to the previous question?

A) Lines 4-7 ("Even his . . . hurt")

B) Lines 16-19 ("That evening . . . still")

C) Lines 26-29 ("We hadn't . . . worked itself")

D) Lines 32-35 ("For years . . . need it!")

6

Which choice best describes what happens in the passage?

A) Two characters reflect on the choices that they have made in their lifestyles and careers.

B) Two characters who had been at odds when younger are reconciled as adults.

C) Two characters discuss the best way to intervene in the troubled life of a third character.

D) Two characters struggle to suppress their unflattering perceptions of one another.

7

As described in the passage, Emil can best be understood as

A) arrogant.

B) irresponsible.

C) idealistic.

D) paradoxical.

8

Which choice provides the best evidence for the answer to the previous question?

A) Lines 35-38 ("Then I went . . . of us!")

B) Lines 42-44 ("It's curious . . . of us")

C) Lines 48-50 ("He shall do . . . worked for")

D) Lines 50-52 ("Sometimes he . . . land")

CONTINUE

Questions 9-16 are based on the following passage.

Adapted from Caitlin Hoynes-O'Connor, "The Crisis of Abundance: Good Economy, Bad Nutrition, and How to Change It All."

Make no mistake: nutrition in America is in a state of crisis. According to the Institute for Food and Development Policy, "The price of fresh fruits and vegetables went up 15%
Line between 1985 and 2000. The price of sugars, sweets, fats and
5 red meat—all based on the overproduction of grain—has been getting relatively cheaper." Because unhealthy food is cheap, poor health is becoming easier to come by. Especially in low-income areas, financial pressures discourage Americans from purchasing fruits and vegetables, the only two food groups that
10 have not yet been associated with obesity.

This situation has created socioeconomic zones that researchers call "food deserts": in such places, only unhealthy food abounds. Often, there is lack of full-service supermarkets in such urban or low-income areas. And while corner stores
15 (which are not lacking at all in food deserts) may be useful for lottery tickets and chewing gum, they are not generally a desirable source of nutritious food.

However, the problem with American nutrition today begins far away from metropolitan "food deserts." Because
20 a career in farming not economically feasible for most, Americans in rural areas have gravitated to other professions. Again, according to the Institute for Food and Development Policy, "Large-scale corporate and non-family farms now control 75% of agricultural production in the U.S." Those
25 mega-farms are far more likely to produce high-yield crops such as corn, which in turn are turned into products such as high-fructose corn syrup, which in turn make their way to food deserts and wreak havoc on public health.

Food reformers recognize these interlocking problems,
30 and their most compelling solutions are those that stress the need for local and regional interdependency. For example, some have championed farm-to-school programs as a way to increase the nutritional value of school meals, foster an awareness of the importance of food production, and use a
35 given school's purchasing power to support local farmers. Many food action plans suggest that hospitals, prisons, and other large institutions reevaluate their procurement processes and food purchasing patterns, with an eye to healthy and balanced choices. Such substantial financial
40 leverage should be used to support smaller farms that are truly bio-diverse. Other reformers point to farmland preservation as key to facilitating local linkages: planning tools like transfer development rights can be used to protect local fields and orchards, even as a community builds
45 up infrastructure. Reconciling healthy food and normal community life, not casting them in opposition, is key: after all, local food retailers (like those corner stores) can become potential partners with nearby farms, leading to both healthier options and a more resilient local economy.

50 If a food desert can result from financial considerations, then surely financial incentives can help to bring healthy food to underserved communities. It should be noted that in low-income areas, federal food assistance in the form of Supplemental Nutrition Assistance Program (SNAP) benefits
55 can be a useful leveraging tool. Only a little SNAP money is needed for a big social payoff: according to a resolution from House of Representatives, just one dollar in SNAP money is capable of generating $1.78 of economic activity. Should this money be spent on products derived from
60 processed grain, or should it be used to support local farmers who sell food in urban areas? The answer, from a public health perspective, is obvious. By increasing benefit viability at farmers markets and other venues for fresh produce, we can both encourage beneficiaries to eat more fruits and
65 vegetables and provide a financial boost to local farmers and fresh food retailers. We can, perhaps, make each "food desert" an oasis of health.

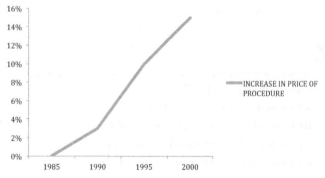

PERCENTAGE OF COMMERCIAL FARMS

INCREASE IN PRICE OF PROCEDURE

CONTINUE

9

As used in line 8, "pressures" most nearly means

A) persuasions.

B) troubles.

C) arguments.

D) strengths.

10

Which of the following approaches to "food deserts" does the author clearly support?

A) Providing additional government assistance to mega-farms

B) Fining businesses that do not provide sufficiently healthy food to their customers

C) Increasing the funding and influence of the Institute for Food and Development Policy

D) Working with existing "food desert" businesses to promote better nutrition

11

Which choice provides the best evidence for the answer to the previous question?

A) Lines 2-4 ("According . . . 2000")

B) Lines 18-19 ("However . . . deserts")

C) Lines 47-49 ("after all . . . economy")

D) Lines 66-67 ("We can . . . health")

12

As used in line 41, "point to" most nearly means

A) emphasize.

B) criticize.

C) gesture towards.

D) give directions to.

13

The author develops her argument that American nutrition is in "crisis" (line 2) by

A) criticizing a single company for its unethical business model.

B) recording the personal experiences of current food activists.

C) explaining why nutrition reformers should abandon their present efforts.

D) analyzing the consequences of specific food industry practices.

14

Which choice provides the best evidence for the answer to the previous question?

A) Lines 13-14 ("Often . . . areas")

B) Lines 24-28 ("Those . . . health")

C) Lines 39-41 ("Such . . . bio-diverse")

D) Lines 41-42 ("Other reformers . . . linkages")

15

The author of the passage would argue that the two graphs are evidence of

A) the improving state of health in America.

B) the deteriorating state of health in America.

C) the effectiveness of food policy reform.

D) the benefits of commercial farming.

16

In what respect do the two graphs differ?

A) One graph considers a shorter time span.

B) Only one graph lists data using percentages.

C) One graph records a trend that the author finds to be positive.

D) Only one graph refers to a topic that was raised in the passage.

CONTINUE

Questions 17-25 are based on the following passages.

These readings are from two recent science articles that consider recent technology developed to aid physicists and astronomers.

Passage 1

Albert Einstein predicted the existence of gravitational waves as early as 1916, but it is only in 2016 that they were detected for the first time. Gravitational waves are a key
Line component of Einstein's theory of general relativity. This
5 theory posits that gravity is best understood as a warping of space itself, and that when objects operating under the force of gravity move, they generate ripples, or waves in space. In most cases, these waves are tiny and therefore impossible to detect; even the orbit of a planet around a star doesn't
10 emit waves strong enough to be detected. The best hope for detectable waves lay with black holes: these remnants of dying stars, whose formation involves extremely strong and rapidly changing gravitational forces, trigger strong gravitational waves.
15 In cases where two black holes coalesce, the waves are stronger still, and it was just such an event that allowed scientists to finally observe this phenomenon. The detection took place using Laser Interferometer Gravitational-wave Observatories or LIGOs, which involve strong laser beams
20 being projected along tubes of 2.5 miles in length, from which air has been evacuated. Mirrors are located at each end of the tube, on which light from the lasers is reflected, and analysis of this light shows tiny variations in the distance between the two mirrors. The changes in the distance between the mirrors
25 demonstrate the presence of gravitational waves because, as space expands and contracts, the seemingly stable distance will alternately increase and decrease, albeit by an amount less than one millionth of an atom. In September 2015, two separate LIGOs, one in Washington and one in Louisiana, both
30 registered changes indicating the presence of gravitational waves caused by the spiral and merger of two black holes. In one stroke, LIGO technology both confirmed the theory of relativity and opened the door to new astrophysical insights.

Passage 2

The successful detection of gravitational waves by
35 two LIGO stations represents a major accomplishment in confirming a century of theoretical work on relativity. LIGO has only just begun to reveal its usefulness to astronomers: even during its initial observation period, it produced large quantities of data needing analysis beyond the data indicating
40 gravitational waves. LIGO and other observatories will, over the coming years, gather information about a wide range of stellar and sub-stellar objects and phenomena, such as neutron stars or pulsars, a type of neutron star that spins and emits a beam of radiation.
45 Only with a series of recent upgrades (such as a vacuum-sealed, background-noise-eliminating chamber for the detector), was LIGO able to complete its mission. Now, the LIGO team is planning to open another, India-based detector possessing all of these upgrades. There are several
50 laser interferometer stations in Europe that will coordinate their efforts with the existing LIGO stations to detect gravitational waves on a regular basis.
One challenge that the existing LIGO stations face is the encroaching noise of urban life. The Louisiana
55 observatory, not far from Baton Rouge, may prove too close to urban noise and activity to detect the most minute cosmic phenomena. For this reason, future interferometers are being planned for remote locations. One example is the Japanese KAGRA detector scheduled to open in 2018, which will be
60 buried deep within a mine to shield it from manmade and seismic disturbances alike.
The possibilities are still unfolding for LIGO and other highly advanced observatories. LIGO team member Rana Adhikari of Caltech, who worked on the recent upgrades,
65 says, "We've just made a machine that has given humanity a new sense, beyond the usual five." As these detectors continue to increase in number, sensitivity, and diversity of design, researchers will gain access to a wholly new means of perceiving and interpreting the universe.

17

Which choice explains the difference between how the two passages discuss the LIGO apparatus?

A) Passage 1 focuses on the successful use of LIGO stations in a single experiment; Passage 2 focuses on future possibilities for LIGO stations.

B) Passage 1 explains how LIGO stations helped scientists form new ideas about gravity; Passage 2 explains why these ideas will be rejected.

C) Passage 1 predicts that LIGO stations will soon be abandoned; Passage 2 predicts that LIGO stations will continue to be useful.

D) Passage 1 praises LIGO researchers for their ingenuity; Passage 2 criticizes LIGO researchers as impractical.

CONTINUE

18

As used in line 15, "cases" most nearly means

A) mysteries.

B) instances.

C) debates.

D) problems.

19

Which of the following could be considered one of the "new astrophysical insights" (line 33) mentioned in Passage 1?

A) A "century of theoretical work on relativity" (line 36)

B) Information about "neutron stars or pulsars" (lines 42-43)

C) The "recent upgrades" (line 45) to the LIGO technology

D) The creation of "future interferometers" (line 57)

20

Unlike Passage 1, Passage 2 does which of the following?

A) Quotes an authority on LIGO technology

B) Mentions Albert Einstein by name

C) Predicts that LIGO will continue to be useful

D) Refers to the theory of relativity

21

According to Passage 1, what event allowed researchers to detect the presence of gravitational waves?

A) The discovery of a new planet

B) The rediscovery of Einstein's theories

C) The interaction of black holes

D) The detection of a new type of atom

22

Which choice provides the best evidence for the answer to the previous question?

A) Lines 1-3 ("Albert . . . time")

B) Lines 9-10 ("even the . . . detected")

C) Lines 15-17 ("In cases . . . phenomenon")

D) Lines 24-28 ("The changes . . . atom")

23

As used in line 62, "unfolding" most nearly means

A) deteriorating.

B) being expressed.

C) being reconciled.

D) emerging.

24

According to Passage 2, which of the following can make the functioning of a LIGO apparatus problematic?

A) Legal restrictions on building LIGO stations

B) Changes in temperature and air pressure

C) Expenses involved in creating the technology

D) Man-made background noise

25

Which choice provides the best evidence for the answer to the previous question?

A) Lines 40-42 ("LIGO . . . phenomena")

B) Lines 49-51 ("There . . . stations")

C) Lines 53-54 ("One . . . noise")

D) Lines 62-63 ("The possibilities . . . observatories")

CONTINUE

Questions 26-34 are based on the following passage.

Adapted from Supreme Court Justice Ruth Bader Ginsburg, "Advocating the Elimination of Gender-Based Discrimination" (2006). Ginsburg's remarks were delivered in Cape Town, South Africa.

In the 1970s, a revived feminist movement blossomed in the United States. I was in those years a law teacher and counsel to the American Civil Liberties Union, an organization
Line committed to the preservation and advancement of human
5 rights in the U.S. It was my good fortune to be in the right place at the right time, able to participate in the effort to place women's rights permanently on the human rights agenda in the United States. I thought you might find engaging a description of what that effort entailed.
10   Unlike South Africa's Constitution, a model fundamental instrument of government for a nation starting afresh, the U.S. Constitution is nearly 220 years old and contains no express provision opposing discrimination on the basis of gender. Equal protection in the United States involves interpretation
15 of the spare command that governing authorities shall not deny to any person "the equal protection of the laws." Those words, inserted into the U.S. Constitution in 1868, were once interpreted narrowly, but over time, they proved to have growth potential. In the 1890s, the U.S. Supreme Court said
20 that racial segregation, mandated by state law, was compatible with the Constitution's equal protection principle. By the middle years of the twentieth century, the Supreme Court came to recognize how wrong that judgment was. Separate, the Court acknowledged, could never be equal. Yet, until 1971, the
25 Court turned away every woman's complaint that she had been denied equal protection by a state or federal law.
    In that year, 1971, the Court turned in a new direction. The Justices began to respond favorably to the arguments of equal rights advocates who urged a more dynamic
30 interpretation of the equality principle, one that would better serve U.S. society as it had evolved since the founding of the Nation in the late eighteenth century.
    However, our starting place for women's rights was not the same as that of advocates seeking the aid of the courts in
35 the struggle against race discrimination. Judges and legislators in the 1960s, and at least at the start of the 1970s, regarded differential treatment of men and women not as malign, but as operating benignly in women's favor. Legislators and judges, in those years, were overwhelmingly white, well-heeled, and
40 male. Men holding elected and appointed offices generally considered themselves good husbands and fathers. Women, they thought, had the best of all possible worlds. Women could work if they wished; they could stay home if they chose. They could avoid jury duty if they were so inclined, or they could
45 serve if they elected to do so. They could escape military duty

or they could enlist.
    Our mission was to educate, along with the public, decisionmakers in the Nation's legislatures and courts. We tried to convey to them that something was wrong with their
50 perception of the world. As Justice Brennan wrote in a 1973 Supreme Court plurality opinion, Frontiero v. Richardson, decided a year and a half after the Court had begun to listen: "Traditionally, [differential treatment on the basis of sex] was rationalized by an attitude of 'romantic paternalism'
55 which, in practical effect put women, not on a pedestal, but in a cage."
    Those with whom I was associated at the ACLU kept firmly in mind the importance of knowing the audience—largely men of a certain age. Speaking to that
60 audience as though addressing one's "home crowd" could be counterproductive. We sought to spark judges' and lawmakers' understanding that their own daughters and granddaughters could be disadvantaged by the way things were.

26

According to Ginsburg, what is one major difference between the United States and South Africa?

A) South Africa does not have an organized feminist movement.
B) South Africa has completely eliminated racial discrimination.
C) South Africa's legal system has actively worked against the interests of women.
D) South Africa's governing principles more clearly oppose gender-based discrimination.

27

Which choice provides the best evidence for the answer to the previous question?

A) Lines 1-2 ("In the 1970s . . . States")
B) Lines 5-8 ("It was . . . States")
C) Lines 10-13 ("Unlike . . . gender")
D) Lines 24-26 ("Yet . . . law")

28

As used in line 9, "effort" most nearly means

A) physical labor.
B) specific endeavor.
C) futile attempt.
D) unpleasant struggle.

CONTINUE

29

The main purpose of lines 10-26 ("Unlike . . . law") is to

A) compare the structure of the American government to the structure of the South African government.

B) compare the American struggle for women's rights to other initiatives.

C) explain how the Constitution of South Africa was created.

D) explain why racial segregation will soon be eliminated worldwide.

30

Ginsburg explicitly states that "Judges and legislators in the 1960s" (lines 35-36) were largely similar in terms of

A) political party.

B) education.

C) personality.

D) ethnicity.

31

For what reason, according to the passage, did judges and lawmakers allow "differential treatment on the basis of sex" (line 53)?

A) It was believed that women were too emotional to serve as judges or as legislators.

B) It was normal for American schools to promote outdated gender stereotypes.

C) It was impossible for women to find ways to publicize their own viewpoints and ideas.

D) It was believed that such treatment actually offered considerable benefits to women.

32

Which choice provides the best evidence for the answer to the previous question?

A) Lines 38-41 ("Legislators . . . fathers")

B) Lines 41-45 ("Women . . . do so")

C) Lines 47-48 ("Our . . . courts")

D) Lines 57-59 ("Those . . . age")

33

As used in line 29, "dynamic" most nearly means

A) rapid.

B) intriguing.

C) effectively adapted.

D) emotionally vital.

34

It can be reasonably inferred that 1971 is significant because during that year

A) the ACLU was founded.

B) South Africa's Constitution was approved.

C) Ginsburg first became interested in the civil liberties of women.

D) the Supreme Court became more sympathetic to women's causes.

CONTINUE

Questions 35-42 are based on the following passage and supplementary material.

Adapted from Nancy Hoffman, "Brain Transplants . . . No Longer Just Science Fiction."

The underlying causes of neurodegenerative diseases such as Parkinson's, Alzheimer's, and ALS had once eluded scientists, although research has made inroads toward treating
Line at least some of the symptoms of these diseases. Such diseases
5 are usually marked by a combination of decline in motor and cognitive abilities; eventually, many of these ailments lead to death. For some patients, symptomatic treatments can significantly improve quality of life and even extend longevity, but for others, these treatments are ineffective.
10 Technological advancements such as enhanced brain-imaging techniques have improved researchers' understanding of the roots of these diseases. Researchers have concluded that in cases of some diseases, like Alzheimer's, neurons in the brain wither and die, leading some to hypothesize that
15 new neurons—for example, transplanted neurons from a healthy brain—could slow, stop, or even reverse the disease's progression.
Transplants of brain cells are theoretically promising, but have been unsuccessful in trials involving transplanting cells
20 from a healthy animal into the brain of a sick animal, since the transplanted cells do not survive after the procedure. This low-survival phenomenon is a risk of all transplants, of all organ types. In fact, even the most successful transplants of external tissues have low survival rates.
25 Transplants from a patient's own tissue have a much higher likelihood of success, and are common in instances when a patient's body can produce new healthy tissue of the same type as the damaged tissue—for example, in the case of skin grafts. However, doctors cannot grow new brain tissue
30 using the same techniques that stimulate new skin growth.
In the case of neurons, a better approach could be to grow the cells in a lab from a patient's own stem cells, the undifferentiated cells that have the potential to mature into almost any type of cell. Converting stem cells into functional
35 neurons has posed a challenge until recently, since matured cells typically lack the physical structure that allows neurons to transmit electrical impulses.
However, researchers from the Robert Wood Johnson Medical School have been able to bridge the gap between
40 stem cell and functional neuron. First, they converted stem cells into neurons in their lab. Once the cells had matured and differentiated into neurons, they created scaffolds on a microscopic scale so that neurons can grow up the scaffold. (The scaffolds themselves were about the width of a human
45 hair, 100 micrometers, and made from a synthetic polymer.) When the scientists injected these lab-grown neurons into the

brains of mice, the transplants survived 100 times better than transplants that relied on the previous best method.
Dr. Prabhas V. Moghe, one of the lead researchers,
50 describes the main challenge that this research confronts as establishing communication between a living brain and transplanted cells. The neurons, which were electrically active pre-transplantation, continued their healthy activity once transplanted. Currently, the team is using the treatment
55 on mice with Parkinson's disease to see if their condition improves, and to what degree if so.
Moghe is optimistic about the applications of this technology, and identifies the next step as increasing the density of the scaffold to better approximate the density of
60 brain tissue. "The more neurons we can transplant, the more therapeutic benefits you can bring to the disease," Moghe says. "We want to try to stuff as many neurons as we can in as little space as we can." He estimates that human trials are as many as 20 years away, but that one day this research may
65 benefit many people suffering from diseases once thought to irreparably damage brain tissue.

35

The author of the passage suggests which of the following about Alzheimer's disease?

A) It was neglected by medical researchers until only a few years ago.

B) It only afflicts people who are elderly and infirm.

C) It appears to be traceable to the decay of brain tissue.

D) It will soon be eliminated through brain tissue transplants.

36

Which choice provides the best evidence for the answer to the previous question?

A) Lines 1-3 ("The underlying . . . scientists")

B) Lines 4-7 ("Such . . . to death")

C) Lines 12-14 ("Researchers . . . and die")

D) Lines 18-20 ("Transplants . . . animal")

37

As used in line 29, "grow" most nearly means

A) expand.

B) popularize.

C) generate.

D) inspire.

CONTINUE

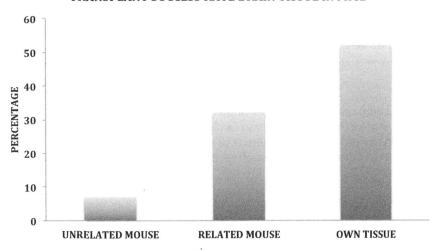

TRANSPLANT SUCCESS RATE BRAIN TISSUE IN MICE

38

It can be reasonably inferred from the passage that brain cell transplants

A) were most successful before the use of cell scaffolds.

B) have not yet been performed on human subjects.

C) are the most expensive method for treating neurodegenerative diseases.

D) have caused the deaths of many test subjects.

39

Which choice provides the best evidence for the answer to the previous question?

A) Lines 25-28 ("Transplants . . . tissue")

B) Lines 44-45 ("The scaffolds . . . polymer")

C) Lines 54-56 ("Currently . . . if so")

D) Lines 63-66 ("He estimates . . . tissue")

40

As used in line 51, "communication" most nearly means

A) productive interaction.

B) consistent dialogue.

C) clear messages.

D) thoughtful collaboration.

41

According to the graph on brain tissue transplants, how does the success rate involving an unrelated mouse compare to the success rate involving a mouse's own tissue?

A) The own tissue rate is slightly higher.

B) The own tissue rate is much higher.

C) The own tissue rate is slightly lower.

D) The own tissue rate is much lower.

42

The data in the graphic

A) support the author's ideas about the high transplant success rate when using a subject's own tissue.

B) contradict the author's ideas about the high transplant success rate when using a subject's own tissue.

C) are directly cited in the first two paragraphs of the passage.

D) are unrelated to the author's main topic.

STOP

Writing Test
35 MINUTES, 44 QUESTIONS

Turn to Section 2 of your answer sheet to answer the questions in this section.

DIRECTIONS

Each passage below is accompanied by a number of questions. For some questions, you will consider how the passage might be revised to improve the expression of ideas. For other questions, you will consider how the passage might be edited to correct errors in sentence structure, usage, or punctuation. A passage or a question may be accompanied by one or more graphics (such as a table or graph) that you will consider as you make revising and editing decisions.

Some questions will direct you to an underlined portion of a passage. Other questions will direct you to a location in a passage or ask you to think about the passage as a whole.

After reading each passage, choose the answer to each question that most effectively improves the quality of writing in the passage or that makes the passage conform to the conventions of standard written English. Many questions include a "NO CHANGE" option. Choose that option if you think the best choice is to leave the relevant portion of the passage as it is.

Questions 1-10 are based on the following passage.

William Shakespeare, Comedian

Of thirty-five plays commonly attributed to Shakespeare, fourteen are comedies. In fact, some of these rank among the best of all the written works Shakespeare **[1]** obtained, even though he is probably better known for his tragedies. Although there are productions of a certain few today, **[2]** they have been regarded, by and large, as plays that have trouble attracting a modern audience, either because of their settings **[3]** or when Shakespeare's puns and ironic language belong to a society far removed from that of today.

1
A) NO CHANGE
B) produced
C) made up
D) had some ideas for

2
Which of the following is the best replacement for the underlined portion?
A) the comedies have been
B) theater-goers have been
C) the setting has been
D) Shakespeare has been

3
A) NO CHANGE
B) or because
C) and when
D) and because

CONTINUE →

[4] Yet the comedies feature some remarkable sequences of fantasy and symbolism. Broadway and Hollywood have gleefully turned them into musicals such as *The Boys from Syracuse* (based on *The Comedy of Errors*) and *Kiss Me Kate* (based on *The Taming of the Shrew*). On the screen, stars such as Denzel Washington, Al Pacino, and Elizabeth Taylor have been eager to show their prowess by tackling some of the toughest roles in Shakespeare's comedies. Today's audience experiences the same feeling [5] by satisfaction as the curtain falls as did the audience of the seventeenth century—perhaps more so, since the feeling that a five hundred year-old play can remain relevant even today is a uniquely refreshing sensation.

[4]

Which choice best introduces the discussion that follows?

A) NO CHANGE

B) Yet the comedies have been studied extensively by Shakespeare scholars.

C) Yet the comedies were revered by Shakespeare's contemporaries.

D) Yet the comedies can be surprisingly rich with possibility.

[5]

A) NO CHANGE

B) to satisfaction

C) of satisfaction

D) for satisfaction

CONTINUE

One comedy in particular—*A Midsummer Night's Dream*—exemplifies clearly the insight and the universality of Shakespeare's writing. While the play appears to be about a single significant wedding, the motif that lies at its heart is [6] when you examine love. Shakespeare defines for the audience the difference between real love [7] or physical love. It is only when his characters have each felt that they are being cheated by love that they can see love as it really is. This is true of the play's fantasy characters: it is only when the forest lord Oberon realizes how selfishly he has treated his mate Titania that he can understand that love includes forgiveness. This is also true of purely human characters: [8] when a self-absorbed weaver named Nick Bottom wakes from his "dreams" of love that he can live in the world and pursue something more enduring.

These themes explain why the play resonates with people today. In all his comedies, Shakespeare investigates that [9] element of our lives that is perhaps most important to us: love, the need to discover it and cherish it, the need to give it and return it. Shakespearean love is a force that elevates—that imparts wisdom and, with it, [10] we laugh.

6
A) NO CHANGE
B) when we examine love.
C) an examination of love.
D) an examination, which is of love.

7
A) NO CHANGE
B) and
C) from
D) as

8
A) NO CHANGE
B) however,
C) it is only when
D) it is only, however,

9
A) NO CHANGE
B) major thing in
C) most important aspect of
D) ideal that is most important in

10
A) NO CHANGE
B) one laughs
C) it imparts laughter
D) laughter

CONTINUE

Questions 11-20 are based on the following passage.

Invest Now, Retire Later

[11] Like the typical investment account today, I often feel that saving for retirement is an uphill battle. This feeling may seem rather unexpected, since I am, after all, only twenty-eight years old and work a well-paying job with a generous benefits package. But even though time is on my side (since, in all likelihood, I will not retire until I am well into my sixties), [12] other factors are certainly not working to my advantage. A sizable portion of each paycheck I earn goes to paying off credit card debt, student loan debt, and basic living expenses such as rent and utilities. In other words, [13] my yearly paycheck of $3500 normally shrinks to $500 or less by the time I have accounted for everything.

11
A) NO CHANGE
B) Like many other young adults today,
C) Like the feelings that many other people have,
D) Like other common jobs,

12
A) NO CHANGE
B) obscure aspects are
C) a large bunch of things are
D) random stuff is

13
Which choice offers the most accurate interpretation of the data in the chart?
A) NO CHANGE
B) my yearly paycheck of $3500 normally shrinks to around $3200 or more
C) my monthly paycheck of $3500 normally shrinks to $500 or less
D) my monthly paycheck of $3500 normally shrinks to around $3200 or more

The Writer's Monthly Expenditures, Maximum and Minimum

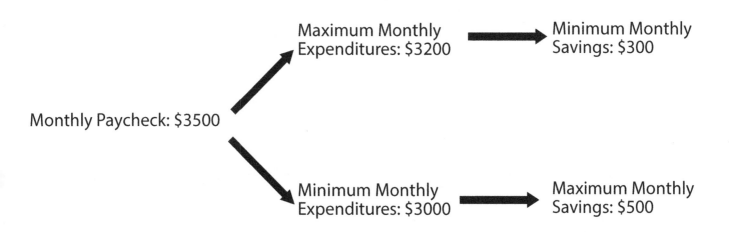

229

CONTINUE

Under circumstances such as these, saving enough to invest in the stock market can become difficult; saving enough to create a retirement account that could last me several decades [14] appears to be unthinkable. [15] Lamentably, the technology industry is aware that there are many young people in situations similar to mine. To help us out, entrepreneurs have spent the past five years or so creating phone apps and computer programs that make it easy for anyone to establish long-term investments— and, perhaps, [16] to gain a better understanding of how the stock market works.

14
A) NO CHANGE
B) appear to be
C) appear being
D) being

15
A) NO CHANGE
B) Fortunately,
C) Shockingly,
D) In addition,

16
Which choice most accurately reflects one of the writer's personal motives for creating an investment account?
A) NO CHANGE
B) to experience the thrill of financial risk and financial reward.
C) to find better-paying job opportunities.
D) to create the retirement savings that we need.

CONTINUE

[1] Of course, it is possible to research stocks, bonds, and other [17] assets, they will increase in value over time: online investment platforms such as E*Trade and Scottrade have simplified this process enormously. [2] But there are other programs that cater to relatively young working adults, or "millennials," such as myself. [3] [18] Every time, I make a credit card purchase Acorns wires a small amount of money to an investment account. [4] I get to choose whether my account will target high-risk or low-risk investments, but a computer algorithm handles most of the other technicalities. [19]

Over time, the tiny investments in a Scottrade portfolio or an Acorns account can gain value— [20] to a multiple of ten over my lifetime, if I am lucky—and give me the retirement fund of my dreams. I don't need to be a Silicon Valley guru or a Wall Street wizard—just a forward-thinking employee with the right technology.

[17]
A) NO CHANGE
B) asset, all of these will increase
C) assets that will increase
D) assets. Increasing

[18]
A) NO CHANGE
B) Every time I make a credit card purchase
C) Every time I make a credit card purchase;
D) Every time I make a credit card purchase,

[19]
The writer would like to add the following sentence to this paragraph.

My personal favorite is an app called Acorns.

To make the paragraph most logical, this new sentence should be placed
A) before sentence 1.
B) before sentence 2.
C) before sentence 3.
D) before sentence 4.

[20]
Which phrase provides the most specific information about how the writer will benefit from making investments?
A) NO CHANGE
B) by a truly enormous amount over my lifetime,
C) by several multiples over my lifetime,
D) by a varying percentage over my lifetime,

CONTINUE

Questions 21-30 are based on the following passage.

My Historical Valentine

So many of us around the [21] world that celebrates Valentine's Day, but most of us don't know how the holiday originated. Why do we give flowers and gifts to our loved ones? And why is the heart so closely associated with Valentine's Day? We all know that Valentine's Day is a day of romance and love, but to answer these deeper questions, [22] they must go back in history and investigate the original Saint Valentine.

[1] The Catholic Church recognizes at least two different saints that were both named Valentine, or Valentinus, and who were both martyred. [2] During this time, the Emperor Claudius II decreed that single men were better soldiers than married men. [3] For this reason, he outlawed marriage for young men in hopes of building a stronger army. [4] Valentine opposed this [23] decision, although he continued to marry young lovers in clandestine ceremonies. [5] Unfortunately, he was discovered, and Claudius had Valentine executed. [24]

21
A) NO CHANGE
B) world where we celebrate
C) world celebrating
D) world celebrate

22
A) NO CHANGE
B) we must go
C) you must go
D) it must go

23
A) NO CHANGE
B) decision; however, he continued
C) decision; he continued
D) decision; continuing

24
The writer wishes to add the following sentence to this paragraph

One story goes that Valentine was a priest who served in third-century Rome.

To make the order of ideas in the paragraph most logical, this sentence should be placed
A) before sentence 1.
B) after sentence 1.
C) after sentence 2.
D) after sentence 3.

CONTINUE

The second Valentine's Day origin story maintains that Valentine helped Christians escape from Roman prisons. He was imprisoned himself, and allegedly [25] heals the blind daughter of his jailer. Before he was executed, he sent the jailer's daughter a note, signed "From your Valentine": this may well have been the first valentine ever to be sent. [26] They say that Valentine cut out parchment hearts and gave them to persecuted Christians and soldiers as a sign of brotherhood. These may be the prototypes of today's Valentine's Day hearts.

But Valentine's Day also has possible non-Christian origins: in fact, the holiday is believed to originate in part from a pagan festival that took place on February 15, [27] it was the feast of the Lupercalia. At the end of a day of elaborate celebrations, young women would place their names in a big urn. [28] These matches generally ended in marriage.

25

A) NO CHANGE
B) healed
C) he can heal
D) he will heal

26

A) NO CHANGE
B) Lots of people say that
C) Legend has it that
D) Someone had the idea that

27

A) NO CHANGE
B) that was
C) so that
D) DELETE the underlined portion.

28

Which sentence, if inserted here, provides the most relevant and necessary information at this point in the passage?
A) It is fairly common, according to historians, for Christian traditions to incorporate some pagan customs.
B) The urn itself was made of a fairly common metal such as copper, but was decorated with fine sculptures and small gold ornaments.
C) Unmarried men would then choose a name and become paired with the woman chosen for the entire year ahead.
D) Whether the historical Saint Valuentine had any exposure to such festivities remains an unresolved question.

CONTINUE

Whichever origin story you prefer—the stoic priest who believed in marriage, the healer and savior of the persecuted, or the pagan [29] celebrants, they granted fertility at festivals— Valentine's Day still holds a special place in our hearts. It is a day of joviality, romance, and (of course) chocolate—the 21st century answer to a [30] centuries-old love feast that has endured for hundreds of years.

[29]
A) NO CHANGE
B) celebrants, those were granted
C) celebrants granted
D) DELETE the underlined portion.

[30]
A) NO CHANGE
B) love feast that has endured for centuries and hundreds of years.
C) love feast, and it has endured for centuries, or hundreds of years.
D) centuries-old love feast.

CONTINUE

Questions 31-40 are based on the following passage.

Mitochondria Power!

Mitochondria are often referred to as the "powerhouses" of the cell, and indeed they are crucial to the **31** body's energy production. Most cells in the human body contain hundreds, if not thousands, of these minuscule battery packs. Yet perhaps the most **32** unfounded myth about mitochondria are that they are not actually human-derived. This idea, referred to as the "endosymbiotic hypothesis," holds that mitochondria were once independent organisms that were absorbed by animal cells. The key bit of evidence for this theory is that mitochondria have their own genome— **33** DNA that's fundamentally different from human DNA.

31
A) NO CHANGE
B) bodys'
C) bodies
D) bodie's

32
A) NO CHANGE
B) fascinating theory
C) weird thought
D) presumptuous notion

33
Which phrase most effectively clarifies the point that the writer is making about mitochondria genomes?
A) NO CHANGE
B) DNA that scientists have yet to study at length.
C) DNA that is unique to each individual mitochondrion.
D) DNA that can be explained by how mitochondria evolved.

CONTINUE

Each human body has enormous numbers of mitochondria: though there's no way to know for sure, **[34]** there is most likely quintillions of them in each person. Mitochondria are a type of "organelle," a specialized subunit of a body cell. **[35]** The name "organelle" comes from the idea that an organelle performs roughly the same function within an individual cell that a specific organ performs within a human body. The function of mitochondria is very specialized: **[36]** their crucial to the cell's production of adenosine triphosphate (ATP), which is used as a source of chemical energy. In fact, mitochondria are responsible for most of the cell's production of ATP.

34

A) NO CHANGE
B) there are
C) they have
D) you have

35

The writer is considering deleting the underlined sentence from the passage. Should the writer delete this portion?

A) Yes, because the sentence contradicts the idea that mitochondria have their own genome.
B) Yes, because the sentence the sentence introduces a concept only loosely related to mitochondria.
C) No, because the sentence anticipates the writer's discussion of organelles other than mitochondria.
D) No, because the sentence both clarifies a term and anticipates the discussion that follows.

36

A) NO CHANGE
B) they're
C) its
D) its'

CONTINUE ➡

How did these diminutive creatures begin, and how did they become part of our bodies? The endosymbiotic theory, first proposed by Lynn Margulis in 1967, postulates that mitochondria were once specialized bacteria. The story goes back millions of years, to a time [37] where the Earth's atmosphere had hardly any oxygen. As life proliferated over the surface of the planet, oxygen [38] begin building up in the atmosphere—as a waste product released by micro-organisms. As oxygen accumulated, it began choking out the first species of bacteria, which are "anaerobic" (poisoned by oxygen). Newer forms of life developed that were "aerobic," which means they can actually convert oxygen into energy.

As more and more oxygen built up in the Earth's atmospheric system, the ability to process oxygen became a major advantage. Mitochondria, which are aerobic (taking energy from oxygen) were absorbed by bacterial organisms [39] which is anaerobic (poisoned by oxygen). In other words, mitochondria confer an enormous advantage to a cell that is usually not capable [40] to process oxygen. In fact, if it weren't for mitochondria, oxygen would even be poisonous to human cells.

37
A) NO CHANGE
B) which
C) when
D) that

38
A) NO CHANGE
B) begins building
C) began building
D) begun building

39
A) NO CHANGE
B) which are
C) and being
D) and from being

40
A) NO CHANGE
B) at processing
C) for processing
D) of processing

STOP

Answer Key: TEST 3

SECTION 1—READING

1. C	9. B	17. A	26. D	35. C
2. A	10. D	18. B	27. C	36. C
3. C	11. C	19. B	28. B	37. C
4. D	12. A	20. A	29. B	38. B
5. C	13. D	21. C	30. D	39. D
6. A	14. B	22. C	31. D	40. A
7. D	15. B	23. D	32. B	41. B
8. B	16. A	24. C	33. C	42. A
		25. C	34. D	

SECTION 2—WRITING

1. B	11. B	21. D	31. A
2. A	12. A	22. B	32. B
3. B	13. C	23. C	33. A
4. D	14. A	24. B	34. B
5. C	15. B	25. B	35. D
6. C	16. D	26. C	36. B
7. B	17. C	27. D	37. C
8. C	18. D	28. C	38. C
9. A	19. C	29. C	39. B
10. D	20. A	30. D	40. D

Made in United States
Orlando, FL
27 September 2024

52034225R00130